VINTAGE

OUR HINDU RASHTRA

Aakar Patel is a syndicated columnist who has edited English and Gujarati newspapers. His translation of Saadat Hasan Manto's Urdu non-fiction, *Why I Write*, was published in 2014. His analysis of India's performance under Prime Minister Narendra Modi, *Price of the Modi Years*, was published in 2021. He is chair of Amnesty International India.

T0307568

PRAISE FOR THE BOOK

'Based on his activism and journalism, Patel aims to help readers understand the meaning of "Hindu Rashtra", its long political and institutional genealogy, and signal how it can still be prevented . . . To the credit of the author, he engages with the Sangh and its texts with all seriousness and provides a comprehensive outlook of foundational ideologies'—*Economic and Political Weekly*

'Lucidly written . . . *Our Hindu Rashtra* is recommended reading not only for Indians but also for Pakistanis interested in understanding how their countries got to where they are'—**Firstpost**

'Aakar Patel builds his case brick-by-brick to substantiate two primary theses. One, that Hindu majoritarianism never had positive aspects but was perpetually "negative and aimed at India's minorities". Additionally, Hindutva is not an ideology but merely an anti-minority (chiefly targeting Muslims and Christians) programme . . . Some of the polemical chapters are well argued'—*Mint*

'Aakar Patel offers a sober analysis of Hindutva ideology from a non-BJP perspective'—***Business Standard***

OUR HINDU RASHTRA

WHAT IT IS.
HOW WE GOT HERE

AAKAR PATEL

VINTAGE
An imprint of Penguin Random House

VINTAGE

USA I Canada I UK I Ireland I Australia
New Zealand I India I South Africa I China

Vintage is part of the Penguin Random House group of companies
whose addresses can be found at global.penguinrandomhouse.com

Published by Penguin Random House India Pvt. Ltd
4th Floor, Capital Tower 1, MG Road,
Gurugram 122 002, Haryana, India

Penguin
Random House
India

First published by Westland Publications Private Limited in 2020
Published in Vintage by Penguin Random House India 2022

ISBN 9780143458517

Typeset in EB Garamond by SÜRYA, New Delhi

www.penguin.co.in

CONTENTS

PREFACE TO THE 2022 PAPERBACK EDITION

This work was first published at the end of 2020. In the two years that have passed since, India has accelerated down the path it has chosen. New and innovative means of torturing its minorities were discovered, and applied, by the State and the mobs it has empowered.

A fierce Hindu nationalism, aimed internally at India's own citizens, became more unhinged and more vengeful. The trauma and distress expressed by minority Indians on social media was shocking to those as yet unaware of the gravity of what was happening. Just as appalling was the apathy of the majority to the pain of the minorities, and seeing many Hindus in fact expressing their satisfaction, if not pleasure, at the persecution. Social media exposed Indians quite thoroughly in a way that may not have been noticeable in previous decades.

Another development of note was the Indian State's devolution of considerable authority to Hindu mobs. In the National Capital Region, the State had designated spaces for Friday prayer in the open. This was for the hundreds of thousands of migrants working in and around Delhi, who had no access to a local mosque for congregation. After mobs disrupted their prayers week after week, the Government of Haryana withdrew its permission in December 2021.

The previous month, in four cities in Gujarat—Ahmedabad, Baroda, Bhavnagar and Junagadh—the BJP-controlled civic bodies forced vendors of meat and eggs, mostly Muslims of course, off the street. This was done without any written order, and the State was complicit or looked away while the vendors were brutalised.

The next month, Karnataka passed an order forbidding students, including adults, to wear the hijab to colleges. The mob quickly took over, heckling young women, and soon, even teachers and professors were forced to remove the garment; many of them were told to disrobe before entering the premises they worked in. The courts sided against individual liberty and minority rights.

In March 2022, Karnataka saw calls for a ban on Muslim traders selling goods near temples and in temple fairs. In April 2022, cities began banning the sale of meat on the Hindu festival of Navratri. Also in April, in the states of Uttar Pradesh, Madhya Pradesh, Gujarat and then Delhi, bulldozers were run over the homes and businesses of Muslims. The vandalism by the State continued in the face of a 'status quo' order from the Supreme Court, which was ignored for an hour and a half.

The violence against Muslims came amid mobs parading outside their mosques and using abusive language. Many so-called 'dharam sansads', or parliaments of religion—they were nothing of the sort—gave open calls for genocide against Muslims. The State did not act firmly against them, and the judiciary looked away. Those who called out the hate-mongering and abuse were themselves jailed, as was the case for the fact-checker Mohammed Zubair.

Starting in 2018, seven BJP states—Uttarakhand, Himachal Pradesh, Madhya Pradesh, Uttar Pradesh, Karnataka, Haryana and Gujarat—criminalised inter-faith marriage. Vigilantism on the issue of 'love jihad', a phantom that Parliament has been told does not exist, was widespread and normalised.

Documented attacks against Christians rose from 127 in 2014 to 142 a year later; then this number went up to 226, and then to 248. It reached 292 in 2018 and 328 in 2019. It was 279 in the pandemic year of 2020, and 486 in 2021. A People's Union for Civil Liberties report on the attacks against Christians in Karnataka found that the police colluded with the mobs in their violence on churches and homes, forcing many places of worship to stop the Sunday Mass.

The vigilante assaults on the propagation of religion (ironically, both a criminal offence and a fundamental right in India) continued, here also enabled by an enthusiastic State.

The world noticed. India was a 'Country of Particular Concern' three years running—2020, 2021 and 2022—for the United States Commission on International Religious Freedom. This bipartisan and independent part of the US federal government recommended sanctions against Indian officials and state agencies in 2022, though these had not yet come. How long India can ignore the world and how long the world can ignore what is happening in India is a question that will likely receive an answer soon. India continues to aspire to a greater role on the global stage, an aspiration incongruous with its present behaviour. Modernity will yank those nations reluctant to leave their medieval mindsets, towards civilization in due time. Those that are unwilling will be dragged into modernity, of this there is no doubt.

There are those who are still hopeful within India during such a dark present. The 2021–22 period was one of our worst in terms of the erosion of pluralist values. And yet, it was also the year in which another great civil rights battle was fought and won by protestors ranged against the State. The farmers of India forced the government to not only take back laws passed without consultation but also sought and received an apology from the prime minister.

Our future is not preordained, and our fate has not yet been written. We retain the ability to influence it in many ways.

Political opposition to Hindutva may be weak, but it exists. In many states, it has electorally prevailed over bigotry. The judiciary is reluctant to deter the State on majoritarian matters (and indeed it can even be seen as complicit), but it is technically and constitutionally independent. The media has voluntarily done the work of the State more enthusiastically and more effectively than official propaganda, and yet it is free. Civil society is under sustained assault, but it still puts up spirited resistance. The Constitution is intact.

Space exists. It must be used.

Bangalore   **Aakar Patel**
15 August 2022

FOREWORD

Majoritarianism is primitive and easy to do. Polarisation is democratically rewarding. Both damage the nation and its individuals but elections sanctify the savagery. When a political force chooses to pursue internal division against India's vulnerable own, it prospers and the history of our parts proves fraternal violence is profitable. Harvesting the dividend of blood requires not genius but viciousness. In authority, it requires mere inaction: charisma will ensue. Someone can claim to possess a chest fifty-six inches around not for an achievement of personal valour or signal bravery but for failing to protect his wards from butchery. This is not questioned, much less ridiculed in our parts, but seen as heroic.

What has happened in India over the last thirty years is the telescoping of a majoritarianism already present. It was not as overtly and as aggressively pursued as it is being now, but it existed. This book attempts to understand how we have arrived here.

A reckoning of the immediate present through this same understanding will require another book and it will come soon. An urgency is being forced on us by this telescoping, and its effects on this country are now clear.

It is unclear what the idea of India is, was or if any such construct existed. We have woven myths around a Constitution few have read. The identity of India on the other hand is a more palpable and less intangible thing. Its brand is more exposed to disfigurement and mutilation. What we are doing to ourselves today comes at a price. It will be paid by us and by the generation we are bringing into this polarised and prejudiced present, before we can move on. And we will, of course, move on.

Majoritarianism is both natural and abnormal. Natural because it is an instinct of our tribal self. Abnormal because it is vestigial: we are no longer Neanderthals and tribalism is unproductive in a nation that sends rockets to Mars.

I'd like to thank the following individuals. At Westland, Deepthi for commissioning this book, and my editor, Karthik. My wife Tushita and Shailesh for reading the chapters as they were being written and for making them more readable. Mahmood for his critique and for his validation.

Bangalore   **Aakar Patel**
31 October 2020

INTRODUCTION

This book is about how India became majoritarian, privileging one community over others. It did so in a different way than its neighbours, but the result was as lethal to its society and its communities as was the majoritarianism of the nations around it.

If we look at the modern history of South Asian nations, India stands out for its constitution. Alone in South Asia, India has not dabbled with constitutional majoritarianism. It did not officially privilege the rights of one community or privilege one religion over the others. This made it unique in the region that comprises Afghanistan, Pakistan, the Maldives, Sri Lanka, Bangladesh, Bhutan, Nepal and India.

Of these nations, India is unique for wanting to be inclusive throughout its independent history. This 'wanting' is best expressed through the Constitution, which is an aspirational document for any nation, but especially so in our part of the world, with its deprivation, poverty and history of social violence. Constitutions represent a map of a better place we can reach from our present if we follow its directions and guidance. The Indian Constitution has attempted to steer us away from the prevalent thinking around us and towards something higher, more universal.

But the Bharatiya Janata Party, and especially since 2014 under Narendra Modi, appears to be pulling India in the opposite direction, away from this constitutional goal being aspired for and towards our lived reality. The facts of existence in India bear little resemblance to the values of the Constitution. Minorities are actively and regularly persecuted, dissent is punished, the judiciary is unable to balance executive overreach, freedoms are restricted often to the point of being absent and the State is vicious. It is a reality that is also reflected, truth be told, in the everyday actions of Indians themselves as the violence and discrimination reported in our newspapers and TV channels daily testify. This pulling away has been achieved by the BJP through selectively emphasising that which is divisive and keeps frozen the present and its antagonisms. And by using the current framework to push its communalism.

This is in keeping with the manner of India's route to majoritarianism. India did not approach the brutalisation of its minorities through constitutional change, but through existing law and policy and, above all, through the issues that parties and governments picked and stayed focused on till the majoritarian impact was achieved. It is clear, as I finish writing this towards the end of 2020, that this impact has taken root and will be with us for a long time. We then owe it to ourselves to examine it honestly and to see how we arrived here.

Let us begin with nomenclature. The Hindutva ideology and its supporters and votaries are referred to as being 'right' and 'right-wing'. Is this accurate and if so, what does it mean? The word 'right' is used because of the seating arrangement in the early French Parliament—they sat to the right of the assembly president's chair. This group of representatives, 'conservatives' as they were known, were trying to preserve or 'conserve' aspects of the monarchy and the social order, and were averse to change or innovation. Their opponents, who were republicans insisting on reform rather than conservation, sat to the left of the president's chair. And so the terms 'right' and 'left' mean conservative as opposed to reformist or liberal.

In American politics, the conservative seeks to preserve what she sees as Christian values and tradition, from encroachment by the State. On such issues as abortion and gay rights, the American conservative seeks a halt to reform.

This is social conservatism rather than political and such a person seeking a halt to reform could be either a Democrat or a Republican, though for the last few decades she has been mostly Republican.

British conservatism rose from its class system and the landed elite, seeking to preserve the social order by supporting the monarchy, the church and the empire. The political opposition to it is called 'Labour', because the working class's interests are fundamentally opposed to conservatism. They are seen as socialist because they push for greater state ownership over ownership by private interests that they feel shut out from. In time, the liberal and conservative ideologies have evolved and expanded, but retain their essential differences.

The question is: if we are to assume that Hindutva is an ideology of the right, what is it trying to conserve? Is it the social order? If so, which aspect of it—the caste system? Or something else?[1]

The answer is not clear according to the ideology's own texts, nor is it readily apparent when one observes Hindutva in action. While we shall explore what its objectives are, at first sight it appears to be the case that it is not trying to conserve anything.

It is therefore not appropriate to refer to the ideology and its supporters and proponents as 'right'. The word 'Hindutva'

---

1. Dictionaries define 'right' in this manner: 'A right-wing person or group has conservative or capitalist views.' (*Collins Dictionary*); 'That section of a political party, assembly, or other body most tending to hold conservative or reactionary views.' (*Oxford English Dictionary*); 'Individuals professing support of the established order and favouring traditional attitudes and practices and conservative governmental policies.' (*Merriam-Webster*); 'Political parties or people that have traditional opinions, and that believe in low taxes, property, and industry being privately owned, and less help for the poor.' (*Cambridge*); 'Considered to be conservative in your political views, not willing to accept much change, especially in the traditional values of society.' (*Macmillan*). These definitions do not align with what the BJP says it is.

implies something unique and distinct, and right and right-wing should not be incorrectly substituted or used as a synonym for Hindutva, because it normalises Hindu majoritarianism and locates it wrongly.

In the political language of our time, the word 'right' has also come to be associated with individual freedoms, a hawkish nationalism, a resistance to immigration, a focus on the military at the expense of other organs of the state and their capacities, and a determination to liberalise the economy. Here it is not easy to separate the policies and outlook of India's two national political parties. On all these subjects, including immigration, both have followed similar trajectories and policies based on an institutional consensus.

The 'right', as understood in the rest of the world, is vehemently against aspects of the welfare state which it sees as handouts. But again, despite the initial rhetoric from some of his supporters when he came to power, even under Modi there was little difference in outlook or policies from the BJP on this front.

We must therefore discard the word 'right' and all of its attendant meanings when we refer to Hindutva. Correspondingly, in India the word 'liberal' has come to be used as a slur. But all understand what it communicates: someone opposed to majoritarianism (Hindutva refers to such an attitude as appeasement) and to ethnonationalism, equating India and Indianness with only one set of its citizens. Both sides agree that this is an acceptable definition. The problem of definition affects only Hindutva.

There is a second difference that makes Hindutva politics distinct from that of the right. The BJP is not like the Republican Party or the Conservative Party in a distinct way. These are political groups that can shift away from adversarial positions against minorities, because broad ideas and principles, and not a particular community, lie at the core of their belief system. This focus on principle over people means that Cuban Americans, who are Hispanic immigrants, often identify as Republican. The Republicans are seen by many opponents as racists but they are also the party of Abraham Lincoln, who chose civil war over letting the South continue with slavery. America's Democrats are seen as liberal and the party of Barack Obama but they were also once the party that supported racial segregation in the South. The point is that on the question of race and identity the outlook of those calling themselves 'Republican' and 'Conservative' can evolve.

Hindutva is however coded rigidly into the BJP. The party is inseparable from a fixed ideology, or to use a more appropriate word a 'fixed prejudice', which is anti-minority and primarily anti-Muslim. This is why the supposedly right-wing BJP and Hindutva can dabble in what would otherwise be seen as socialism and handouts, without internal resistance or discomfort. It can indulge in anti-libertarian economics (for instance, through the Swadeshi Jagran Manch or Narendra Modi's own Aatmanirbharta thrust), or effortlessly warm towards gay rights and change many of the other positions that it has held over the years. It has no core interest in any of these things that define ideology and political division in other democracies. What it does not do and will not do is to give up its minority-focused agenda because that sits at the heart of the Hindutva project.

The third difference between the BJP and other extremist or right-wing parties is its absolute lack of ideology. This might come as a surprise since the BJP claims to be an ideological party.[2] It will also puzzle those who fear the BJP as an ideological

---

2. On its website, the BJP says it is 'an organisation built on certain principles. Its strength is its cadre. It is not centred around any individual, leader, family or dynasty. Its driving force is national approach to all issues rising above caste and religion. We draw our strength from "Bharat Mata ki Jai". This is our central theme. "Bharat" (our land), "Mata" (our heritage and culture) and "Jai" (people's aspirations) are expression of our deep commitment to the nation. Nation emerges from the union of land, people and culture. We have faith in cultural nationalism.')

party or at least a party wanting to follow an ideology, and a rather strong and well-defined one, namely, Hindutva. But the definition of an ideology is a system of ideas and ideals that form the basis of a political theory. What is the theory of Hindutva? If it is Hindu Rashtra, then what is it intended to achieve? We shall have a look at it in the following chapters, but an important aspect of Hindutva is that at the level of theory it is merely a definition. It means 'Hinduness' and its author Vinayak Savarkar was careful to specify that even the word 'Hindu' here did not mean, or meant more than, just the Vedic or Puranic faith that is known to the world as Hinduism. It meant to Savarkar the history of the Hindus' engagement with those who were not Hindu.

Hindutva makes no demands on the State, and doesn't require it to significantly change in the way that socialism or fascism or even capitalism might require. At the level of practice, Hindutva has come to be associated with the three primary political demands of the BJP.

Firstly, Muslims must surrender their mosque in Ayodhya (Ram Janmabhoomi). Secondly, Muslims must surrender their personal law and assent to a Uniform Civil Code. Thirdly, Muslims must surrender their constitutional autonomy in Kashmir (Article 370). On taking power, other issues have been added to these: that Muslims give up their diet (ban on cattle slaughter), that Muslims must prove their identity in Assam or be disenfranchised (National Register of Citizens) and so on.

This is not an ideology. There is no political theory underlying these demands, nor does the Hindutva ideology claim to produce or foresee any utopia. However, the valid fear in our time in the minds of many is that that extended rule at the Centre by the BJP will produce a Hindu Rashtra in India.

But does the BJP seek a Hindu Rashtra? And if yes, what changes does it foresee in the State that will bring about Hindu

Rashtra from the present secular legal order? This is the worry that has come to occupy the minds of many.

The answer to the second question is: none. The BJP does not seek any changes regarding the secular nature of the Indian Constitution. We know this for a fact because the BJP's membership form requires the taking of a pledge that contains the line: 'I subscribe to the concept of a secular state and nation not based on religion.' This language, continued below, was inserted into the BJP's constitution years before the law required all parties to do so. It was done voluntarily in 1980, as we will see.

The BJP does not campaign for a constitutional shift or for a change in the secular contours of the State.[3] In fact, it pledges rigid adherence to the Constitution of India. At the very beginning of its party constitution, the BJP promises it will 'bear true faith and allegiance to the Constitution of India as by law established and to the principles of socialism, secularism and democracy...'

The party's membership form also requires the BJP and its members to be 'committed to nationalism, national integration, democracy, Gandhian approach to socio-economic issues leading to the establishment of an egalitarian society free from exploitation, positive secularism (Sarva Dharma Samabhav) and value-based politics.'

The BJP also says that 'Integral Humanism' is the basic philosophy of the party. The phrase is in upper case because it refers to some specific ideas.

This appears strange, because if it is a philosophy Integral Humanism also does not suggest a change in the State. Is it

---

3. The BJP says it has five principles ('Pancha Nishthas') guiding its politics:
   1. Commitment to nationalism and national integration
   2. Commitment to Democracy
   3. Commitment to Gandhian Socialism (Gandhian approach to socio-economic issues leading to the establishment of a society free from exploitation)
   4. Commitment to positive secularism (sarva dharma samabhav)
   5. Commitment to value-based politics

then the case that the BJP does not seek to move away from the present constitutional order? If so, then what is Hindu Rashtra? What does it offer, and what has it already provided in the years that it has been in charge of the State, by way of change to Hindus in this Hindu Rashtra?

The book seeks to explore this theme. To get a grasp of what it has done to itself, we should also consider what India has not done. How did the other states in South Asia become majoritarian differently from us? This is easy to see. All of them, at some stage in their modern history, have inserted language that discriminates against minorities, and that privileges the majority, into their laws.

Afghanistan is an Islamic state. Both its 1964 and current (2004) Constitution open with 'Bismillah ir rehman ir rahim'. Article 1 declares it to be an Islamic republic and Article 2 says that Islam is the state religion. Article 3 says no law can contravene the tenets of Islam, and this is the usual formulation of Islamic states. It limits the rights non-Muslims can enjoy and ensures that reform is difficult because religious tenets are often codified and usually interpreted in conservative ways.

Article 62 says that only a Muslim can be the president, and the oath of office requires the person to swear allegiance to 'obey and protect the holy religion of Islam'. The two vice-presidents and all ministers are also required to take this oath and therefore presumably can only be Muslim. Supreme Court judges also take an oath swearing to 'attain justice and righteousness in accordance with tenets of the holy religion of Islam'. Article 149 locks in the Islamic nature of the state and specifies that this cannot be amended.

Pakistan is an Islamic republic that also opens its Constitution with 'Bismillah'. Of all the modern South Asian Islamic nations, none has had as full and long a debate on what the nature of the State should be as did Pakistan in the years leading up to 1947 and in the years since. We shall look more closely at how the

Islamic nature of the State was given form over the decades in a later chapter.

Like Afghanistan, Pakistan constitutionally can only be led by a Muslim. Both the president and prime minister must profess the Islamic faith. The oath of office to the president and prime minister also opens with the Bismillah phrase. It contains the line, 'I,————, do solemnly swear that I am a Muslim and believe in the Unity and Oneness of Almighty Allah, the Books of Allah, the Holy Quran being the last of them, the Prophethood of Muhammad (peace be upon him) as the last of the Prophets and that there can be no Prophet after him, the Day of Judgment, and all the requirements and teachings of the Holy Quran and Sunnah.'

The unusual phrasing regarding the prophet is present because Pakistan has an abhorrence of a Muslim sect found mainly in India and Pakistan, which it has apostatised, the Ahmadis.[4] This community had not voted in thirty years because Pakistan had separate electorates for non-Muslims and forced Muslim voters to declare they were not Ahmadi. For Ahmadis, acceptance of their 'non-Muslim' status is problematic and hence, they have chosen to not vote. Passports are also issued only to those Muslims who testify in writing that 'I consider Mirza Ghulam Ahmed Qadiani to be an imposter nabi (prophet) and also consider his followers whether belonging to the Lahori or Qadiani group to be non-Muslim.' Needless to say, Ahmadis do not have any religious freedom and are often killed in targeted violence.

---

4. The Ahmadis (or Ahmadiyyas) belong to a movement that was founded in the late 19th century by Mirza Ghulam Ahmad (1835–1908). Owing to the controversial nature of some of his teachings, including an apparent claim to prophethood, Ahmadis have been at daggers drawn with conservative Muslims. Since the creation of Pakistan, the Ahmadis have been singled out for discrimination. 'Qadiani', meaning from Qadian, the Punjab town (now located in India), where the movement was centred in its initial years has since become a slur in Pakistan.

Maldives is an Islamic state. The 2008 Maldives Constitution says the country 'is a sovereign, independent, democratic Republic based on the principles of Islam'. Article 10 says that 'the religion of the State of the Maldives is Islam. Islam shall be the one of the basis of all the laws of the Maldives.' And that 'no law contrary to any tenet of Islam shall be enacted in the Maldives.' The Constitution gives rights and freedoms conditionally, provided these rights are not 'contrary to any tenet of Islam'. Conduct and activity must also be that which 'is not expressly prohibited by Islamic Shari'ah or by law'.

All parliamentarians (the assembly is called Majlis) must be Sunni Muslims. The president, ministers and all judges must also be Sunni Muslims. While Maldives in the recent past has gone through a process of reform, this aspect has not changed. The 1998 Constitution of Maldives also identified it as an Islamic republic. The attorney general had to be Sunni Muslim and judges were also required to be Muslim. The Constitution said that 'the word "law" also includes the norms and provisions of Shari'ah established by the Noble Quran and the traditions of the Noble Prophet, and the rules derived therefrom.'

Sri Lanka is officially a democratic socialist republic and there is no reference to a state religion. However, the Constitution (Chapter 2) specifies that the 'Republic of Sri Lanka shall give to Buddhism the foremost place'. And because of this, 'accordingly it shall be the duty of the State to protect and foster the Buddha Sasana'. This has led to the government having a ministry of Buddha Sasana, which oversees the affairs of the majority community's religion. The ministry's functions are to act and evaluate policies that 'enhance religious values among the people for building a virtuous society'. It is also charged with implementing programmes and projects that 'protect, foster and enhance Buddha Dhamma'. It must plan and develop sacred areas and it must 'take action to propagate Theravada

Dhamma internationally'. It was set up as the Sri Lanka Arts Council in 1952 because the country's leaders felt that economic development should be accompanied by cultural development. In 1988, a department for Buddhist Affairs was set up to 'promote Buddhism and Buddhist activities'. The ministry was renamed and reformed several times over the decades to include cultural affairs and national heritage, at one time being called the Ministry of Religious Affairs and Moral Upliftment, before acquiring the name, the Ministry of Buddhasasana, cultural and religious affairs in 2010. This appeared to include other faiths in it. In 2015, other religions were removed from its purview and it was meant to promote only Theravada Buddhism.

The Constitution of Bangladesh opens with the phrase 'Bismillah ir rahman ir rahim'. Article 2A says that 'the state religion of the Republic is Islam, but the State shall ensure equal status and equal right in the practice of the Hindu, Buddhist, Christian and other religions'. Article 25 says that 'the State shall endeavour to consolidate, preserve and strengthen fraternal relations among Muslim countries based on Islamic solidarity'. A 2010 order from Bangladesh's Supreme Court apparently restored secularism. It said that the 'preamble and the relevant provisions of the Constitution in respect of secularism, nationalism and socialism, as existed on 15 August 1975, will revive'. However, it left the text on the State's religion untouched. And so, we have the unusual situation of a nation whose Constitution opens with a Quranic verse in the name of Allah, the preamble pledges 'that the high ideals of nationalism, socialism, democracy and secularism shall be the fundamental principles of the Constitution' but there is also a state religion, which is Islam.

Like Dubai, Bangladesh has its weekly holidays on Friday and Saturday and is one of the few nations that works on Sunday. This is a practice that even Pakistan does not follow.

Bhutan is possibly the most theocratic nation in the world. India identified and singled out the two Islamic states of Afghanistan and Pakistan when it justified the passing of the Citizenship Amendment Act in 2019, and threw in Bangladesh for good measure. But Bhutan has escaped attention because it is Buddhist and therefore acceptable to the BJP, though it is more of a religious state than any other in India's neighbourhood.

The hereditary Buddhist king controls both the religion and the State. The Constitution says that 'His Majesty the Druk Gyalpo is the Head of State and the symbol of unity of the Kingdom and of the people of Bhutan' and that 'the Chhoe-sid-nyi of Bhutan shall be unified in the person of the Druk Gyalpo who, as a Buddhist, shall be the upholder of the Chhoe-sid'. Chhoe-sid-nyi is a phrase meaning 'religious and material', and the Druk Gyalpo is the king. He is the person who appoints the Chief Abbott.

Other than the king, no other religious figure can dabble in politics.

The Parliament has no power to amend any of this, per section 26 of Article 2. The king 'shall not be answerable in a court of law for His actions and His person shall be sacrosanct' (Article 2, 15). The primary check on the king is the instruction that he step down at age of sixty-five and pass the power on to the next hereditary ruler.

Religion is introduced with the line: 'Buddhism is the spiritual heritage of Bhutan, which promotes the principles and values of peace, non-violence, compassion and tolerance.' The king is also the 'protector of all religions'.

Till 2008, Nepal was a Hindu Rashtra, the only one in the world. Why was it a Hindu Rashtra? Because executive power flowed from a Kshatriya (Chhetri) king as prescribed in the Manu Smriti. Nepal's 1959 Constitution identifies the head of State as an 'adherent of Aryan culture and Hindu religion'. The

Constitution has no religious freedom as such and 'no person shall be entitled to convert another person to his religion'. A citizen may only 'practice and profess his own religion as handed down from ancient times', meaning no propagation was allowed, a principle still followed in Nepal.

The 1962 Constitution defines Nepal as an 'independent, indivisible and sovereign Hindu State' and repeats the formulation of the king as being Aryan and Hindu. The Raj Sabha or governing council includes the head Brahmin (Bada Gurujyu) and the officiating priest (Mool Purohit). The ban on conversion was rephrased to close the loophole: 'No person shall be entitled to convert another person from one religion to another.'

Nepal's 1990 Constitution defines the country as being 'multiethnic, multilingual, democratic, independent, indivisible, sovereign, Hindu and constitutional monarchical kingdom'. It restates the 'Aryan-ness' and 'Hinduness' of the king and the prohibition on conversion. The Raj Sabha was now called Raj Parishad and the Mool Purohit excluded though the Bada Gurujyu remained.

This is what a Hindu Rashtra is. It is a form of government different from a modern republic and shows in the way that the State and society must adhere to Hindu textual prescription. The government is led by a Kshatriya king guided by Brahmins in his court. Nepal was only to this extent a Hindu Rashtra. No other parts of the prescribed caste hierarchy were applied to the State in Nepal and they could not have been. It would have gone against the Universal Declaration of Human Rights and every single modern law and practice that gives individuals liberty and equality and freedom.

This is also why there will not be any Hindu Rashtra in India either: it is an impossibility. The modern State is defended by a professional army. It is not and cannot be the preserve of one caste, as the Hindu Rashtra desires.[5] The twenty-first century economy must not only include traders, manufacturers and financiers who are not twice-born Vaishya, it also requires economic exchange with foreigners: 'mleccha' in the language of the Hindu texts. Education, science, literature and knowledge outside of the world of rituals is not the monopoly of Brahmins today. We cannot go back to such a state of affairs even if ordered to. Nepal had a warrior ruler by caste, India doesn't. To become a Hindu Rashtra, even merely a formal one such as Nepal was, India would have to dismantle its political and judicial system and hand over executive authority to a hereditary king that it doesn't have. To become a proper Hindu Rashtra as prescribed the State will have to take away from all individuals their freedom of association and all sexual agency.

And then there is the question of acceptance. Even if we were to dismiss or disregard, as the Indian middle class generally tends to do, the resistance of the Dalit and the Adivasi, together a quarter of the Indian population, the majority of the remaining Hindus, the peasantry drawn from the Shudra varna who are today politically the most powerful Indians, would be excluded from power, knowledge and the economy in a real Hindu Rashtra. Meaning that the Patel, Jat, Reddy, Patil, Gowda, Yadav would till their land and stay away from political and economic power. That is not going to happen.

Hindu Rashtra is an illusion. It is also a lie. The name promises something reality will never deliver. When the phrase 'Hindu Rashtra' is used by the Sangh parivar and its adherents, something else is meant. Not the Nepali model of Hindu Rashtra or something along those lines.

---

5. The Dalit activist and writer Chandrabhan Prasad has observed that in the golden age of Hindu Rashtra, the Kshatriya was in charge of defence—but India was the most conquered land in the world, the Vaishya managed the economy—but India was the poorest nation in the world, the Brahmin monopolised learning—but India was the most illiterate place in the world.

The true meaning of Hindu Rashtra is not to be found in a theory of State or a return to some golden age or a change in the Constitution. It is purely about the exclusion and persecution of India's minorities, particularly Muslims. That is the only meaning of Hindu Rashtra in India. It imagines India as a Hindu nation where the Muslim and Christian exist on sufferance. That is all there is to Hindu Rashtra in the way Hindutva desires. It is hollow and bankrupt as an idea once its content of hate and prejudice is emptied out. The acquisition of authority in Hindu Rashtra is not towards bettering the lives of Hindus but damaging, excluding and handicapping those who are not born Hindu. That is the creeping Hindu Rashtra that we are living in and have lived in for decades.

Nepal became a republic in 2008 after the monarchy ended. The law on freedom of religion in the new Constitution, effective from 2015, continues with the ban on conversion. Article 26(3) says: 'While exercising the right as provided for by this Article, no person shall act or make others act in a manner which is contrary to public health, decency and morality, or behave or act or make others act to disturb public law and order situation, or convert a person of one religion to another religion, or disturb the religion of other people. Such an act shall be punishable by law.'

Aligning their constitutions and laws to privilege the majority was presumably to achieve something in particular. But majoritarianism does not seem to have brought India's neighbours the desired results: Pakistan is on its third constitution, Maldives, by some counts, on its sixth, Nepal on its seventh and Sri Lanka on its second. The road is long, and there is never any satisfaction at having finally arrived at whatever utopia the exclusion of minorities is meant to deliver.

This is the story of how India is taking a different route to also reach nowhere. This book is structured in four parts. The first looks at Pakistan and how it became the majoritarian State it is today. This is less obvious than might appear and we hope to introduce new arguments by looking at the same set of facts through a different lens.

The second part is about the core individuals behind the Hindutva ideology and their intellectual output, which has been examined and connected to its politics. This chapter tracks the Rashtriya Swayamsevak Sangh's entry into politics and the elements it introduced into India's democracy leading to the triumph of the Bharatiya Janata Party.

The third part, the longest, is the manner in which the democratic, secular republic of India has become majoritarian by law over time. India has done so in more devious fashion than Pakistan, by privileging Hindutva and discriminating against and restricting the rights of its minorities, while pretending to be secular and pluralist. This book will show how.

The fourth part, the final chapter, is about more recent events. It looks at the way in which brute force majoritarianism was successfully resisted in democratic and peaceful ways in our time. It also examines how the Constitution handicaps the individual freedoms of Indians and how, despite these handicaps, those standing for pluralism and secularism can fight back against what has happened and is happening to the Indian State under Hindutva.

1

PARTITION WITHOUT EMOTION

Our story must begin with the Partition. The division of India and the creation of Pakistan in 1947 is understood by Hindutva as the result of Congress weakness and the perfidy of Muslims. Such an oversimplistic understanding holds that Muslims were insistent on division and that mere resolve to keep the country together in the face of Muslim separatism would have been sufficient to thwart them. Had someone with more backbone been in charge then, he would have kept Bharat Mata intact or so goes the thinking. This version has not been challenged in the popular media and has found wide currency in a voting population that has been indoctrinated through phrases like 'tukde tukde gang', meaning those who want India deliberately broken up. It may surprise them to know that Lala Lajpat Rai, the lion of Punjab and part of the Lal-Bal-Pal nationalist trio, was also a member of the tukde tukde gang.

The reality of the events of 1947 was that they sprang out of Congress strength and not its weakness. It was the refusal of the Congress to give India's Muslims their reasonable share in power, especially at the Centre, that ultimately led to Partition. A fairer and more honest way of looking at the sequence of events would be to accommodate what happened in the decades leading up to 1947. Aware that the British rule would give way to some form of autonomy and eventually independence, India's communities began positioning themselves for the future. Those were the years when it was not obvious that a break up of India was the only solution to the communal problem, and many of those years were times when reasonableness and compromise on both sides heralded the promise of a future that was ultimately not to be.

Let us examine this period.

In 1905, the British under Lord Curzon partitioned Bengal. The Bengal of that time was a large province comprising in addition to today's West Bengal and Bangladesh, large parts of Bihar, Orissa, as also Assam and other areas conquered by the colonial State. This meant that it was a large and fairly unmanageable unit. The administrative separation was justified but it was resisted, especially by the Hindu landlords of what had become East Bengal, because they would be separated from Calcutta where they had residences.

The Hindu majority of West Bengal centred in Calcutta would now dominate a much smaller Bengal, and feared they would face competition for their jute industry from East Bengal through a rival port at Chittagong and the creation of jute factories there. Under the Indian National Congress, Hindus retaliated with a swadeshi call. This involved a boycott by the public of British goods and involved large numbers of people: it transformed the Congress into a mass organisation from a mostly middle-class grouping. The movement forced the British to undo Bengal's partition a few years later, in part because they wanted to avoid the accusation of 'divide and rule'. Bengal's Muslims resented the undoing, because under the partitioned status they had their own capital and a larger say in affairs since Calcutta, the capital of this large province (and British India at that time) had been separated from them. It was also during this movement against the partition of Bengal that Vande Mataram, the Hindu nationalism trope, became popular as the anthem of Indian nationalism.

The Muslim League was formed in 1906 in Dhaka, the capital of the new province of East Bengal and Assam that they had secured, and this was also the year in which Muslims made their first formal demand for political representation as a community. In 1909, reforms were put in place that for the first time allowed elections at the provincial level and gave Indians some limited say in government (though not at the Centre). These were known as the Morley-Minto reforms under which Muslims were given a separate electorate. This meant reserved seats in which only Muslims could vote, ensuring that they would be proportionally represented.

In 1915 and 1916, the Indian National Congress and the Muslim League met jointly, first in Bombay and then in Lucknow. The second meeting produced an agreement, called the Lucknow Pact. The Congress agreed formally to separate electorates for Muslims and both parties then jointly demanded from the British a greater say in running India. The power dynamics within the Muslim League (which was controlled by a Muslim elite drawn largely from north India) were reflected in this agreement. It gave Muslims in the United Provinces (roughly today's Uttar Pradesh and Uttarakhand) half the seats, though they were only 14 per cent of the population in those parts. And it took away the majority that Muslims enjoyed in the number of seats in Bengal and reduced the majority to parity in Punjab.

Mohammad Ali Jinnah, then a barrister practising in Bombay, was one of the negotiators of the Lucknow Pact, and one of the few people to be a member of both the Congress and the Muslim League at the time. It is important to note that of the registered members of Congress in this period and the years to follow, the number of Muslims was miniscule. The 1914 Congress had a total of 856 delegates, in 1915 there were 2190 and in 1916 there were 2249. Of these, the number of Muslims was less than 1 per cent in 1914, 2 per cent in 1915 and 3 per cent in 1916. In a speech on 19 September 1926 in Kanpur, Motilal Nehru had said: 'I can go one step further and say that even the Congress is a Hindu body. Some Muhammedans had certainly joined it in 1920-21, otherwise it has been a purely Hindu body from its very start.' The numbers show that the Congress before independence was the party of Hindus, just as the League was that of Muslims, though formally the Congress, as it continues to do today, claimed wider representation.

M.K. Gandhi's arrival from South Africa in 1915 resulted in a series of actions from the Congress with mass public participation, some of which were meant to unite Hindus and Muslims in civic action. One such was the Khilafat movement (1919-23), which sought to insert India's Muslims into the Turkish conflict with the West. The Khilafat movement's aim was to restore the leadership of the Ottoman Caliph or khalifa, who considered himself the leader of all Sunni Muslims, as an effective political authority in Istanbul. It was also a protest against the sanctions placed on the Caliph and the Ottoman Empire after Turkey's defeat in the First World War. Jinnah, who had marginal interest in such an issue, warned against religion mixing with politics, but was overshadowed by Gandhi in this period even in gatherings that had a large Muslim presence. This movement produced some Hindu-Muslim unity, and made Gandhi a national leader. However it came to an end in 1923 when the Turkish warrior-statesman Mustafa Kemal 'Ataturk' (who was irritated by the Indian interference) abolished the caliphate and expelled the Western powers from areas controlled by Turkey.

Gandhi's non-cooperation movement, which Jinnah as a Congressman had opposed and for which he was booed by Gandhi's supporters, also ended in 1922 when protestors burnt alive twenty-two policemen in Chauri Chaura, near Gorakhpur. Gandhi had suspended the movement since he believed that non-violence as an article of faith could not be compromised with. This movement was in opposition to the British government's use of preventive detention in cases of sedition, though it was used more moderately by the British than it is in India today.

For many Hindus, including those inside Congress, the idea that Muslims had separate electorates was unacceptable. In November and December 1924, Lala Lajpat Rai wrote a series of articles on the 'Hindu-Muslim problem', which were published in the *Hindustan Times*, the *Tribune*, *Bombay Chronicle* and *Swarajjya*. He was convinced that the continuation of separate electorates for Muslims was inconsistent with Indian nationalism and could not be allowed to continue. Muslim leaders like Jinnah who spoke in favour of separate electorates were not nationalists. Separate electorates were wrong to Rai's mind because they could never be abolished except through civil war.

Hindus opposed the empowerment of Muslims because they suspected Muslims were planning to establish Muslim rule in India with the help of foreign states. So long as the Muslims insisted on separate electorates, the British would never leave India. This was the crux of the Hindu-Muslim problem, according to Rai. On 14 December, 1924, he published his solution in the *Tribune*: 'My suggestion is that the Punjab should be partitioned into two provinces, the Western Punjab with a large Muslim majority to be a Muslim-governed province; and the Eastern Punjab with a large Hindu-Sikh majority to be a non-Muslim governed province."

He did not think it imaginable that the 'rich and highly progressive and alive Hindus of Bengal' would ever agree to work with Bengali Muslims. And so he proposed to divide Bengal along communal lines also. 'Under my scheme, the Muslims will have four Muslim states: 1) The Pathan Province or the

North-West Frontier; 2) Western Punjab; 3) Sind; and 4) Eastern Bengal.' He concluded: 'It means a clear partition of India into a Muslim India and a non-Muslim India.' Remember that this was 1924, almost a quarter century before Partition and years before even the word 'Pakistan' had been coined.

Historian K.K. Aziz wrote that 'in clarity, detail and firmness this proposal is a landmark in the evolution of the idea of Pakistan. There is no vagueness or confusion about the situation. This is the first clear scheme of Partition.' In his four-volume *History of Partition of India*, Aziz has recorded the growth of the idea of Partition between 1858 and 1940. A majority of the proposals even as late as the 1931-40 period (eighteen out of thirty-three) were from non-Muslims. Of a total of fifty-six different proposals for partitioning India (such as Lala Lajpat Rai's) recorded between 1858 and 1940, when the Pakistan Resolution was finally moved, the majority (thirty-four) came from non-Muslims.

On 20 March 1927, Jinnah called an all-Muslim parties meeting to discuss the possibility of giving up separate electorates and under what conditions Muslims would be willing to accept a joint electorate. These became known as the Delhi Proposals. They proposed that: 1) Muslims would give up separate electorates in favour of joint electorates with reserved seats for Muslims. 2) One-third representation to Muslims in the Centre. 3) Reserved representation to Muslims in Punjab and Bengal in proportion to their population.4) Formation of three new Muslim majority provinces—Sindh, Baluchistan and North-West Frontier Province.

Jinnah's Delhi Proposals were accepted by the Congress, but were vetoed by the Hindu Mahasabha led by Madan Mohan Malaviya, which did not want Muslim majorities in Bengal and Punjab. The Congress succumbed to the Hindu Mahasabha, even though Maulana Abul Kalam Azad backed Jinnah's proposals.

In 1928, an all-parties conference resulted in the Nehru Report, authored by Motilal Nehru, Jawaharlal Nehru's father. It proposed a comprehensive makeover of the existing system of government. It was progressive in many ways, including on the matter of gender equality and fundamental rights. However, it was a step back for the Muslims from what they had negotiated with the Congress in Lucknow. The Nehru Report took away their separate electorates, replacing them with reserved seats for Muslims (in proportion to their numbers) under joint electorates, with the right to contest the general seats. It rejected reserved seats for Muslims in Punjab and Bengal (point no. 3 of Jinnah's proposals). And it made no reference to his most crucial point about one-third representation to Muslims at the Centre. The Congress leadership accepted these recommendations, and did not even acknowledge Jinnah's proposals, creating a major fault-line that would remain all the way to Partition.

Motilal Nehru wrote to Gandhi on 14 August 1929, urging him to work with the Hindu Mahasabha to sabotage Jinnah's proposals: 'We (Nehru and the Hindu Mahasabha leadership) agreed that the Hindu opposition to the Muslim demands was to continue and even be stiffened up by the time the Convention was held... You will see that the stumbling block in our way is this question of one-third Muslim representatives and on this point even the most advanced Musalmans like Dr. M.A. Ansari, Maulana Abul Kalam Azad, Mr. T.A.K. Sherwani and others are all very strongly in favour of the concession. I would therefore ask you to direct your attention now to the Mahasabha leaving Ali Brothers and Mr. Jinnah to stew in their own juice.'

The Muslim League rejected Motilal Nehru's report and in response Jinnah proposed fourteen points under which an agreement could be made. His primary demands were:

a) A federal India with residuary power in the provinces.

b) Uniform autonomy to all provinces.

c)   Effective representation of minorities. A continuation of the separate electorates, with the option to abandon them in favour of a joint electorate at any time, if the community so desired. (Jinnah, a liberal South Bombay lawyer with a Gujarati background that brought him into contact with Hindus, Parsis and others, had himself not originally been a strong proponent of separate electorates but came to recognise that Muslim rights would not be automatically be conceded.)

d)   No territorial redistribution of provinces that would affect existing majorities in Bengal, the North West Frontier Province (NWFP, today known as Khyber Pakhtunkhwa) and Punjab.

e)   Freedom of religion and constitutional safeguards for the protection of Muslim personal law, language, culture and charitable institutions.

f)   One-third representation of Muslims in all Cabinets, Central as well as provincial.

g)   No changes in the Constitution at the Centre without the consent of the states.

The main differences between the League, particularly Jinnah, and the Congress, particularly Jawaharlal Nehru, emerged at this point and were never to be fully resolved.

The same year (1929), the British announced that India could not have unrepresentative central government forever and that dominion status (as a self-governing territory, like Australia and Canada even today) was the ultimate goal. The views of Indians would be sought on this and this was to be enabled through the Round Table conferences to be held between 1930 and 1932. These did not produce any agreement among the Indians and it was left to the British to make reforms on their own. This resulted in the Communal Award of 1932.

Under it, Muslims were again given separate electorates, along with reservations and special constituencies for other communities. Gandhi went on a fast to resist the awarding of separate electorates to the depressed classes (Dalits in today's parlance) and a protracted negotiation with B.R. Ambedkar produced the Poona Pact. Ambedkar agreed to give up separate electorates for Dalits in favour of reserved constituencies, an act he would regret.

The next step was the Government of India Act of 1935 which was a sort of constitution and in many ways quite similar to the present Indian Constitution. It retained a strong Centre and set up some of the structures under which legislation and the dispensation of justice would take place. The Congress and the Muslim League did not fully approve of the 1935 Act but decided nonetheless to participate in the scheme. In 1937, elections were held under the new rules and the Congress secured majorities in Bombay, Bihar, Central Provinces, Madras, Orissa, United Provinces and the North West Frontier Province. The last win was due to the fact that the charismatic Pashtun leader Dr Khan Sahib (the older brother of Gandhi's associate, Khan Abdul Ghaffar Khan or Frontier Gandhi, who was also in the Congress) was a Congressman in a Muslim-majority province.

Perry Anderson ('Why Partition', *London Review of Books*, 19 July 2012) writes that: 'Nehru's first real test as a political leader came with the elections of 1937. No longer an adjutant of Gandhi, who had withdrawn to the wings after 1934, he was president of Congress in the year of its triumph at the polls and the formation of its first regional governments. Crowing over the results, Nehru announced there were now only two political forces that mattered in India: Congress and the British government. There is little doubt that, with fateful self-deception, he believed this. In fact, it was a confessional victory. By this time, the membership of Congress was 97 per cent Hindu. It could not even find candidates to run in close to

90 per cent of Muslim constituencies across India. In Nehru's own province, Uttar Pradesh, then as now the most populous in India, Congress had swept the board of Hindu seats. But it had not won a single Muslim seat.'

Jinnah was open to cooperation and offered to be part of a coalition. However, Nehru insisted that the League dissolve itself and its members join the ministries as Congressmen. This was not acceptable to Jinnah. Congress ministries made Vande Mataram compulsory in the legislative assemblies they won and also prohibited cow slaughter. The sense of compromise and progress that was promised in Lucknow seemed to have come to an end by this time.

In 1940, feeling marginalised by the way in which the Congress had operated, the Muslim League resolved to resist any plan for a new constitution that would not specify that the North West zones (Punjab, Sindh, the NWFP) and the East (Bengal) in which Muslims were a majority should be designated as independent states, which would be autonomous. The minorities of these places would be given religious, cultural and other rights in consultation with them. Reciprocally, they would hope that Muslim minorities in other parts of India would get the same rights through consultation.

This resolution was made in Lahore in 1940, and it was here that Jinnah announced that India's Muslims were not a minority but a nation. From now the political division between Hindus and Muslims was bitter and communal. The Lahore Resolution was adopted in the second year of the Second World War, at a time when the British were still sitting it out in France and refusing to join battle against the Nazis. Over the next couple of years, prime minister Winston Churchill would come under enormous military pressure from Germany and the British were vulnerable in India to mass mobilisation by the Congress. A few months after the Lahore Resolution, Gandhi launched the

Civil Disobedience Movement and the empire, less tolerant in a time of crisis, put him in jail for long periods, along with senior members of the party like Nehru, Azad and Patel. The Congress had by then resigned its ministries stating that the British had not taken the consent of Indians before declaring war on Germany and Japan on India's behalf.

Jinnah benefitted from this absence of the Congress. The British took over the functioning in provinces where the Congress had resigned and the Muslim League in any case had ministries in some states including Assam, Bengal, Punjab and Sindh.

In 1942, the British proposed a Constituent Assembly comprising of elected representatives from provinces and nominated ones from the princely states. Both Congress and the Muslim League rejected this.

In August that year, Gandhi launched the Quit India Movement seeking independence and calling for non-violent civil disobedience. In 1944, as Stalin's Russians had vanquished the Nazis and allied victory was around the corner, Gandhi was released.

After the end of the world war, elections were held in India in 1945-46. Across India, Muslims voting in separate electorates chose Jinnah unanimously as their leader over Nehru and Gandhi. Of the 495 Muslim seats in the provinces, the Muslim League won 446, losing only the North West Frontier Province though it did well (17/36) even there. In the Central Assembly it took all the Muslim seats. Congress swept the general seats of course, winning over 900 seats. The Hindu Mahasabha contested a few seats and lost all. It was clear after this election that Congress under Nehru and Gandhi represented India's Hindus and Jinnah India's Muslims.

That year, 1946, came the final proposal which could have helped preserve an undivided India. This was the Cabinet Mission

Plan. It rejected Jinnah's demand for two states and instead offered a federal structure with the Centre only controlling defence, foreign affairs and communications.

The rest would be decided later by the constituent bodies. British India would be divided into three zones. Zone A was more or less what is today India, Zone B what is today Pakistan and Zone C what is Bangladesh but including Assam. These three zones would first work on their provincial constitutions and then their representatives would meet with those of the princely states situated within their zones to hammer out the Union constitution.

The central government would have an executive and legislature drawn from the three zones and the princely states. All questions concerning major communal issues would require the minority to be present and voting before a decision could be taken.

Jinnah felt Muslim interests had been provided sufficient safeguards in this plan and accepted it, giving up Partition and moving away substantially from the Lahore Declaration. The Congress, under the presidentship of Maulana Azad, accepted as well. But Nehru, who soon became Congress president, said that he was free to alter or modify the Cabinet Mission Plan once the British were gone.

This effectively sabotaged the agreement and Jinnah backed out.

What followed was communal violence, especially in Bihar and Bengal as Jinnah called for 'Direct Action'. In July 1946, elections were held again, this time for the Constituent Assembly in which the Congress alliance won 212 seats. The Muslim League won 73 seats, again cementing its position as the voice of India's Muslims. Wary after the Cabinet Mission experience, Jinnah did not join the Constituent Assembly and instead demanded Partition.

In March 1947, Mountbatten arrived as the last British Viceroy of India and after a failed attempt at reconciliation, announced that the British would partition the country. Members of those provinces which had boycotted the Constituent Assembly (meaning the Muslim League ones) would vote on whether they wanted to join that Assembly or another. In effect, this was a choice between India and Pakistan. Bengal's and Punjab's assemblies would meet in two parts, Muslims separately from Hindus, to vote independently. All the Muslim provinces chose Pakistan.

Bengal, with a Muslim majority of 56 per cent and Punjab, with a Muslim majority of 51 per cent per cent would be partitioned with one wing each to India and Pakistan. Jinnah was expecting a division that would leave the west (Punjab, Sindh, NWFP) and all of Bengal including Assam as intact units that would go to Pakistan. He objected, but had no leverage at this stage when things were rapidly unfolding and the British wanted out.

Thus came the Partition of India. It happened three decades after Jinnah had first hammered out an agreement with the Congress in Lucknow to share power proportionately. It was not the whim of an individual, the weakness of a party or the desire of Muslims to break up Bharat Mata that produced Partition and Pakistan.

It was the inability of India's Hindus, led by the Congress, to arrive at a power-sharing mechanism that would grant political rights to the world's largest religious minority.

Had Congress not rejected separate electorates, Pakistan would not have happened. Had Jinnah's proposals in 1927 for one-third representation at the Centre not been rejected by Congress after being accepted, India would have not been partitioned. Had Congress not sabotaged Jinnah's compromise formula, the communal divide would not have been as bitter.

Had Nehru accepted the Cabinet Mission plan, with a federal structure and a relatively weak centre, India would have come into freedom intact.

But Nehru wanted a strong Centre, as India continues to have and as the RSS have always insisted on, with states having little power or voice in Union affairs. Any assertion of independence of action by the federating units is seen as secession. In effect, an aggressively expansionist colonial State was overnight renamed independent India. Those areas which had been subdued by the gun, such as the Northeast, continued to be in turmoil and remain so even today.

Jinnah's concerns about how India would treat its minorities on achieving independence have been fully validated. His insistence on separate electorates with the option of voluntary integration was eminently sensible.

A.G. Noorani writing in *Frontline* ('Assessing Jinnah', 26 August 2005) quoted him as saying that 'the only hope for minorities is to organise themselves and secure a definite share in power to safeguard their rights and interests'. And that 'all safeguards and settlements would be a scrap of paper unless they were backed up by power'. In Britain, the parties alternate in holding power. 'But such is not the case in India. Here we have a permanent Hindu majority.'

That is the case. In 2019, the party running the Indian government had 303 Lok Sabha MPs of whom none was a Muslim. In 2014, this ruling party had 282 Lok Sabha seats, of whom none was a Muslim. That is 585 Lok Sabha seats with zero Muslims. This is the permanent Hindu majority Jinnah spoke about and which has always existed in India and only been made obvious in our time.

Noorani says of Jinnah that he 'was an Indian nationalist who did not believe that nationalism meant turning one's back on the rights of one's community. The Congress stipulated that, virtually. Its shabby record on Muslims in the Congress bears recalling.' He recalled that Sarojini Naidu did not change her opinion of the man even after he began to advocate Partition. At a press conference in Madras on 18 January 1945, she described him as the one incorruptible man in the whole of India. 'I may not agree with him, but if there is one who cannot be bought by title, honour or position, it is Mr Mohammed Ali Jinnah.'

It is incorrect and cruel therefore to say that Muslims partitioned India when their every attempt under Jinnah was to try and preserve the Union. It is equally wrong to assume that a weak Congress capitulated. It is the strength and backing received from over 90 per cent of the Hindus, that gave Congress the arrogance to go it alone and dismiss the legitimate demands of India's Muslims. Noorani notes that Jinnah's communal politics after 1940 cannot erase his brave attempts at compromise and reconciliation in the decades before that. And Nehru's brave defence of secularism after independence cannot take away from his actions or those of the Congress before Partition. This is the background to the events that led to the breaking up of India.

2

THE HOUSE THAT JINNAH BUILT

Having secured an independent nation for his community, what sort of State did Jinnah want in Pakistan? Was he in favour of a secular constitution as is sometimes suggested and if so, what is the evidence for that? Or was Pakistan envisaged as a theocratic nation for the Muslim community?

In a famous speech made to Pakistan's Constituent Assembly on 11 August 1947, Jinnah said that the task before it was to deliver a provisional constitution, act as a legislative assembly and draft the permanent constitution. In his mind, Jinnah saw an inclusive Pakistan. He said: 'If you change your past and work together in a spirit that every one of you, no matter to what community he belongs, no matter what relations he had with you in the past, no matter what is his colour, caste, or creed, is first, second, and last a citizen of this State with equal rights, privileges, and obligations, there will be no end to the progress you will make.'

He goes on: 'I cannot emphasise it too much. We should begin to work in that spirit, and in course of time all these angularities of the majority and minority communities, the Hindu community and the Muslim community—because even as regards Muslims you have Pathans, Punjabis, Shias, Sunnis and so on, and among the Hindus you have Brahmins, Vaishnavas, Khatris, also Bengalees, Madrasis and so on—will vanish.'

Jinnah says divisions of identity have held India back: 'Indeed if you ask me, this has been the biggest hindrance in the way of India to attain freedom and independence, and but for this we would have been free people long, long ago. No power can hold another nation, and specially, a nation of 400 million souls, in subjection; nobody could have conquered you, and even if it had happened, nobody could have continued its hold on you for any length of time, but for this.'

He continues: 'Therefore, we must learn a lesson from this. You are free; you are free to go to your temples, you are free to go to your mosques or to any other place or worship in this State of Pakistan. You may belong to any religion or caste or creed—that has nothing to do with the business of the State. As you know, history shows that in England, conditions, some time ago, were much worse than those prevailing in India today. The Roman Catholics and the Protestants persecuted each other. Even now there are some states in existence where there are discriminations made and bars imposed against a particular class. Thank God, we are not starting in those days. We are starting in the days where there is no discrimination, no distinction between one community and another, no discrimination between one caste or creed and another. We are starting with this fundamental principle: that we are all citizens, and equal citizens, of one State. The people of England in course of time had to face the realities of the situation, and had to discharge the responsibilities and burdens placed upon them by the government of their country; and they went through that fire step by step. Today, you might say with justice that Roman Catholics and Protestants do not exist; what exists now is that every man is a citizen, an equal citizen of Great Britain, and they are all members of the nation.'

Jinnah says this is also the ideal that he is reaching for: 'Now I think we should keep that in front of us as our ideal, and you will find that in course of time Hindus would cease to be Hindus, and Muslims would cease to be Muslims, not in the religious sense, because that is the personal faith of each individual, but in the political sense as citizens of the State.'

This speech, made four days before Partition and Independence, is the one that liberal Pakistanis use most often to make their case that the founder of Pakistan wanted a secular constitution. This is the only such instance that can be produced, and Jinnah had qualified his remarks earlier in the speech by cautioning: 'I cannot make any well-considered pronouncement at this moment but I shall say a few things as they occur to me.'

Also the speech was a brief and rambling one in which Jinnah was formally thanking the assembly for electing him its president. He speaks of other things also, for instance the evils Pakistan would have to guard against, listing corruption, black-marketing and nepotism. He ends by reading out a letter sent to him by the United States Secretary of State George C. Marshall. The bit about the nature of the constitution is in the middle of the speech.

However it cannot be denied that in a few words, Jinnah addressed some fundamental issues and tells us what he envisaged when it came to Pakistan's minorities. He specified that he saw for them equal rights, freedom of religion and no discrimination. And the reason he brought this up comes earlier in the speech, where he said of Partition that "'... in this division it was impossible to avoid the question of minorities being in one Dominion or the other. Now that was unavoidable. There is no other solution. Now what shall we do? Now, if we want to make this great state of Pakistan happy and prosperous, we should wholly and solely concentrate on the well-being of the people, and especially of the masses and the poor.'

Over the years leading up to Partition and in the months after it, Jinnah appears to have never used the word 'secular' in describing what he thought Pakistan's Constitution ought to be. He may not have been pressed particularly hard to use the word. The Indian Constitution's Preamble did not use the word secular either till it was introduced in the 1970s. And the only other place in India's Constitution the word 'secular' is used (in Article 25A) is in the meaning of the word as temporal, separating it from the religious. Not in the sense of inclusion as is intended in the Preamble.

On the other hand, Jinnah appeared to have been convinced that Pakistan's Constitution would reflect Islamic principles in some form. And on this issue he had spoken several times.

Addressing the Karachi Bar Association on 25 January 1948, Jinnah said he 'could not understand a section of the people who deliberately wanted to create mischief and made propaganda that the constitution of Pakistan would not be made on the basis of Shariat ... Islamic principles today are as applicable to life as they were thirteen hundred years ago ... Non-Muslims have nothing to fear ... Islam has taught us democracy. Let us make it (the future constitution of Pakistan). We shall make it and show it to the world.'

At the Shahi Darbar in Sibi, Balochistan on 14 February 1948, Jinnah said: 'It is my belief that our salvation lies in following the golden rules of conduct set for us by our great lawgiver, the Prophet of Islam (peace be upon him). Let us lay the foundation of our democracy on the basis of truly Islamic ideals and principles.'

He said it was the job of the Constituent Assembly to draft the constitution, but even here he was careful to address religion.

On 26 February 1948, in a broadcast from Karachi he said: 'The Constitution of Pakistan has yet to be framed ... I do not know what the ultimate shape of this Constitution is going to be, but I am sure that it will be of a democratic type, embodying the essential principles of Islam. Today, they are as applicable in actual life as they were 1300 years ago. Islam and its idealism have taught us democracy. It has taught equality of men, justice and fair play to everybody. We are the inheritors of these glorious traditions and are fully alive to our responsibilities and obligations as framers of the future constitution of Pakistan. In any case, Pakistan is not going to be a theocratic state—to be ruled by priests with a divine mission. We have non-Muslims— they are all Pakistanis. They will enjoy same rights and privileges as any other citizen.'

On 18 April 1948 at Edwards College in Peshawar, he said: 'What more can one really expect than to see that this mighty land has now been brought under a rule, which is Islamic, Muslim rule, as a sovereign independent State.'

On 28 March 1948, he made a speech on Radio Pakistan's Dacca station where he said: 'Pakistan is the embodiment of the unity of the Muslim nation and so it must remain.' Two days before that in Chittagong, he described Pakistan as 'this biggest Muslim State'.

On 26 November 1945, Jinnah had said at Peshawar: 'You have asked me in your welcome address what would be the law in Pakistan. It is an absurd question. Muslims have faith in one God, one Holy Prophet and one Book. This is the only law for the Muslims. Islam will be the basic law of Pakistan and no law repugnant to Islam will be enforced in Pakistan.'

What were these principles, laws, and rules of conduct? This was not apparent. Jinnah was not a scholar of Islam, but even if he had been it would not have been easy to derive from the politics of early Islamic history ideas and principles that would help create a specific constitution. Prophet Muhammad had a written covenant in the city of Medina which can be seen as a law. It specified some tribal codes with regard to blood money and the duties of the city's Jewish population. But it is not a constitution in the sense that we understand the word to be.

Even history and practice were unable to provide concrete direction. Prophet Muhammad had no successor on the religious side, and Muslims say he is the last prophet and the Quran is a complete book needing no sequel or revision. On the temporal side, he was succeeded by members of his tribe, the Quraish. The four caliphs who came after him were chosen by a sort of tribal consensus. After them, the Ummayad dynasty, whose members were also Quraish, seized power and they were also recognised as legitimate by Sunni Muslims. There had never been an ideal Islamic model of the State even in its early history. This is why no two Muslim nations had the same constitution, no agreement of what the ideal Islamic State should be like and no settled method of succession.

Jinnah appeared to be alert to the nature of the problem of Islamic law: the fact that what Islamic democracy actually consisted of was vague, while the danger to its minorities was concrete. This is what his August 11 speech was meant for.

Jinnah died in Karachi on 11 September 1948 at the age of seventy-one, with Pakistan's Constitution unwritten. He had been suffering from tuberculosis, a fact kept secret from the world by his physician, Dr Jal Patel. Six months later, on 7 March 1949, Jinnah's heir Liaquat Ali Khan introduced to the Constituent Assembly a resolution called the 'Aims and Objects of the Constitution', later to be popularly referred to as the Objectives Resolution.

This is the document that began the formal Islamising of Pakistani law and took the country towards a particular direction. The text of Liaquat's resolution was as follows:

'In the name of Allah, the Beneficent, the Merciful;

Whereas sovereignty over the entire universe belongs to Allah Almighty alone and the authority which He has delegated to the State of Pakistan, through its people for being exercised within the limits prescribed by Him is a sacred trust;

This Constituent Assembly representing the people of Pakistan resolves to frame a Constitution for the sovereign independent State of Pakistan;

Wherein the State shall exercise its powers and authority through the chosen representatives of the people;

Wherein the principles of democracy, freedom, equality, tolerance and social justice as enunciated by Islam shall be fully observed;

Wherein the Muslims shall be enabled to order their lives in the individual and collective spheres in accordance with the teachings and requirements of Islam as set out in the Holy Quran and the Sunnah;

Wherein adequate provision shall be made for the minorities to freely profess and practice their religions and develop their cultures;

Wherein the territories now included in or in accession with Pakistan and such other territories as may hereafter be included in or accede to Pakistan shall form a Federation wherein the units will be autonomous with such boundaries and limitations on their powers and authority as may be prescribed;

Wherein shall be guaranteed fundamental rights including equality of status, of opportunity and before law, social, economic and political justice, and freedom of thought, expression, belief, faith, worship and association, subject to law and public morality;

Wherein adequate provisions shall be made to safeguard the legitimate interests of minorities and backward and depressed classes;

Wherein the independence of the Judiciary shall be fully secured;

Wherein the integrity of the territories of the Federation, its independence and all its rights including its sovereign rights on land, sea and air shall be safeguarded;

So that the people of Pakistan may prosper and attain their rightful and honoured place amongst the nations of the world and make their full contribution towards international peace and progress and happiness of humanity.'

Having introduced the resolution, Pakistan's prime minister made a speech in which he explained why it was important for the nation's laws to have a religious orientation. Liaquat, educated at Oxford, was the most prominent Muslim League leader after Jinnah. It is clear from his speech that he anticipated some pushback on the text of the resolution.

The following is a summary of how he justified it.

Jinnah had spoken on the issue of the future constitution several times in unmistakable terms and his views had been endorsed several times through the Muslim League's electoral victories. Pakistan had been founded not only because undivided India's Muslims wanted to build their lives in alignment with Islam but also to put into practice a new form of Islamic government.

This project would address the problems that had crept into humanity. Material and scientific development had leapt ahead of the development of the human individual. The result was that man was able to produce inventions that could destroy the world and society (atomic weapons had been used against the Japanese only a few years earlier). This had happened only because man had chosen to ignore his spiritual side and if he had retained more faith in god, this problem would not have come up.

It was religion that tempered the dangers of science and as Muslims, Pakistanis would adhere to Islam's ideals and make a contribution to the world. This was why the preamble began by surrendering all authority to god. The Pakistan project was to be in contradiction to modern political ideas going back to Machiavelli, separating ethics from the State and from governance. It was a positive instrument of beneficence and not negative. Misuse would be prevented because Pakistanis would ensure that power was exercised in accordance with Islam's standards.

The first principle of preventing misuse was that this power would be exercised through elected representatives and not through dictatorship. The Objectives Resolution's specification that State authority would be in the hands of 'chosen representatives' also eliminated the danger of theocracy, which was the rule of priests. In any case, theocracy was impossible in Islam because it had no priesthood or religious authority like the papacy. Therefore those who suspected that Pakistan was headed down the path of theocracy were wrong.

The question would arise that why was this new thing called Islamic democracy being introduced through the Objectives Resolution. It spoke of democracy, freedom, equality, tolerance and social justice, but as they had been expressed in Islam. It had been necessary to qualify the words because democracy was not understood uniformly around the world. The United States and the Soviet Union both claimed to be republics and democracies but they were not alike.

Pakistan's democracy would be one where not just the government but society would also be democratic in the idea of being one of equals. Even in its decadent period Islam was free of the prejudices of discrimination which affected other societies. Muslim states had a great record of tolerance even in the Middle Ages and didn't have such things as the Inquisition. Minorities had always been treated well by Muslims because of a legal obligation arising from religion.

The evidence of this was that there was no Muslim nation without a strong minority population, where they had the freedom to keep their religion and culture. The best example of this was in fact India. It was under Muslim rule that religious texts were translated from Sanskrit to the regional languages.

Islamic social justice in Pakistan would not be that of forcible regimentation. It would ensure on the basis of its laws that people would be free of material need as well as free in other ways. The State's enabling of Muslims to lead their lives in alignment with Islam did not concern non-Muslims so obviously they should not have a problem with the reference to that.

On the other hand, Jinnah and other leaders of the Muslim League had made it clear in the struggle to achieve Pakistan that their demand was based on the fact that Muslims had a particular code of conduct and way of life. Islam was not just a relationship between the individual and god, but a contract also with the State.

The new state could therefore not just be a neutral observer allowing Muslims to merely freely practise their faith. Pakistan had been formed so that the State would enable the practice of religion for Muslims in the correct manner.

Islam sought to guide society through prescribing and enforcing specific social behaviour. It would direct the activities of Muslims which in turn would produce a new and better society. All Muslim sects agreed that the Quran and the life of the prophet (his customs and practices, collected in the Sunnah) were the basic sources of inspiration. Because of this, no Muslim sect should fear the State to come, because it would not be sectarian.

The State would try to unite all Muslim sects, though it would not curb the freedom of any sect to practice the faith as it wanted. The sect of the majority (in this case, Hanafi Sunni) would not be allowed to dictate to others. The State that would be produced would be something of a laboratory. The experiments conducted in it would demonstrate to the world that Islam was progressive and provide remedies for humanity's problems.

It would not be the ideal State if it ignored the rights of minorities. It would be unIslamic to do so. Islam was firmly opposed to imposing itself where it wasn't wanted. Minorities would in no way be hindered from professing and protecting their religion and developing their culture. Pakistan's Muslims were aware of the fact that the minorities could make a contribution, and minorities should look forward to a period of full freedom.

The State would be federal because its two units (East and West Pakistan) were separated by 1600 kilometres and so a unitary State was impossible. The Assembly would figure out how best to distribute subjects between the Centre and the two units of East and West Pakistan.

Fundamental rights would be given without restrictions else that would make them meaningless. The government would be truly liberal. Everyone would be equal before the law, but personal law would remain protected. Islamic principles would also be applied to the economy to better distribute wealth and eradicate poverty. Minorities from the backward classes would be given special protection because their plight was not the result of their own doing.

The Objectives Resolution was the first step towards the creation of an environment which would do all of the above. It was not often that a great nation was created with a clean slate and such a clear opportunity for a renaissance was presented. This opportunity had to be used with wisdom and foresight.

This was Liaquat's defence of the text of his resolution. After Liaquat spoke, a Hindu member from East Pakistan, Prem Hari Barma proposed that a few weeks be given for the motion to be circulated for eliciting public opinion before it was voted on and adopted. Barma was supported by another Bengali member, Siris Chandra Chattopadhyaya who made a speech setting out the objections that the Hindu minorities had to Liaquat's resolution. He said that the implications of some of the words, such as the handing over of sovereignty to Allah, would need to be studied, which they had not had the time to do. He reminded the Constituent Assembly of Jinnah's August 11 speech and raised other points of concern.

India had also had an Objectives Resolution, but that had happened in 1946 before Independence and it was necessary to map out what the constitution would be like when British rule ended. There was no need for one here, Chattopadhyaya argued, because it was the constitution itself that mattered. The committee looking at fundamental rights had made final their report even before the Objectives Resolution, so it was unclear what purpose it would now serve.

Liaquat opposed the motion for time to study the resolution, and it was put to vote that very day, 7 March 1949, and defeated. The next few days saw a discussion in which the Hindu members of the Constituent Assembly, Bhupendra Kumar Datta, Professor Raj Kumar Chakravarty, Prem Hari Barma, Kamini Kumar Datta and Birat Chandra Mandal raised objections to the Resolution. They moved amendments that sought to omit the line handing over sovereignty to Allah and the line containing the words 'as enunciated by Islam'.

They sought to add 'and other religions' into the line ending 'as enunciated by Islam' and also tried to insert the word 'democratic' after the word independent in the line 'sovereign, independent state of Pakistan'. They tried to insert the words 'but not inconsistent with the Charter of the Fundamental Human Rights of the United Nations Organisation' after the words 'as enunciated by Islam'.

In the line enabling Muslims to order their lives in accordance with Islam, they tried to add the words 'Muslims and non-Muslims shall equally'. In the same line they also sought to add 'in perfect accord with non-Muslims residing in the state and in complete toleration of their culture and social and religious customs'.

Having moved these amendments, the minorities made some points to justify them. Birat Chandra Mandal said that Pakistan was unusual in introducing elements of religion into its Constitution. Other Muslim majority nations like Turkey did not have constitutions based on Islamic principles. India had not produced a Constitution based on Hindu ideas and the nations of Europe and America did not have Christianity guide their constitutions. What Pakistan was about to do, they said, was unprecedented and would be a blunder.

The world was secularising rapidly and there would come a time when religion would not be relevant, as Jinnah had said in his address, and it may even disappear. It would not therefore be wise to have a State based on religion. Faith and reason should be allowed to develop separately to reach their full maturity and what Pakistan was attempting was a forced blending. This was problematic because politics belonged to the domain of reason. Political institutions benefited from criticism, when it was free and frank and even when it was severe and bitter. The risk in mixing faith and politics was that religion would become exposed to criticism. Laws based on religion would be challenged and exposed and possibly repealed for not belonging in the modern era. This would be resented as being sacrilegious.

The fear was also that someone in future might find a justification in the preamble to become a dictator. The line delegating Allah's authority to the State through its people needed only a further link till it was delegated by the State to an individual, who would name himself ruler.

They also spoke of other specific problems that may be produced. For example, the obligatory alms tax of Zakat did not fit in with the modern structure of direct taxes. If the State were to be guided by the Objectives Resolution, such a conflict on taxation would come in future. A demand may be made for the institution of the Caliphate, or for a system of moral policing, and even for the abolition of the banking system. These were the objections the minorities made in moving their amendments.

In response to this, the Muslim members defended the Objectives Resolution. Dr Ishtiaq Husain Qureshi insisted that the real guarantee to the minority lay not in the inclusion of some words in the Resolution or even in the final Constitution but in the behaviour of the majority. Another member, Maulana Shabbir Ahmed Usmani, offered the orthodox reasoning for why it was required that Pakistan introduce religion into its constitution. He said Islam had never accepted the view that religion was a private affair between man and his creator and as such has no bearing upon the social and political relations of human beings. He quoted a letter to Gandhi in August, 1944 in which Jinnah wrote: 'The Quran is a complete code of life. It provides for all matters, religious or social, civil or criminal, military or penal, economic or commercial. It regulates every act, speech and movement from the ceremonies of religion to those of daily life, from the salvation of the soul to the health of the body; from the rights of all those of such individual, from the punishments here to that in the life to come. Therefore, when I say that the Muslims are a nation, I have in my mind all physical and metaphysical standards of values.'

Quoting other instances of Jinnah saying similar things, Usmani said it was not appropriate to say that the Objectives Resolution would not have been introduced had Jinnah been alive. Sardar Abdur Rab Khan Nishtar, who was a close associate of Jinnah, said that separation of religion and politics was in fact the fundamental difference that separated Hindus from Muslims on the subcontinent. No such separation was allowed in Islam.

The fear of capture of the State by an individual was unfounded because one of the principles of Islam was that the ruling authority in a Muslim country could never be a dictator. He added that while it was true that Jinnah had given assurances to the minorities, he had also given assurances to the majority. Pakistan was demanded and founded on the basis of a particular ideology and a particular purpose, with which the Objectives Resolution was aligned. Chaudhry Muhammad Zafarullah Khan, the foreign minister of Pakistan, said no exception could be taken to the opening line handing over sovereignty to Allah because man had been made in the image of god.

Ending the debate five days after the resolution was tabled, Liaquat tried to reassure the Hindus again by saying that their fears were unfounded. On the matter of discrimination, Liaquat responded to a Hindu member who had heard from the ulema that a non-Muslim could not head an Islamic state. He said: 'My friend said that these people told him that in an Islamic state, that means that a state that is established in accordance with this Resolution, no non-Muslim can be the head of the administration. This is absolutely wrong. A non-Muslim can be the head of the administration under a constitutional government with limited authority given under the Constitution to a person or an institution in that particular state. So here again these people have indeed misled him.'

Liaquat said that even if the Hindus did not believe them, the Muslims were determined to do the right thing for the minorities because their religion asked them to do so. And the reason was that they were trying to build up the State on morality and on higher values of life that what materialism could provide.

He said while the personal law of Muslims was not to be recognised in India, in Pakistan minorities would be guaranteed religious freedom and equal opportunities. To Mandal, he said: 'My honourable friend, Mr B.C. Mandal, told me that posterity will curse me for bringing forward this Resolution. Let me tell my friend, if we succeed in building Pakistan on the basis of this Resolution, we shall be able to create conditions that posterity instead of cursing me, will bless me.'

At the conclusion of the speech all the amendments proposed by the non-Muslim members were put to the vote of the Constituent Assembly. These amendments were rejected by the house by ten against twenty-one. Speaker Maulvi Tamizuddin Khan put the first question to vote: 'That the paragraph beginning with the words "whereas sovereignty over the entire universe..." and ending with the words "... is a sacred trust" be omitted.' The names of the members voting are printed on Page 98, Volume 5, issue 5 of the Constituent Assembly of Pakistan Debates. The members voted in this fashion:

AYES–10
Mr Prem Hari Barma
Prof. Raj Kumar Chakraverty
Mr Sris Chandra Chattopadhyaya
Mr Akshay Kumar Dass
Mr Bhupendra Kumar Datta
Mr Jnanendra Chandra Majumdar
Mr Birat Chandra Mandal
Mr Bhabesh Chandra Nandy
Mr Dhananjoy Roy
Mr Harendra Kumar Sur

NOES–21:
Mr A. M. A. Hamid
Mr Maulana Mohd Abdullah-el-Baqui
Mr Abul Kasem Khan
Maulana Mohd Akram Khan
Mr Fazlur Rahman
Prof. Ishtiaq Husain Qureshi
Mr Liaquat Ali Khan
Dr. Mohammad Husain
Mr Nur Ahmad
Mr Serajul Islam

Maulana Shabbir Ahmed Osmani
Khwaja Shahabuddin
Begum Shaista Suhrawardy Ikramullah
Mr Nazir Ahmad Khan
Sheikh Karamat Ali
Dr Omar Hayat Malik
Begum Jahan Ara Shah Nawaz
Sir Mohd Zafarullah Khan
Sardar Abdur Rab Khan Nishtar
Khan Sardar Bahadur Khan
Pirzada Abdus Sattar Abdur Rahman
'The motion was negatived', the record reads. As can be seen, all ten Hindus voted for the amendments and all twenty-one Muslims voted against. The Objectives Resolution was put before the Constituent Assembly and adopted on 12 March 1949.

With this vote, Jinnah's Pakistan officially went down its road to majoritarianism.

3

BURNING DOWN THE HOUSE

Pakistan's intentions, that is to say those of the people leading it, when it began Islamising itself were positive. They were not aimed at discrimination and the references to the minorities in their constitution came as we have seen with assurances that their rights would be safeguarded. It was the majority, the Muslims, who were objects of the ideology and they were to be influenced by the new orientation and future Islamic laws.

The second important element was that the ideological intentions were placed outside the Constitution proper. They were reflected in the Objectives Resolution which later became the preamble and they were in the Directive Principles. Meaning that they were not justiciable and were not actual laws: they merely signalled intent. Most of post 1947 Pakistan's laws remained the same that the British had left behind and are common to the subcontinent, going back to the Penal Code written by Thomas Macaulay in the 1830s and enforced from 1862 onwards.

Even in 2020, the Indian Penal Code and the Pakistan Penal Code remain identical. The changes that came in after 1947 are few on either side. The natives of Lahore know what the number 144 (Section 144 which criminalises assembling of people under certain circumstances) means in law just as well as those of

Chennai. For Pakistanis, just as for Indians, the law that deals with punishing murder is called 302 and the one for cheating is 420. These are numbers that Macaulay left behind and have been the ones that the subcontinent has been governed under even after 1947. They were familiar and they were functional. Everyone from the thanedar and the constable to the citizen knew them. The challenge in Pakistan was to Islamise the nation and introduce new laws that would reflect the intentions set out in the Constitution.

In 1956, almost a decade after independence and six years after the Indian Constitution came into effect, Pakistan produced its first Constitution. It assured all Pakistanis equality before law (Article 5), said there would be no discrimination including on grounds of religion (Article 14, which was the same number as the one in the Indian Constitution guaranteeing equality) and, while offering the guarantee of positive discrimination through reservations or affirmative action, said everybody was qualified for appointment to office irrespective of faith (Article 17).

It secured for minorities through Article 18, two important rights. First that 'every citizen has the right to profess, practise and propagate any religion' and that 'every religious denomination and every sect thereof has the right to establish, maintain and manage its religious institutions.'

These rights the government and courts could not violate or diminish and were permanent. Laws that contradicted these rights would be void. So far, the Pakistani Constitution was not dissimilar to the Indian one.

There were laws that seemed to anticipate what would actually come ahead and what we shall look at later. Article 21 said: 'No person shall be compelled to pay any special tax the proceeds of which are to be spent on the propagation or maintenance of any religion other than his own.' Article 13(4) said: 'In respect of any religious institution, there shall be no discrimination against any community in the granting of exemption or concession in relation to taxation.'

Article 27 said, 'The State shall safeguard the legitimate rights and interests of the minorities, including their due representation in the Federal and Provincial Services.'

The Constitution took on the task of introducing religion not through justiciable laws but through the Directive Principles, which offered only guidance for future laws. Their most striking provisions called for:

1) Enabling Muslims to order their lives according to the Quran, prohibiting prostitution, gambling, drinking and to take steps for the State to better enable the organisation of mosques.

2) Providing housing, food, clothing, education and medicine to the poor.

3) Discouraging parochial, tribal and racial feeling among Muslims.

4) Protection of the rights of non-Muslims.

5) Eliminating riba (interest) from the banking system as early as possible.

The Directive Principles also called for parity between West and East Pakistan, the part that was to break off and become Bangladesh fifteen years later. These principles, just like India's Directive Principles on prohibition, a uniform civil code, banning cow slaughter and encouraging arbitration in international disputes, were to guide lawmaking but could not be enforced by a court.

The difficult and challenging part of introducing religion into the modern state, the Pakistani leaders appeared to have left to the future. There had been some debate about whether the parliamentary form of government accurately reflected the way power was transferred in early Islam (through tribal consensus), and it was decided that it did not oppose it sufficiently for it to be changed. The laws did specify, however that the office of head of State, a president indirectly elected as in India, could only be held by Muslims. This was a necessary condition if the ideas of the Objectives Resolution, vesting sovereignty in Allah and making Pakistan an Islamic Republic were to be met. This was the only element of discrimination in the 1956 Constitution. Since the president was only a figurehead, as in India, it was not seen as particularly important. Also, the Constitution provided that in the absence of the president, the speaker would play his role and there was no restriction on non-Muslims becoming speaker. Similarly, there was no restriction on non-Muslims becoming prime minister, the operating head of the executive.

Another feature, allowed through Article 145 was that East Pakistan (now Bangladesh) could have a joint electorate, though West Pakistan would have separate ones with non-Muslims voting for separate candidates. This was later given up but the problem would never leave Pakistan fully. Non-Muslim Pakistanis, including the rump of the Congress that now found itself in Pakistan, wanted joint electorates, which would ensure that non-Muslims would have some element of influence with Muslim lawmakers who would have real power. This was the original idea Jinnah had proposed, leaving it to the minority to choose if it wanted to give up its separate electorate. But some of the conservative Muslims in Pakistan opposed the joint electorate.

Meanwhile, outside the constituent assembly, there was action on both the side of the acquisition of power as well as in the sphere of religious majoritarianism. The army already had considerable influence at this point, after a brief skirmish with India that left Kashmir divided and in time would put the military inside the Cabinet. It was also the recipient of aid from and wooed by the Americans at the period when the Cold War began to intensify. And lastly, the Muslim League after Jinnah began to fragment.

In 1953, the army had gotten rid of the government in Punjab after a food shortage and rioting against the Ahmadi community. This group of Muslims followed a spiritual leader, Mirza Ghulam Ahmad who died in 1908, whose claims of visions clashed with the orthodox Muslim view of Muhammad being the last prophet of mankind. The ulema (the clerics), wanted Ahmad's followers, the Ahmadis, to be declared apostates and non-Muslim.

The violence of 1953 led to the establishment of a commission. This body was led by the chief justice of Lahore High Court, Muhammad Munir and it spoke to various schools of Islamic thought to figure out who actually was a Muslim and who was not. The report concluded, having heard the views of the different Sunni and Shia groups that nobody was a real Muslim in the eyes of the other group. It concluded that, 'The net result of all this is that neither Shias nor Sunnis nor Deobandis nor Ahl-i-Hadith nor Barelvis are Muslims, and any change from one view to the other must be accompanied in an Islamic State with the penalty of death, if the government of the State is in the hands of the party which considers the other party to be kafirs. And it does not require much imagination to judge of the consequences of this doctrine, when it is remembered that no two ulema have agreed before us as to the definition of a Muslim.'

They concluded that,'... keeping in view the several definitions of a Muslim given by the ulema, need we make any comment except that no two learned divines are agreed on this fundamental. If we attempt our own definition as each learned divine has done and that definition differs from that given by all the others, we unanimously go out of the fold of Islam. And if we adopt the definition given by any one of the ulema, we remain Muslim according to the view of that alim but kafirs according to the definition of everyone else.'

Having determined that they could not answer the question, nor could anyone else, as to who was a Muslim, the judges said that '... if democracy means the subordination of law and order to political ends—then Allah knoweth best and we end our report'.

This question about the status of Ahmadis would remain unanswered in the 1956 Constitution also. Other than the stipulation that the presidency be held only by Muslims, it had no element that could be seen as discriminatory. And it kicked the can down the road on the matter of Islamisation by keeping the phrasing open and vague, and also by consigning it in the preamble and the non-justiciable part. India's constitution makers also played a similar game with the difficult question of cow slaughter in a secular Constitution: they left it to the future and couched it in scientific terms. More on that in a later chapter.

On 16 October 1951, Liaquat Ali Khan was killed, shot while addressing a rally in Rawalpindi. In the seven years following his death, Pakistan had six prime ministers till the army formally took over. The Constitution was abrogated and Gen. Ayub Khan made himself Pakistan's ruler in 1958. In his autobiography, *Friends Not Masters*, he reproduced a note he had written the following year on his reflections on the new Constitution. It sketched out the following points:

1) Something was needed urgently to unite Pakistan else the country would be lost.

2) Man yearned for an ideology that he could die for, and such an ideology in this situation was Islam.

3) Islam was the unity of god, and the equality of all humans before him.

Khan got this far and then had questions for which he says he did not have answers. These were:

1) How would religion have a say in matters that were temporal and secular?

2) What is the definition of the believer?

3) What would fundamental rights be which were 'wholesome for the individual as well as for the state'?

4) How could Pakistanis—'a collection of so many races with different backgrounds ... be welded into a unified whole'?

He said that the task of answering these was beyond him and that he would send it to a committee. Something similar had been present in the 1956 Constitution also, through Article 197 of the Islamic Provisions, which read: 'The President shall set up an organisation for Islamic research and instruction in advanced studies to assist in the reconstruction of Muslim society on a truly Islamic basis.'

Khan pointed out that the ulema were insisting on an Islamic constitution but could not produce one themselves. He also observed that throughout the Muslim world there was no single document that a nation had produced as an ideal for the others. That led him to conclude that, 'Islam had not prescribed any particular pattern of government but had left it to the community to evolve its own patterns to suit its circumstances.'

The Constitution Commission Gen. Ayub Khan appointed came back saying that secularism could safely be rejected in favour of an Islamic form of government which would be based on the early period of Islam. Its most important recommendation was that no law should be legislated which was in conflict with the injunctions of Islam and that existing laws be brought into conformity with these injunctions. This again was an echo of what was also there in the 1956 Constitution, through Article 198.

The Commission also recommended the appointment of yet another committee which would engage other Muslim nations and answer the question as to whether the instructions given by the Prophet Muhammad with reference to local conditions should be followed literally, regardless of local custom, or only their principle was to be taken.

The Constitution that was produced at the end of this, in 1962, offered little enlightenment on Islamic law in the modern era but it did give Ayub sweeping powers over the executive and the legislature. This was of course his primary intent. It again limited, through Article 10, the office of president to Muslims, the first exclusionary step against its minorities Pakistan took by law. This time the exclusion was from real power, with the presidency under Ayub Khan having become the primary executive office.

Ayub Khan's bespoke document like the previous one, consigned Islam to the Directive Principles. From the earlier preamble, the words 'within the limits prescribed by God' were deleted from the line specifying how the people would exercise their authority. This removed the difficulty of wrestling with what these limits were and who would determine them.

The Directive Principles sought the teaching of the Quran and of Islamiat (the history and beliefs of the Islamic faith) to all Pakistan's Muslims, the promotion of unity and Islamic moral standards among the Muslims, and the ensuring by the State of the proper organisation of mosques, zakat and waqf.

Zakat is the giving of alms and one of the five pillars of Islam. Waqf is the body looking at charitable endowments. The mention of zakat, also present in the 1956 Constitution, would bring trouble later.

Ayub Khan ruled for about a decade till the close of the 1960s. He was overthrown by his fellow generals after a war with India in 1965 over Kashmir that ended in a stalemate.

An election followed in which East Pakistan voted overwhelmingly for the Bengali Awami League party under Sheikh Mujibur Rahman, while the West voted mostly for Zufikar Ali Bhutto's Pakistan People's Party. The Bengalis had won more seats overall but the Punjabis were unwilling to cede power. A conflict ensued in 1971 between the two wings into which Indira Gandhi inserted the Indian Army and Bangladesh was formed.

West Pakistan (or now, all of Pakistan) was led by Bhutto, who produced a third Constitution, adopted in 1973.

This document extended the Islamic nature of the previous ones through four major changes. Firstly, it restricted the office of the prime minister also to Muslims. Secondly, it added into the oaths of office for the president and the prime minister, lines affirming the finality of the prophethood of Muhammad. This effectively excluded Ahmadis from holding either of these offices.

Thirdly, it again postponed the question of aligning existing laws and bringing them in conformity with Islamic injunctions by setting up a committee, but introduced a deadline giving Parliament nine years to act. And fourthly, Bhutto's Constitution made Islam the state religion of Pakistan.

It is in this Constitution that contradictions begin to appear, and the problems that were raised and dismissed during the debate over the Objectives Resolution begin to manifest. The same document also guaranteed equality before law, freedom from discrimination and said that all qualified citizens 'irrespective of religion' were eligible for appointment in the service of the state. These three fundamental rights were in conflict with the Islamic changes listed above and represented the difficulty of reconciling religion with modern government.

The most significant and discriminatory part of this Constitution came through its second amendment which was legislated the following year. It followed an incident similar to that in Godhra, which sparked the Gujarat riots in 2002. In May 1974, a train stopped at the Ahmadi headquarters of Rabwah in Punjab. It was carrying 160 students from Multan to Peshawar and the students apparently shouted offensive slogans against the Ahmadis. A few days later, the train returned carrying these students back and the Ahmadis attacked them, wounding about thirty.

This created a scandal nationally and unleashed extreme violence against the Ahmadis, with the destruction of several of their properties. An agitation began which ended after the National Assembly amended the Constitution to declare Ahmadis as not Muslims. Bhutto had little interest in religion and if his Pakistan Peoples Party had any ideology, it was socialism. He just had no defence against the conservatives who pushed the religious aspects already present in the Constitution.

The act of apostatisation also effectively disenfranchised Ahmadis permanently. They were told to contest from and vote only for seats reserved for non-Muslims. Ahmadis could not contest from or vote in the Muslim (general) constituencies. Since they still considered themselves Muslims, the entire community was thus removed from active politics.

Another change, which came a little later, redefined Muslims. Pakistan's Constitution now contains these lines:

'"Muslim" means a person who believes in the unity and oneness of Almighty Allah, in the absolute and unqualified finality of the Prophethood of Muhammad (peace be upon him), the last of the prophets, and does not believe in, or recognise as a prophet or religious reformer, any person who claimed or claims to be a prophet, in any sense of the word or of any description whatsoever, after Muhammad (peace be upon him); and 'non-Muslim' means a person who is not a Muslim and includes a person belonging to the Christian, Hindu, Sikh, Buddhist or Parsi community, a person of the Qadiani Group or the Lahori Group who call themselves "Ahmadis" or by any other name or a Baha'i, and a person belonging to any of the Scheduled Castes.'

The trajectory of the Islamic state project of Pakistan and where it would go was now in full view. The way in which the ideology was manifesting itself was in negative terms. The people who would get a taste of it were not the Muslims, for whom Liaquat and others in the Constituent Assembly said the Islamic aspects of law were necessary, but the minorities.

The Islamic republic was different from another state not in its structure which, with its written Constitution, president and prime minister and legislature, seemed to be that of just another modern state. It was not different in its rights-based approach and limiting the intrusion of the State into the liberties of the individual. Fundamental rights, including those of equality and non-discrimination, were values the Pakistani state and Constitution stated that they adhered to.

The Islamic-ness was expressed in the way in which minorities were treated. They could not access high office and they did not, in the case of the Ahmadis who would face increased levels of persecution, have freedom of religion.

The positive expression of the religious state, meaning its ability to 'enable Muslims to order their lives in the individual and collective spheres in accordance with the teachings and requirements of Islam as set out in the Holy Quran and Sunnah' was not easy. This task had been farmed out to committees and given years to figure out.

Bhutto set up a ministry for religious affairs, appointing a man named Maulana Kauser Niazi to head it. In 1976, he mandated the placing of copies of the Quran in hotel rooms. And in 1977, under pressure from a militant opposition that was led by the clergy, Bhutto banned alcohol. There was reference made in this period to the 'ideology of Pakistan' a phrase that would become common in the media later, and more substantial changes were still to come.

They would appear with the next phase of Pakistan's constitutional development and the ascent to power of its next military ruler, Gen. Muhammad Zia-ul-Haq.

Born in Jalandhar and educated in Delhi's St Stephen's College, Zia-ul-Haq was elevated to the position of army chief over other senior claimants to the post by Bhutto, whom he would later depose in a military coup and hang on a criminal charge. He was from the Arain community of Punjabis who are not classified as being a martial race, unlike the Jats and Rajputs, the castes which dominated the mostly Punjabi Pakistan Army. Bhutto's logic in elevating Haq was probably that being an Arain, he was less likely to conspire with them against him.

As chief of the Pakistan Army, Zia changed its motto. From the secular 'Ittehad, Yaqeen aur Tanzeem' (unity, faith and discipline) it now became 'Imaan, Taqwa, Jihad fi Sabilillah' (faith, piety and jihad for Allah).

Bhutto was charismatic and able to attract support from large parts of Pakistan. However, he was also quite despotic and harsh with the opposition. When his government was approaching the end of its term, he succumbed to rigging an election which he might have most likely won in any case. The opposition, led by the clergy, was incensed and organised a series of protests, refusing to accept the results. Bhutto was unable to recover fully from the pressure the opposition had put him under, and Zia used the ensuing turmoil to carry out an army coup in 1977 and ultimately got the judiciary to hang Bhutto.

The army was again in charge, this time under a general who had, or at least pretended to have, a religious bent of mind.

In February 1979, Zia changed the Constitution, adding Islam to the legal process. Each high court would have a Shariat Bench, and laws would be examined for their conformity to the Quran and the Sunnah, the customs and practices of the Prophet Muhammad which were to be followed as a model. If the laws were found to be in violation, they would be struck down and rewritten. The Supreme Court would have a bench of three Muslim judges who would be the appellate authority. In time, another body, the Federal Shariat Court of five judges would be set up.

Two days later, Zia added what he considered to be Islamic laws, altering Macaulay's penal code which Pakistan had so far shared with India. Drinking was punishable by public lashing (the culprit was to be administered eighty 'stripes'), and evidence of this was to be produced by two male witnesses. This was the first time that gender was made relevant in testimony. These ordinances used Arabic words but did not quote any Islamic law as a precedent.

The one on 'zina' (fornication, having sex without being married) starts with the lines:

'Whereas it is necessary to modify the existing law relating to zina so as to bring it in conformity with the Injunctions of Islam as set out in the Holy Quran and Sunnah;

And whereas the President is satisfied that circumstances exist which render it necessary to take immediate action ... (and) is pleased to make and promulgate the following Ordinance.' From here, it jumped straight into the law and its punishments.

The punishment for theft and robbery was chopping off of the right hand from the wrist. In case of a second offence by the same person, his foot from the ankle down was to be amputated. The law for adultery was conflated with that for rape. The adulterer was to be stoned to death, the fornicator (someone who has sex before marriage) was to be given 100 lashes. This was a Quranic injunction, from verse 24:2, which reads: 'The woman and the man guilty of adultery or fornication—whip each of them with a hundred stripes. Let not compassion move you in their case, in a matter prescribed by Allah, if you believe in Allah and the Last Day: and let a party of the Believers witness their punishment.'

One can remember the visuals published forty years ago in the *Illustrated Weekly of India* of individuals who were lashed in public when these laws were introduced. However, the judiciary was not comfortable with the laws even though amputation was a Quranic injunction. Verse 5:38 says, 'As for the thief, the male and the female, amputate their hands in recompense for what they committed as a deterrent from Allah.' Pakistan has never stoned anyone or amputated anyone's limbs under these laws. Though judgments were sometimes delivered, the conviction was overturned or the punishment reduced on appeal.

Zia ran into trouble with the clergy when the Federal Shariat Court struck down the punishment of stoning. He was forced by the clergy to appoint three ulema to the Federal Shariat Court and the decision on stoning was then reversed. This was the Hazoor Bakhsh case of 1981 in which a man was convicted of adultery and sentenced to be stoned to death. The petitioner challenged the ordinance, saying that the Quran did not prescribe the death penalty and made no reference to stoning. The closest it comes is in Verse 27:58 which talks about Sodom and Gomorrah. The Quran says that god sent down upon the sinners 'a torrent of rain'. This is interpreted by some as stoning through a metaphor. The court concluded that stoning was not mandatory but discretionary and asked the government to amend the law. One judge dissented and said the Islamic law did not use only Quranic verses but could also use other sources and stoning was mandatory. The ulema were angered by the majority decision and Zia was compelled to appoint ulema to the Shariat Appellate Bench, raising its strength from three Muslims to a bench of five.

Zia also separated the electorates. Non-Muslims, divided into Hindus, Christians, Ahmadis, Parsis and others could elect ten members but they could not vote in the general constituencies. This alienated the minorities from Muslim legislators, who held the power.

Separate electorates have always been a part of Pakistan's history, of course. The 1956 Constitution did not specifically mandate non-Muslims voting separately for their own candidates, but left it for Parliament to decide. The same year, in its Dhaka session, the National Assembly approved separate electorates in West Pakistan but a joint one in the east. This was mainly because the Christians in Punjab wanted a separate electorate while the Hindus in Bengal wanted a joint one.

In 1960, Gen. Ayub Khan had appointed a commission on the issue which concluded that the desire of Hindus 'for a joint electorate seems clearly to be for some ulterior purpose other than the welfare of Pakistan'. Ayub disregarded this and Pakistan voted in a joint electorate in his basic democracies scheme through which he was indirectly elected.

The 1973 Constitution also initially saw joint electorates, but the religious parties in opposition to Bhutto felt that the minorities usually sided with Bhutto's PPP (perceived to be liberal and socialist) which gave it the edge in tight contests. They also wanted the Ahmadis out and so six reserved seats were created for non-Muslims.

The separate electorates on the subcontinent had always existed on the principle that it was a demand of the minorities and if and when they so wanted, they could merge into the joint electorate. This time it was forced on them.

Zia next extended his Islamisation programme to the economy. Previously, Bhutto had executed radical reforms in this sphere. However, the PPP ideology was influenced to a large extent by socialism. Many of the intellectuals around Bhutto, people like the Bengali J.A. Rahim, were communist in orientation. The PPP's nationalising of not just banks, as was happening in India at the same time under Indira Gandhi, but also cotton ginning plants and neighbourhood flour mills, oil mills and rice mills which Pakistan's bureaucracy was tasked with running can be seen in this light.

Zia's reforms in the economic sphere were less radical and ultimately less meaningful but stamped with religiosity. Interest was forbidden and banks were told they would instead have to share their profit (or loss) with the account holder. Predictably, the banks continued as usual, renaming the interest they were paying out as 'profit'. Similarly the word 'loan', because of its assumption of interest payments, was replaced with the word 'finance'.

Zakat, the giving of alms, is as noted previously one of the five pillars of Islam, believed by many Muslims to be mandatory. Zia instituted the Zakat Ordinance, forcing Muslims to pay this charity tax through an automatic debit of their bank accounts. Zakat was deductible at source and to not pay it, one had to prove that one was not Muslim.

A report by the *Associated Press* from 2012, headlined 'During Ramzan, Pakistanis dodge tax collectors' showed what has happened. It said: 'During the Muslim holy month of Ramzan, Muhammad Tashfeen Khan does what millions of other Pakistanis do: tries to keep his money from the government's religious tax collectors.

'The wealthy businessman pulls all his savings from his bank account right before Ramzan starts so the government cannot deduct 2.5 per cent as zakat, the annual donation many Muslims are religiously required to make as a basic tenet of the Islamic faith.'

The report said that the money the government debited went to charities including the Jamaat-ud-Dawa, which was the front of the Lashkar-e-Taiba. Between lack of trust and dodging of the tax, most of the money was lost. Instead of 2.5 per cent of the deposits, what the government got was 0.3 per cent, the report said.

The Zakat law also ran into trouble with the Shias, who are the only Muslims with a hierarchical religious leadership to whom they pay a tithe. After their protests, the Shias were exempted from the Zakat debits, if they could prove that they were Shias. This led to some Pakistani Sunnis also claiming to be Shia when Ramzan and the day of debit arrived.

Through another ordinance, Zia introduced State intervention in Ramzan fasting, which in any case, the majority of Muslims around the world and especially on the Indian subcontinent follow quite diligently. The law prohibited eating in public places and criminalised the violation. The ordinance read: 'No person who, according to the tenets of Islam, is under an obligation to fast shall eat, drink or smoke in a public place during fasting hours in the month of Ramazan' and that, 'whoever contravenes the provisions of sub-section (1) shall be punishable with simple imprisonment for a term which may extend to three months, or with fine which may extend to five thousand rupees, or with both'.

Restaurants and cafes were forbidden from serving Muslims during the fasting hours for the entire month or its owners would face three months in jail. Cinema halls also had to be shut and the State given powers to enter establishments and make arrests. Even in recent times, there have been protests from the owners of multiplexes and restaurants that this law is problematic.

Zia ratcheted up the persecution of the Ahmadis. In 1984, the form Pakistanis had to fill out to apply for a passport was amended to add a declaration for Muslim applicants. It read:

'1: I am Muslim and believe in the absolute and unqualified finality of the prophethood of Muhammad (peace be upon him) the last of the prophets.

2: I do not recognise any person who claims to be a prophet in any sense of the word or of any description whatsoever after Muhammad (peace be upon him) or recognise such a claimant as prophet or a religious reformer as a Muslim.

3: I consider Mirza Ghulam Ahmad Qadiani to be an imposter nabi and also consider his followers whether belonging to the Lahori or Qadiani group to be Non-Muslim.'

This declaration still exists and so Pakistan's Ahmadis must either self-declare as non-Muslims, or endorse the words above and denounce their faith, or not apply for a passport.

More was to come. Section 298 of the Indian Penal Code reads: 'Whoever, with the deliberate intention of wounding the religious feelings of any person, utters any word or makes any sound in the hearing of that person or makes any gesture in the sight of that person or places, any object in the sight of that person, shall be punished with imprisonment of either description for a term which may extend to one year, or with fine, or with both.'

Zia altered this by criminalising the use by Ahmadis of certain words. They could not refer to their places of worship by the name 'masjid' or the call to prayer as 'azan' and if they did, they would face three years in jail. They could not call their faith 'Islam' and their leaders could not be referred to as 'emir' or 'khalipha'.

Today, when the Pakistani media refers to an attack on an Ahmadi mosque, it refers to it as 'Ahmadi place of worship'. The writing and passing of such laws produced and spread and intensified religious hatred and the laws were misused even by ordinary citizens to harass and persecute the Ahmadis. Sixty-two Ahmadis were booked under discriminatory religious laws in 2017 and more than 2,500 anti-Ahmadi news items appeared in Pakistan's Urdu-language newspapers, according to an Ahmadi group that publishes findings of their community's persecution in Pakistan.

Zia also amended the law on blasphemy, which in India criminalises attacks on all religions, and added an Islam-specific element: 'Whoever wilfully defiles, damages or desecrates a copy of the Holy Quran or of an extract therefrom or uses it in any derogatory manner or for any unlawful purpose shall be punishable with imprisonment for life.'

A second amendment was added: 'Whoever by words, either spoken or written, or by visible representation or by any imputation, innuendo, or insinuation, directly or indirectly, defiles the sacred name of the Holy Prophet Muhammad (peace be upon him) shall be punished with death, or imprisonment for life, and shall also be liable to fine.'

This was an unnecessary law on the face of it. Only seven cases of blasphemy had been registered in undivided India and Pakistan from 1927 to 1986. But in the quarter century after Zia made the punishment for blasphemy death, 1,058 cases of blasphemy were registered. Of the accused, 456 were Ahmadis, 449 were Muslims, 132 were Christians and 21 were Hindus. The death penalty was used to settle personal enmities and disputes and to go after minorities. Many of those accused, especially Ahmadis, were lynched by mobs before they could be put on trial.

In Zia's other changes, the requirement of two male witnesses or one male and two female (consigning a woman's testimony to half that of a man's) was introduced into the Evidence Act.

When Zia had to legitimise his dictatorship, he did so through a referendum which sought endorsement of his Islamist reforms. The question voters had to answer was: 'Whether the people of Pakistan endorse the process initiated by Gen. Muhammad Zia-ul-Haq, the President of Pakistan, for bringing the laws of Pakistan in conformity with the injunctions of Islam as laid down in the Holy Quran and sunnah of the Holy Prophet and for the preservation of the ideology of Pakistan for the continuation and consolidation of that process, and for the smooth and orderly transfer of power to the elected representative of the people.'

A vote in the affirmative gave Zia another five years in office.

In 1988, Zia passed the Shariah ordinance seeking to Islamise the State and judiciary further, but he died a few weeks later. Zia's passing did not end the drift towards a more ideological state. Two years after his death, an ordinance under his successor added another aspect of Shariah law, called 'qisas' and 'diyat' to the criminal justice system. The concept of qisas is the Biblical eye for an eye.

It is defined in the ordinance as 'punishment by causing similar hurt at the same part of the body of the convict as he has caused to the victim or by causing his death if he has committed qatl-i-amd (murder), in exercise of the right of the victim or a wali (heir of the victim, or the provincial government if there is no heir)'.

This could be the dismemberment, amputation or severance of any limb or organ of another person, the destruction or permanent impairment of the functioning, power or capacity of an organ of the body of another person, or causing permanent disfigurement. Or a wound to the head or face of another person, in which bone is exposed but not fractured. A report by Amnesty International in 1991 said that this was the first time that torture had been introduced into the penal code.

Diyat is blood money, where the party convicted of murder compensates the victim's family. An Amnesty International report in 1995 gave an example of one such case.

'On 17 October 1994, Rehan, aged forty-five, was executed in Central Jail, Peshawar, North West Frontier Province. A sessions court in Peshawar had sentenced him to death in June 1991 for murdering another man in the context of a family feud in 1988. Appeals to the Peshawar High Court and the Supreme Court were rejected in October 1991 and April 1993 respectively. A mercy petition addressed to the President was rejected in early October 1994.

'Officials of Peshawar Central Jail reportedly stated that the noose was put around Rehan's neck on 17 October at 5.00 a.m. in the presence of the jail superintendent, a magistrate and a medical officer. They waited for half an hour while the families of the prisoner and of the heirs of the victim argued outside the jail gate over a pardon and payment of compensation or diyat. Jail officials reportedly sent a messenger to the gate to keep them informed if a compromise was reached at the last minute. When no agreement could be found, Rehan was hanged at 5.30 a.m.'

The report said that in another case, a judge ordered that a man, sentenced to hang for shooting a woman on a school playground in Swabi, was in fact to be taken to the same place and shot there by a relative of the dead woman.

Doctors were trained to administer qisas mutilations, the Amnesty International report said, though they were not ultimately carried out. As with all of the actions aimed at making the Muslim society more pious, this also remained an action on paper, a law at odds with the modern world.

How much Islam was sufficient? There was always more needed. In 1998, the Pakistan National Assembly passed a piece of legislation, the 15th amendment, which made Shariah the supreme law in Pakistan, overriding all previous legislation. Specific mention was made of making the population pray regularly, paying zakat and being controlled by a moral police. This did not become law because it could not clear the Senate.

In 1991, the Shariat bench of the Supreme Court decided that riba (interest) was illegal and could not be charged, giving the government seven months to eliminate it. This of course could not happen and the government appealed. In 1999, the court ruled against the government, insisting on implementation, an act which would have caused economic collapse. The problem remains and has to be managed by the Pakistani executive which has to be pragmatic and find ways to survive, while being goaded on by the clergy, the opposition and sometimes the judiciary into taking the next step towards a pious state.

The Pakistani human rights activist I.A. Rehman has observed that the 'Objectives Resolution gave rise to a concept of two sovereignties and a Muslim's right to defy/violate man-made laws by invoking the superior commandment of Allah'.

In the text of the original Objectives Resolution, non-Muslims were given 'adequate provision' to 'freely profess and practise their religions and develop their cultures'. In 1985, the word 'freely' was removed. In 2010, it was reinserted.

Despite what we have seen, Pakistan remains insufficiently Islamised unlike Iran. The primary reason is that there is no mechanism to Islamise the State in Pakistan fully and make it theocratic. The majority of Muslims of Pakistan, like those in India, are Sunnis, who have no hierarchical clergy. Iran is Shia, which does have a clerical hierarchy, with the Grand Ayatollahs on top. And the Shia's relation to the cleric is much deeper than the Sunni's is to the qazi who marries him or the mufti who gives a fatwa, which is only an opinion, not a binding law.

What Jinnah had said on 28 February 1948 about Pakistan 'not going to be a theocratic state—to be ruled by priests with a divine mission' was correct because it was not possible in a Sunni majority state. Liaquat speaking the following year in the Objectives Resolution debate said the same thing. He said, 'The people are the real recipients of power. This naturally eliminates any danger of the establishment of a theocracy. It is true that in its literal sense, theocracy means the government of God; in this sense, however, it is patent that the entire universe is a theocracy, for is there any corner in the entire creation where His authority does not exist? But in the technical sense, theocracy has come to mean a government by ordained priests, who wield authority as being specially appointed by those who claim to derive their rights from their sacerdotal position. I cannot overemphasise the fact that such an idea is absolutely foreign to Islam. Islam does not recognise either priesthood or any sacerdotal authority; and, therefore, the question of a theocracy simply does not arise in Islam. If there are any who still use the word theocracy in the same breath as the polity of Pakistan, they are either labouring under a grave misapprehension, or indulging in mischievous propaganda.'

What Liaquat is referring to is Sunni Islam. Even Saudi Arabia, the most religious of the Sunni Muslim states, is ruled not by clerics but those who militarily captured the country. On the other hand, Iran is different because the Shia do have a scholar clergy.

Ayatollah Khomeini's revolution in 1979 took the country's executive from the hands of the Shah, a hereditary king and handed it to the Shia clergy, which had captured the state. In Pakistan, the cleric remained on the sidelines and power stayed with the landed and wealthy and then later, the army. The most popular clerical politicians have come from Khyber Pakhtunkhwa, where the Deobandi ulema have a stronghold. But religious parties like their Jamiat-ul-Ulema-e-Islam and the more radical Jamaat-e-Islami of Abul Ala Maudoodi, do not have and have never had a large share of the vote. Pakistan has in fact also de-Islamised in some ways.

In 2006, President Pervez Musharraf passed the Protection of Women Act. It returned some of the offences from Shariah back to the Pakistan Penal Code, including rape. It criminalised marital rape (which is still not an offence in India) and made sexual intercourse with a woman of under sixteen as rape, regardless of consent.

Adultery and fornication were also taken out of Shariah and sent to the penal code, punishable by jail of five years and not stoning. False accusations of fornication would also attract five years in jail. Adultery was retained in the Zina Ordinance but the definition of confession was changed to one that was made before a judge rather than before the police.

Unlike Zia's law on Zina, Musharraf's had a Statement of Objects and Reasons and a short essay on why the law was being amended. It said the Quran did not mention punishment for rape, only for fornication or for a false accusation. Lumping them with rape had led to abuse. Women who were raped and couldn't prove that they were (because it required four live witnesses) were jailed for fornication.

This could not happen any longer by law after the amendment and another change said that complaints of rape could not be converted into those of fornication. Adultery complaints could no longer be made at the police station and required the complainant to go to court, giving the judge discretion to dismiss the case without registering it.

False accusations of adultery would result in automatic invocation of 'qazf', the law on bearing false witness. The accuser unable to prove his accusation would get eighty lashes. This has helped make the law irrelevant.

In May 2009, the Federal Shariat Court ruled that whipping people for the drinking of alcohol was un-Islamic and observed that Islam did not actually have any prohibition against drinking.

Prohibition continues but the government allows licensed wine shops. Alcohol is freely available in Pakistan as anyone who has visited it knows. The law says consumption is only for non-Muslims but there is no check (the author has personal experience of such a shop in Karachi).

An article published by the website *scroll.in* ('The curious history of prohibition in Pakistan') excerpted a book, *Points of Entry: Encounters At The Origin-Sites of Pakistan*, by Nadeem F. Paracha which said:

'In late 2016, a group of petitioners in Karachi moved the Sindh High Court against the continuing growth of "licensed wine shops" in the city. The court ruled in favour of the petitioners and ordered Sindh's provincial government to immediately close down all liquor stores in the province because they were not operating according to the dictates of the 1979 Prohibition Order. The court pointed out that these stores were openly selling liquor to Muslims.

An organisation of wine shop owners in Karachi hired one of Pakistan's leading lawyers and judicial activists, Asma Jahangir, to submit an appeal in the Supreme Court against the SHC's ruling. Jahangir told the court that thousands of people belonging to Pakistan's non-Muslim communities were employed at the shops and would lose their livelihood. She said that the shops were working exactly according to the 1979 Ordinance and that it wasn't their fault that a majority of their customers were Muslim. The Supreme Court struck down the SHC ruling and ordered the re-opening of the shops.'

The forcing of fasting on Muslims during Ramzan, something that the majority of them were particular about in any case, has not come without resistance. *Dawn*, a leading Pakistani newspaper reported on 7 May 2019 that 262 petitions by eateries had been rejected by the Sindh High Court. The judges disagreed with the petitioners that since their hotels and restaurants were situated at bus stops they were exempted under Section V and said that it was not the case because Section V used the word 'bus stand' instead of 'bus stop' and did not refer to stops outside terminals. On 9 May, two days later, the court rejected another 356 petitions on similar grounds.

On 3 June 2016, *The Independent* carried photographs of an eighty-two-year-old Hindu man bloodied by the beating given by a constable in Sindh for eating during Ramzan. On 9 May 2019, an advocate, Yasser Latif Hamdani, wrote for *Naya Daur* that 'the application of this law (Ehtram-e-Ramzan) has more often than not targeted non-Muslims because, in practical terms, it is impossible to tell whether a person is "under obligation" to "fast" just by looking at the person.'

A report in *Dawn* on 6 May 2020 spoke of an opinion placed on record in the Supreme Court with respect to Zakat's continuation. The opinion, that of Mufti Muhammad Taqi Usmani, an Islamic scholar who was a former Supreme Court justice of the Shariat Appellate Bench said:

'If the Zakat system cannot be replaced with a fresh system, then it would be better to forego the idea that the government manage distribution of zakat.

'Let the people pay their zakat with confidence to the poor directly and be satisfied that their zakat has reached those who deserve it,' the opinion stated.

Mufti Usmani regretted that the people had lost confidence in the system of zakat and try to avoid paying zakat to the government, either by drawing the bulk of their money from the bank before Ramzan or giving a declaration that their 'fiqh' (sect) does not allow them to pay zakat on certain items.

The Islamic punishment laws have not reduced crime in Pakistan. And they have had the opposite effect on punishment. Pakistan has four murders per lakh people per year, according to the World Bank data on intentional homicides. India has three. (2.2 according to the National Crime Records Bureau).

The qisas and diyat laws allow the powerful to force victims' families to 'settle' after murders.

An AFP report in November 2015, said that: 'According to "The application of Islamic criminal law in Pakistan" by scholar Tahir Wasti, Pakistan's murder conviction rate dramatically declined from 29 per cent in 1990 to just 12 per cent in 2000 after the enactment of the Qisas and Diyat law.

'The percentage of cases that were cancelled before they were brought to court meanwhile more than doubled in the same period as police "availed the loopholes in the new law".'

Interest, by whatever name, remains in Pakistan's banking system and pragmatism from both the executive and the judiciary has kept the constitutional injunction at bay. Even the great Islamiser Zia only introduced cosmetic changes here because real reform was not possible, even if religion demanded it. From his Federal Shariat Court's jurisdiction, Zia tactfully removed for a period of ten years any law relation to finance, banking and the collection of taxes.

After this period ended, the judiciary immediately took up the matter and in 1992 found twenty laws to be violative of the Quranic principle banning interest (or usury).

The court ruled that '"riba" means any "addition, however slight, over and above the principal", and includes both usury (excessive interest), as well as market-based or government-regulated interest' and that the prohibition against riba was absolute. The executive under Nawaz Sharif appealed and the appeal lay dormant for five years. Pakistan's leaders have managed in creative ways to fend off a judiciary that has been inclined towards banning interest.

Another judgment in 1999 was again appealed, this time under Gen. Musharraf, and the judgment was reversed. This was on the grounds that it made no distinction between interest and usury, made no attempt to exclude non-Muslim Pakistanis and, most important, the ban on riba was not practical or feasible and did not take into account the destruction of Pakistan's economy should the judgment be implemented. Pragmatism had overtaken piety.

The Islamic state has been reaching for piety but has not been able to achieve it through the instrument of ideology. Meaningless and absurd things have been introduced to modern law. To become a Pakistani legislator one must be 'not commonly known as one who violates Islamic injunctions' (Article 62-1d), must have 'adequate knowledge of Islamic teachings and practise obligatory duties prescribed by Islam' (Article 62-1e).

The positive aspects of Islamisation have faded away, and the attempts to create the utopia described in the Objectives Resolution debate have largely come to an end. What has remained embedded is majoritarianism. Gen. Musharraf joined the electorates for minorities and gave them reserved seats, but the office of president and prime minister remain reserved for Muslims.

Unable to make much headway in any of the constructive changes through religious law, whether in the criminal justice system or in the economy or even in public morality, the State has however remained effective in going after its minorities.

Pakistani children are taught in Class V that 'The Hindu has always been an enemy of Islam' and 'Hindus worship in temples, which are very narrow and dark places, where they worship idols'. In Class VI: 'Hindus live in small, dark houses' and Partition happened because the Congress 'demanded that the Muslims should either embrace Hinduism or leave the country' (taken from A.H. Nayyar and Ahmed Salim's work *The Subtle Subversion*).

The State has made it hard for minorities to practise religion freely. Zia meddled with the Christian law of divorce, making it impossible for Pakistani Christians to divorce except by accusing the women of adultery. To get around this, couples would have to convert to Islam and then divorce, giving up their faith. This was undone only in 2016 by the Lahore High Court.

Society has also pushed the State back when it has attempted reform. A report in *Dawn* ('Forced conversions', 12 April 2020) spoke of the problem of minor Hindu girls who were converted through marriage: 'Twice, the Sindh government attempted to outlaw forced conversions and marriages, including laying guidelines for the court process in the Protection of Minorities Bill, placing an age limit of eighteen years upon conversions and enabling better due process. In 2016, the bill was unanimously passed by the Sindh Assembly, but religious parties objected to an age limit for conversions, and threatened to besiege the assembly if the bill received approval of the governor, who then refused to sign the bill into law.

'In 2019, a revised version was introduced, but religious parties protested once again. A sit-in was organised by Pir Mian Abdul Khaliq (Mian Mithu), a political and religious leader and a central character in many cases of forced conversions of underage Hindu girls in Sindh. He and his group claim the girls are not forced, but fall in love with Muslim men and convert willingly. In March 2019, nearly 2,000 Hindus staged a sit-in to demand justice for two sisters, Reena and Raveena, who they claimed were forcibly converted and married. The Islamabad High Court ruled the girls had willingly converted and married the men.' The report said once the girls converted, there was no going back, as apostasy would mean a death sentence. 'In many cases, women are also told that their families are "kafirs" and they cannot meet them. This impedes their access to justice as they remain in the clutches of powerful men.'

On 15 July 2015, *The News* reported from Karachi ('1,000 girls forcibly converted to Islam in Pakistan every year') that large numbers of Christian and Hindu girls and women were converted through forced marriage or bonded labour. In 2012, the Human Rights Commission of Pakistan said twenty or more Hindu girls on an average a month were forcibly converted in Sindh (where most of Pakistan's Hindus live).

The 2015 data was according to a report by the Aurat Foundation which said that many of the girls were under eighteen and married to someone without their consent. When the girl's family filed an FIR, the abductor often filed a counter-FIR accusing the parents of harassing the converted girl.

The girl remained in the custody of the abductor and the case closed once she testified to being converted. A common factor in the cases, the report said, were 'threats to the victim regarding her 'reconversion to her original religion'. Victims are told time and again that they are now Muslim and if they try to continue practising their original religion, they will be considered apostates, the punishment for which was death.'

There was no law that identified and criminalised forced conversions. In October 2019, the PPP rejected a proposed bill against forced conversions. A report ('Bill against forced conversion', *Express Tribune*, 15 October 2019) said that the bill was unexceptionable and provided for judges and the police receiving sensitisation training on the issue of forced conversions, and that women be placed in a shelter, or in the custody of their parents during court proceedings in which the conversion and subsequent marriage was under challenge. The most important element of the bill was that it prohibited someone from changing their religion until they were eighteen years of age. The report said that 'all of this was welcome, and it would have sent a message of solidarity to religious minorities throughout Sindh. But the zealots mobilised, and the PPP buckled.'

The polity's religiosity has manifested itself most viciously against the Ahmadis. In 2018, cases were registered against thirty-three Ahmadis, and another twenty-nine unnamed ones, under the blasphemy law and the other various religious laws targeting the community. The annual reports filed by the community about the persecution against them are collected on the website persecutionofahmadis.org and detail the violence and humiliation of the community by the State.

The most famous instance of what Pakistan has done to Ahmadis is the case of Dr Abdus Salam, who won the Nobel Prize for Physics in 1979. He died in 1996 and his gravestone read that he 'became the first Muslim Nobel Laureate for his work in Physics'. The BBC reported on 14 September 2014 that on the order of the government the gravestone was defaced and the word Muslim removed. The line now reads: 'became the first Nobel laureate', which is of course not true.

A Constitution carries a seed which sprouts in the direction of the code written into it. The code in the instance of Pakistan was written not by Jinnah but those who came after him. They wanted to contribute to modernity through their faith, to try and find a response to some of the problems of our time through reinterpreting religion. In this they did not succeed and while the modifications they made added little to mankind's development, they did affect Pakistan negatively.

Their reforms took their country rapidly away from the

direction its founder wished in his speech a few days before independence.

Jinnah looked into the distant future of mankind and foresaw the falling away of all religious differences. In Pakistan, the angularities of majority and minority did not in fact vanish in the course of time. They became sharper and divided and harmed Pakistanis and Pakistan in the process.

4

HINDUTVA'S GARBLED MANTRAS

Pakistan's majoritarianism was constitutional and overt. It also tried, and failed, to achieve something that it felt would be positive through its majoritarianism: the increased piety of its mostly Muslim citizens which would bring blessings from above. The Pakistani State would help citizens develop their spiritual side and bring it level with their material and scientific side. What happened instead, we have observed.

India's Hindu majoritarianism never had any positive aspects. It was not aimed at Hindu reform or piety. From the beginning it was negative and aimed primarily at India's minorities.

Three twentieth century men laid out the intellectual framework of the majoritarianism that finally produced the BJP. They were Deendayal Upadhyaya of the Jana Sangh, M.S. Golwalkar of the Rashtriya Swayamsevak Sangh and Vinayak Savarkar of the Hindu Mahasabha. The first authored the BJP's philosophy, the second was the leader under whom the RSS conceived the party and staffed it and the third coined and defined the ideology of the BJP, Hindutva.

The word 'Hindutva' was popularised by Vinayak Savarkar's book of the same name. In it, Savarkar claims the word is of common currency, though it was probably first used only around the 1870s and has no history before that. In the 1990s, as we shall see in a later chapter, the Supreme Court would endorse the word, conflating it with Hinduism and then saying that Hindutva was 'a way of life' in the same way that Hinduism, the faith, is loosely described.

Savarkar proposed in the 1920s that the Hindus constituted a unified nation, that this Hindu nation was geographically inseparable from India, and that India's Muslims and Christians did not constitute a part of this nation. This is what Hindutva means in theory. Savarkar famously said, 'Let us bravely face unpleasant facts as they are. India cannot be assumed today to be a unitarian and homogenous nation, but on the contrary there are two nations in the main, the Hindus and the Muslims in India.' The RSS takes Savarkar's view on this issue of what is called the two-nation theory. Savarkar developed it much before the Pakistan movement did and the RSS have pushed it consistently in independent India through the phrase 'Hindu Rashtra' or Hindu nation when referring to the republic.

Born in 1883 in a Chitpavan Brahmin family, Savarkar held a bachelor's degree in arts and went to England to study law. He was an admirer of the Italian nationalists who reunified their nation around his time and who inspired his burning patriotism. He wrote a biography of Giuseppe Mazzini, the Italian leader who helped unified Italy. In his twenties, Savarkar was in London and wrote a book in Marathi on the 1857 mutiny, ascribing its causes above all to a nationally felt sentiment among Hindus for 'swaraj' or independence.

He was also part of a group that dabbled in, or at least discussed, violent revolution for which Savarkar was arrested by the British and was deported to India. While under arrest, on 8 July 1910, Savarkar made a failed attempt to escape by jumping ship at Marseille, for which he was valourised and called 'Veer', though beyond jumping ship and swimming to the shore, it is unclear what his act of valour actually was.

During his incarceration first in the Andamans, and later in Ratnagiri Jail, he wrote an essay published under a pseudonym ('A Maratha') that came to be his most important work, *Hindutva*. After he submitted mercy petitions and promised loyalty to the Raj, he was freed in January 1924. Savarkar was tried for the assassination of Gandhi, before being acquitted. He died in 1966, while in his eighties.

His essay is formally called *Essentials of Hindutva*, and was published as a booklet in May 1923. Savarkar was about forty when this book was written and had no access to sources in jail. It is a sort of polemic in which he offers a version of India's history over the millennia and how it was 'conquered'. And he also grapples with two problems of Hindu majoritarianism: how to resolve Hinduism's problems of caste and discrimination, and how to engage with Indian Muslims. This is a summary of what his essay says regarding Hindutva.

The word 'Hindu' originated from India and was not externally given. The Aryans called themselves 'Sindhus', and one usually knows the name of a place from its original inhabitants. And so it is likely that even before the Aryans, the word 'Hindu' existed and was used by the natives, which in the Sanskrit of the Aryans became Sindhu. Hindus were therefore present in India before the Aryans.

India was in fact a unified nation far before the name India existed. It was first united by Ram, the prince of Ayodhya, who also conquered Sri Lanka. Under the rule of another king, Bharat, the nation adopted the name 'Bharatvarsha' from top to bottom, because the earlier word 'Aryavarta' had excluded the south. This was evidence of India's ancient unitary form.

To protect the caste system and to maintain its purity, the national border was fixed at the Indus, according to the Puranas. The word 'Arya' therefore included all those on this side of the Indus, whatever their caste. The word 'mlechchha' was reserved for foreigners.

Buddhism collapsed in India because it was passive and lacked sufficient virility to resist invasions, particularly from other Buddhists who were non-Indian. For this reason the people of India themselves overthrew it. India acted as a nation and thought in unison. Buddhism was too universal for Hindus and didn't have a geographical centre of gravity, like Mecca and Jerusalem. India's early invaders were Buddhists and so it was necessary for Buddhist Indians to sever ties with their religion to be able to defend their nation.

Hindus were defined not as the followers of what is known as the Hindu faith but as those who collectively had three things in common: land, shared ancestry and culture. Culture (sanskriti) was religious festivals and its associated rites and rituals. This is why Sikhs, Lingayats and Jains and atheists were Hindus, but not Muslims or Christians. Shared culture could not include music, food, language, art, clothing, dance, poetry, architecture, medicine, science and such things.

India's Muslims were disloyal citizens by birth because one's 'holy land' was always a greater and more appealing idea to individuals than their homeland. For this reason Muslims must surely prefer Mecca to India in their love and allegiance. German Americans had been disloyal to the United States during the First World War. Similarly African-Americans were more loyal to Africa than America.

Hindutva was not a word but a history. Not just the spiritual or religious history; a history in full of the nation of Hindus. That is why it was possible to accommodate Sikhs, Jains, atheist Hindus and Lingayats into Hindutva. Hinduism was only a derivative, a fraction and a part of Hindutva. The root meaning of the word Hindu, like Hindi, could only mean an Indian. However it was not possible to call a Muslim a Hindu merely because of his being a citizen of India, just as it was impossible to call an American or African an Indian. An American or an

African could become an Indian citizen. However, if he did not adopt Indian culture (religion), mixed his blood with that of Hindus and come to worship India, he was not a Hindu.

Indians who were Muslim or Christian had originally been forcibly converted. They inherited along with Hindus, a common fatherland and a greater part of the wealth of a common culture—language, law, customs, folklore and history. However, they could not be recognised as Hindus and therefore real Indians. Hindustan to them may be the fatherland but it was not their holy land as well. Their holy land was Arabia or Palestine. Their mythology and godmen, ideas and heroes were not of India's soil. Consequently, their names and outlook were foreign and their love was divided. Some of India's Islamic communities were patriotic but even they lacked one of the essential qualifications of Hindutva and that was that they did not look upon India as their holy land.

Hindus were a brotherhood because they believed the same blood that was in Ram and Krishna, Buddha and Mahavir, Nanak and Chaitanya, Basava and Madhava, Ravidas and Tiruvalluvar was in their veins. Hindus felt they were a 'jati', a race bound by blood: they did not feel divided by caste.

The rigidity of caste and endogamy was actually bogus. The existence of various jatis (sub-castes) was the proof of this. These came into existence through incessant, unauthorised intermingling, producing new jatis. All that the caste system had done was to regulate bloodlines. Upper caste blood could contribute to enriching what was barren and poor, while not polluting itself. This was a good thing because it introduced 'good' blood to the lower castes.

Intercaste marriage had actually been quite common in ancient India. Evidence of this came from the Mahabharata. In the Pandava family, Parashar married a fisherwoman and produced Ved Vyas who in turn fathered sons with Kshatriya women. Later, Pandu allowed his wives to have children with men of unknown castes.[6]

In the modern period also, intercaste marriages were common. Chandragupta Maurya married a Brahmin girl who gave birth to the father of Ashoka the Great. Ashoka married a Vaishya maid and Harsha was a Vaishya but gave his daughter in marriage to a Kshatriya prince.

Individuals could gain and lose caste by their actions. A shudra could become a Brahmin and vice-versa. A Hindu believing in any theoretical or philosophical or social system, orthodox or heterodox, provided it was indigenous and founded by a Hindu, was safe and could not be excluded from the nation.

A Hindu could thus lose caste but not lose his Hindutva. On the other hand the Muslim could never gain it through action because he was disqualified at birth. All who loved India and were locally descended possessed two of the most essential requisites of Hindutva. But the third, which was devotion to India, could never be felt by Muslims.

Muslims could not feel Indian culture because Indian culture was sanskriti. All that best and worth preserving in India was sanskriti and it was because of it that Hindus were a nation— they had a common sanskriti, which was civilisational culture. For this reason even if a Muslim would come to love India as much as a Hindu, he could not be recognised as a Hindu.

The celebration of Dussehra, Diwali, Rakshabandhan, the Jagannath rath yatra, the Kumbh mela and Baisakhi were sanskriti and were common to Hindus, Sikhs and Jains. This was the only form of sanskriti that qualified as being culture. And it was because Muslims did not participate in these that their culture was not sanskriti and not Indian.

Bohras and Khojas (the Ismaili Shias of Gujarat) were patriotic and loved India. They were recent converts and shared common blood with Gujarati Hindus. Even their personal law was Hindu.

---

6. V.D. Savarkar, *Essentials of Hindutva*, p. 87.

So they satisfied the essential conditions of common land, blood and even of sanskriti. However, they stood disqualified because they did not regard India as their holy land. We can have Sanatan Dharma, Sikh Dharma, Jain Dharma, Buddha Dharma but not Islam Dharma or Isai Dharma.

This is the message of Savarkar. His Hindutva is not an ideology—it is a theory of exclusion. Savarkar frames the etymology such that Indian means Hindu and Hindu can never mean Muslim or Christian.

His convoluted rules for Hindutva mean that even the Muslim who lights a lamp on Diwali, who shoulders the corpses of Hindus abandoned by relatives, who knows more about the Hindu faith and custom through scholarship than most Hindus, can never be acceptable as Indian. On the other hand the Hindu, even the atheist who spits on his faith, or the believer who betrays his nation, who prefers another land and its passport, will always be Indian. Savarkar does not accommodate the Christian or Muslim who is agnostic or atheist or the one born Christian and Muslim who knows little or nothing about his faith, much less his holy land.

Being born into a faith or not born into one is all there is to belong to the Indian nation that he has imagined. Savarkar writes up a contradiction that is not resolvable. But then he himself resolves it for an Irish woman, who was devoted to Swami Vivekananda. He writes: 'In one case alone it seems to offer some real difficulty. Is, for example, Sister Nivedita a Hindu?'

He accepts she is Irish and fails his first test of fatherland, but says that if India had been free 'we' would have given her citizenship. 'So the first essential may, to some extent, be said to hold good in her case,' he says, because she adopted India and 'truly loved it'.

'The second essential of common blood of Hindu parentage must, nevertheless and necessarily, be absent in such cases as these. The sacrament of marriage with a Hindu which really fuses and is universally admitted to do so, two beings into one may be said to remove this disqualification.'

But she did not in fact marry an Indian. He gives her a pass here also, saying: 'But although this second essential failed either way to hold good in her case, the third important qualification of Hindutva did entitle her to be recognised as a Hindu. For she had adopted our culture and come to adore our land as her holy land. She felt, she was a Hindu and that is, apart from all technicalities, the real and the most important test.'

He recognises that this might be seen as dissembling so he concludes that recognising Sister Nivedita as Hindu '... should be done as an exception to the rule. The rule itself must neither be too rigid nor too elastic.'

Who administers this test Savarkar speaks of? Hindutva disqualified Sonia Gandhi, who was constitutionally qualified to hold the office of prime minister but was opposed by the BJP in 2004 despite taking citizenship, marrying an Indian, wearing a sari and bathing in the Ganga. Sushma Swaraj threatened to tonsure her head if Gandhi took office. What is the difference between Gandhi and Nivedita? Gandhi even married an Indian unlike Nivedita and gave up her Italian nationality to become Indian unlike Nivedita.

Savarkar's definition is not law and it is not even custom. He says that foreigners who convert to Sikhism are not Hindu and so not part of the Indian nation because they fail the test of fatherland and of blood. Even if they take Indian citizenship, they fail his second test of blood. The fact is that many of the faiths he forcibly includes as Hindu themselves seek minority status today.

Savarkar thought that the ideal nations other than India were Saudi Arabia (founded 1932, he calls it Arabia) and Israel (founded 1948, he calls it Palestine). He saw India in their image.

He explains why: 'The ideal conditions, therefore, under which a nation can attain perfect solidarity and cohesion would, other things being equal, be found in the case of those people who inhabit the land they adore, the land of whose forefathers is also the land of their gods and angels, of seers and prophets; the scenes of whose history are also the scenes of their mythology. The Hindus are about the only people who are blessed with these ideal conditions that are at the same time incentive to national solidarity, cohesion and greatness. Not even the Chinese are blessed thus. Only Arabia and Palestine, if ever the Jews can succeed in founding their state there, can be said to possess this unique advantage. But Arabia is incomparably poorer in the natural, cultural, historical, and numerical essentials of a great people; and even if the dreams of the Zionists are ever realised into a Palestine State still they too must be equally lacking in these.'

This is a primitive way of looking at a nation. Any move towards idealism in a modern nation state can come only from equality under law. Savarkar understands that at some level. He writes: 'We are trying our best, as we ought to, to develop the consciousness of and a sense of attachment to the greater whole, whereby Hindus, Mohammedans, Parsis, Christians, and Jews would feel as Indians first and every other thing afterwards.'

It would be the Indian Constitution and not Hindutva that would ultimately achieve this.

It is not clear how Savarkar reached the conclusions that he has. And it is not certain whether Savarkar was familiar with Sikhism and knew that over hundred of the verses in the Guru Granth Sahib have been written by a Muslim, Fariduddin Ganj-i-Shakar of Multan. The verses were included by the fifth Sikh Guru Arjan himself. Where does that leave the holy scripture of the Sikhs, a work they regard as their living Guru according to Savarkar's rules of what is Indian?

His argument runs into trouble also in the modern era. To the Gujarati in England, is the Swaminarayan temple of Neasden any less holy than the one in Ahmedabad? And if he considers it as being superior or more responsive to his prayer, does that mean he has changed his holy land? And is his visiting it a sign of disloyalty? Savarkar does not appear to have explored the meaning and facets of his assertion.

He does not tell us, even if it is true that an individual holds religious allegiance abroad, when or how a contradiction or choice arises.

How is this love and allegiance to the holy land and the homeland expressed? By paying taxes? By seeking citizenship? By joining its army and police? By speaking the language? By supporting the cricket team? By identifying as Arab and not Indian?

To Savarkar, the shrines in Gulbarga, Agra, Kashmir, Nizamuddin, Ajmer, Sindh and Lahore—more frequented by and more familiar to South Asian Muslims than Mecca—are apparently of no consequence to them. Certainly they are of no consequence to him. It is the Arab world of his suspicions that has possessed all of India's Muslims.

He says that he has heard that Indian Muslims fail his test of loyalty: "If some of them be really believing what they profess to do, then there can be no choice—they must, to a man, set their holy land above their fatherland in their love and allegiance. That is but natural. We are not condemning nor are we lamenting. We are simply telling facts as they stand.'

These are of course not 'facts', even by his own telling: he himself qualifies his sweeping statement with the words—'if some of them be really believing what they profess to do'. These are prejudices.

The qawwali sung at shrines in India goes back to Amir Khusro who died in 1325 in Delhi, more than a century before the birth of Guru Nanak but it is not by Savarkar's definition sanskriti. Hindustani music is mostly devout but is the product of Indian pluralism. For this reason it is not culture according to Savarkar.

The Christian belief in Kerala goes back to St Thomas and the first century AD. Christianity is older in India than many of the Puranas, and the worship of Jesus in India is as old as anything today that is recognisably Hindu but it is in Savarkar's eyes, foreign.

The other problem of the exclusion is who and what it actually excludes. If the definition of who is Indian is linked irrevocably to Dussehra, Diwali, Holi, Baisakhi and Kumbh Mela, India will have to admit that parts of its territory are not Indian. The majority of Nagaland and Mizoram have no interest in such things and by Savarkar's definition they automatically remove themselves from the Indian nation.

Like the other two men we will take a look at, Savarkar insisted on nation-worship and the demotion of the individual and her rights as the starting point. The collective religious identity overwhelmed all else and it alone was meaningful in the relationship with nation, and the worship of the nation alone worthy of individual effort.

Savarkar was himself not particularly devout and by some accounts, was agnostic or even atheist. If he had a religion, it was his devotion to the abstract Bharat Mata figure. This lack of personal belief may be why he had to finesse his definition of Hinduism and demote it below his religious nationalism, characterising all Hinduism as being less important than Hindutva, the cultural history of Hindus as he understood it. Savarkar.org, the website put up with his collected works, tells us that he ate meat.

Perhaps because of this relative absence of dogma, he was also more willing to engage with caste and try and normalise its segmentation. This theory that caste is not all bad, a modern distortion and not particularly discriminatory in its origins, will be familiar to readers. This is because Savarkar's views on this have been made popular by the RSS among the Hindu urban middle-class.

Finally, Savarkar's contribution to Hindutva is only its definition. His text is not prescriptive because, written a quarter century before 1947, it does not anticipate the end of the Raj and independence. Savarkar does not tell us here what Hindutva is meant to do when it takes power and control of the government. He has no theory of the Hindu Rashtra state. He does not say whether on the basis of his definition of what is properly Hindu and therefore, Indian, there should be some hierarchy of citizenship.

Savarkar does not make, in this work, any demands of India's minorities. He only excludes them from his nation. It is the RSS and the BJP that have taken his work and definition further and developed the majoritarian ideal.

Does Hindutva really follow the ideology of Savarkar? No, just like it doesn't follow the philosophy of Deendayal Upadhyaya as we will see. On 19 December 2019, the RSS Sarsanghachalak Mohan Bhagwat said: 'The son of mother India, whether he may speak any language, from any region, follow any form of worship or not believing in worship of any is a Hindu... In this regard, for Sangh all the 130 crore people of India are Hindu society.'

However, this definition did not come with any explicit rejection of Savarkar's text or his ideals. Nor did it address and engage with the Muslims and Christians in any meaningful way because that is not the Sangh's intention. It was a casual assertion of inclusion keeping in place all the bigotry against Muslims and Christians the Sangh routinely continues to express.

So where does this leave Savarkar's *Essentials of Hindutva*? Nowhere. It is an ossified text. It has not been worked on, improved upon, expanded, studied and it is not relevant, including to the people who claim to own it. The ideology and founding text of Hindutva without its hatred of Muslims is empty of content and has been recognised as being so.

Savarkar lived till 1963 but after his trial and acquittal for the assassination of Gandhi he became a peripheral figure in the Hindutva movement. The man who would take charge of the Savarkarian thesis that India was a cultural monolith and that that culture was Hindutva was M.S. Golwalkar of the RSS. He would operationalise the exclusionary idea of Hindutva and popularise the term 'Hindu Rashtra'.

The second figure characterised as a twentieth century Hindutva thinker after Savarkar, Madhav Golwalkar (born 1906) was the second sarsanghachalak, meaning supreme head, of the RSS. He was also its longest serving leader: he took over in 1940 and he died while still sarsanghachalak in 1973, meaning his role stretched from before Independence and Partition through to the death of Nehru, the rise of Indira and the creation of Bangladesh. His term also saw the entry of Hindutva into India's democratic politics through the formation of the Jana Sangh.

Golwalkar was the most important head of the RSS, because under him the RSS was able to spread and grow, from being a provincial and largely Marathi body into one of the largest non-governmental organisations in the world. He formulated and expressed what passes for RSS ideology. The RSS reveres him and calls him Guruji (he also looked the part, with his beard and long hair). Like Savarkar, Golwalkar was a Brahmin, as was his predecessor Keshav Hedgewar, his successor Madhukar Deoras and current RSS head Mohan Bhagwat. His being Brahmin was important. Golwalkar believed that only Brahmins possessed the necessary qualities for guiding India and we will see why he thought that.

Golwalkar did not write on anything at length and the primary work attributed to him is a compilation of speeches and observations called *Bunch of Thoughts*, published twenty-five years after he took over the RSS. All of Golwalkar's and his organisation's themes are represented here. While his writing (or speaking) is simple and transparent, it is not easy to engage with *Bunch of Thoughts* as an intellectual work because that is not Golwalkar's intent or interest.

He sets great store by feeling and sentiment, because thinking takes away from the strong sense of identity and communitarianism that is his passion. Reason also takes away from the fierce emotion he feels, and the RSS feels, for the enemy, which is India's minorities. The following is a summary of what Golwalkar says in his *Bunch of Thoughts*.

India was special in the world because it offered something nobody else could and that was Hindu thought. The excellence of Hindu thought was that it alone knew something about the nature of the soul. This could be proved because it was only in India that from ancient times individuals rose to unravel the mystery of human nature, the 'science of spirit'.

Jesus only saw Satan. Muhammad only met Gabriel. It was only in India that sages saw god. Westerners, no matter how much they understood the science of matter, would remain ignorant of the science of spirit.

This unique offering was under threat because Hindus were abandoning their ancient wisdoms and it was the RSS which must revive them within India and organise Hindu society. It would do this by reversing the things that were damaging Hindus. Progressive societies were permissive. This led to licentious behaviour with respect to sex, food, drinks, family life and free social intercourse. These things did not produce real happiness. The individual must subsume himself into the larger nation, else the social fabric would be destroyed. This was what Hindu philosophy promoted and that was what would make Hindus happy.

All Hindus did not have this special Hindu knowledge, only some did. The common mass of people needed to be properly educated and enlightened. Making them merely literate would not serve the purpose because this special knowledge would still be absent. People were not equal in other ways also. Democracy was flawed because it excluded experts and preferred politicians. Panchayats functioned best when run along caste lines, to represent the interests of society as a whole. Elections should not be competitive but unanimous. (If this sounds disjointed and rambling, it is because that is how *Bunch of Thoughts* is put together).

India was the nation from the oceans to the Himalayas. Not just the edge of the mountains but beyond them, which is why the ancients had places of pilgrimage (Kailash Mansarovar) on the northern side, making these regions 'our live boundary'. Tibet was the abode of the gods and the Hindu epics also give Hindus possession of Afghanistan, Burma, Iran and Lanka. Bharat Mata, for thousands of years, had dipped her arms in the two seas, from Iran to Singapore, with Sri Lanka as a lotus petal offered at her sacred feet.

Bhoomi poojan was done because the entire earth was sacred, but Bharat Mata was the most sacred. She needed total devotion, and not engagement through the intellect. Partition was unacceptable because it was not a division of property between brothers: one does not cut up one's mother as settlement.

The concept of Hindu Rashtra was not a mere bundle of political and economic rights. It was essentially cultural and not political or legal. It revealed itself through the urge for realisation of God: a 'living' god and not an idol or immaterial form.

'Our People Are Our God' is what the ancients had said. But they had not meant all our people. Ramakrishna Paramhans and Vivekanand said, 'Serve man.' But man in the sense of humanity was too wide and cannot be grasped. It should be an Almighty with certain limitations. Man here meant only the Hindu people. The ancients did not use the word 'Hindu' but they did say in the Rig Veda that the sun and moon are his eyes, the stars and skies created from his navel and that Brahmin is the head, King the hands, Vaishya the thighs and Shudra the feet.

The people who had this fourfold arrangement were the God. Service to and worship of this caste-defined society was then service to God. All individuals in Hindu society were part of the divine whole and equally sacred and worthy of service. Any sense of discrimination amongst them was reprehensible. Defining people as Scheduled Caste and Scheduled Tribe produced separatism.

Tyranny was difficult in Hindu Rashtra because of caste. Hindu thought and practice kept economic power away from the hands of the state. It deprived the people producing wealth (Vaishya) of all political power (which was the right only of the Kshatriya). And above all, these two powers, political and economic, were subjected to the supervision of such selfless men as had no axe to grind: the Brahmins.

It was the continuous tradition of Brahmins holding the sceptre of spiritual authority, ever alert to undo the injustices perpetrated by either the ruler or the merchant, while themselves remaining above all temptations of power or riches, that had kept India glorious and immortal.

Social order through caste hierarchy was not discrimination. The feeling of high and low in caste was of recent origin, and a product of the scheming Britisher and his divide-and-rule policy. The Gita said that individuals who did their assigned caste duty were worshipping god. Saints and heroes came up from all castes—from Brahmins to peasants, weavers, cobblers and manual scavengers.

The caste system was not responsible for India's downfall. Prithviraj Chauhan was defeated by his own caste-relation

Jaichand. Rana Pratap was hounded by his fellow Rajput, Man Singh. The defeat of the Hindus at Poona in 1818 was under a fellow caste man of the Peshwas, named Natu, who hoisted the British flag. India was able to withstand the onslaught of Islam. But Afghanistan which was Buddhist and caste-free became Muslim. It was caste which had ensured the survival of Hinduism and Hindus in India.

The stress of the nation should be on duties of the individual rather than on rights. This society's individuals were imperfect, but when merged into a corporate whole could give rise to a perfect society. This catholicity of spirit was the unique Hindu contribution to world thought. What should be aimed for was harmony and the worship of society and motherland. Movements, agitations and other activity for rights were born of ignorance.

The problem of temple entry was not that of discrimination but of maintaining anonymity. If people who are Dalit did not announce their identity, or reveal they were Dalits, then the Brahmins of the temple would not know who they were and allow them to pray. Reports of upper caste attacks on Dalits in the media which were published with regularity were exaggerated and false. The attacks of Muslims on Dalits were being passed off as caste discrimination and caste atrocities and were likely the rest of a foreign hand. The fact that newspapers chose to display such reports in prominent fashion was in itself suspicious and possibly, propaganda.

Culture was not singing and dancing, nor was it cinema and theatre, all of these were cheap entertainment. Hindu cultural ambassadors should be like Rama and Sita and Vivekananda. Hindu wives and husbands did not display their love openly. The Hindu wife did not express her love through tears, embraces or screams, while Hindu men did not express their feelings verbally but their face would be aglow with love. And their love continued forever.

The ultimate vision of all the RSS's organisational efforts was a perfectly organised state of Hindu (male) society where each individual had been moulded into a model of ideal Hindu manhood and made into a living limb of the whole. This required many years and thousands of dedicated missionaries. It also required strong individuals who would not give in to sexual and material temptation. It was to mould them that the RSS laid utmost stress on its members attending daily gatherings at a particular hour, at a particular place, day after day, year after year, for their lifetime.

National reorganisation meant fostering those traits in individuals which built up national character and cohesion. It was directed towards awakening a passionate devotion to the motherland, a feeling of fraternity, a sense of sharing in national work, a deeply felt reverence for the nation's ideals, discipline, heroism, manliness and other noble virtues. This work could not be done through sermons or the taking of pledges. It required daily gatherings in an environment congenial to this passion's growth. The RSS framework for it was designed by its founder K.B. Hedgewar.

The RSS shakha was usually held at an open playground and under a saffron flag, and young men were absorbed in 'Bharatiya' games like kabaddi. The leader's whistle or order had a magical effect on them; there was instant and perfect order and silence. Exercises then followed—wielding the lathi, Suryanamaskar and marching. They then sat down and sang patriotic songs in chorus. They also held discussions in which they delved deep into the problems affecting national life. Finally, they stood in rows before the flag and recited the prayer 'Namaste sada vatsale matrubhumi' (Oh Mother [Bharat Mata or Mother India] who is forever affectionate to her children—salutations to thee). They shouted 'Bharat Mata ki Jai', the final line of the RSS prayer.

Muslims and Christians were born in India, but they were not true to their salt. They were not grateful to India. They did not feel that they were the children of India and its traditions and did not feel that to serve India was their good fortune. They felt no duty to serve. Together with the change in their faith, gone was the spirit of love and devotion for the nation. Muslims still thought they had come to India only to conquer and establish their kingdoms.

Muslims who had inherited names like Sheikh and Syed were participating in treason. They had joined the camp of the enemy leaving their mother nation in the lurch. Muslims were like jackals raised by a lioness. Mere common residence of Hindus and Muslims in a particular territory could not forge a nation with common character and qualities.

German citizens resident in England had been locked up during the First World War lest their attachment to Germany be roused. This was the mature thing to do and the correct understanding of nationalism. India's Muslims had been converted by trickery and deception. It was the duty of Hindus to call their forlorn brothers, suffering under religious slavery, back to their ancestral home. The RSS sought not only political and economic unity but also cultural and religious unity.

The gratuitous antagonism of the Muslim towards the Hindu was so deep-rooted that whatever Hindus believed in, the Muslim was wholly hostile to. If Hindus worshipped in temples, Muslims would desecrate them. If Hindus carried out bhajans and car (rath) festivals, that would irritate Muslims. If Hindus worshipped the cow, the Muslims wanted to eat it. If Hindus glorified woman as the symbol of motherhood, the Muslims wanted to molest her.

Hindus were told by their leaders to forget the past. That if their processions irritated Muslims, then they should discontinue. And if their wives and daughters were carried off by Muslims then they should not be stopped, else there would be violence. The direct result of this was that Muslims defeated Hindus in 1947. This was the worst-ever defeat suffered by India because these were Muslims who had been converted forcibly or through temptation. Hindus had succumbed, and accepted the division of Bharat Mata.

This defeat was the worst-ever suffered by Hindus because these Muslims were those who were converted to Islam at the point of sword or by temptations of power and pelf. They were the progeny of that section of Indian society, which had not the mental stamina or the self-respect to stand up in defence of their swadesh and swadharma but preferred to join the enemy camp to save their skin.

Hindus were the children of heroic ancestors of peerless valour who for centuries had braved and stamped out waves of invading Muslim hordes, but in 1947, they had accepted defeat. Even in the times of Akbar and Aurangzeb not a day passed without a Rana Pratap, a Guru Gobind Singh or a Shivaji challenging them and asserting India's national freedom. The same inspiring tradition of freedom struggle had continued unabated during the rule of the British. However, for the first time in 1947, Hindus gave up the fight, putting an ignoble end to the glorious one thousand-year-long struggle for national freedom, surrendered all their rights and acquiesced in an unchallenged domination of the aggressor over huge portions of their land.

Pushing for unity of Hindus and Muslims in modern India was humbug nationalism. It was also unnatural, unscientific and a lifeless hybrid concept as opposed to the natural, living nationalism of the RSS. Hindus would have to stop being fooled into seeing Hindu nationalism as communal, medieval and reactionary. They must assert that Hindus were the national society of Bharat and elevate the Hindu national life in Bharat.

The RSS called itself the Rashtriya Swayamsevak Sangh and not the Hindu Swayamsevak Sangh. This was because 'Rashtriya' naturally means Hindu and therefore the word 'Hindu' need not be used. The first RSS head Keshav Hedgewar had said: 'If we use the word Hindu it will only mean that we consider ourselves only as one of the innumerable communities in this land and that we do not realise our natural status as the nationals of this country.' Savarkar's Hindu Mahasabha was wrong in once having passed a resolution that the Congress should not give up its nationalist position by holding talks with the Muslim League but instead asking the Hindu Mahasabha to do so. This ceded equal position to the Muslims and was a perversion of the reality that India was wholly and only a Hindu Rashtra.

Both the secularist and the communal Hindu were agreed that the Muslim was always the aggressor. However, the secularist indulged in appeasement. India's response to its Muslim citizens must be touched with the awareness that he was the aggressor and hostile. Instead of saying that Muslims would be given 5 per cent of the seats or 15 per cent seats or parity, or allowing them to partition the land, what should instead be said was, 'Come on, and let us settle accounts.'

Federalism was a problem and the only way out was to be courageous enough to declare a unitary type of government by amending the Constitution. The country was one, the people were one, and therefore India ought to have only a single government and a single legislature. Executive authority could be distributed, but legislative authority should be one and not devolved to the states. One central legislature for the whole of the country should satisfy the demands of democracy.

These were the views of Golwalkar. The name *Bunch of Thoughts* was given to the work after it was compiled, because they present his views in random order on a variety of subjects. Of these some of the most striking are those on caste and the ones on India's minorities, especially Muslims. The intensity of the hatred approaches and likely crosses the limits of sanity.

Golwalkar understands, as B.R. Ambedkar did, that Hinduism was little without caste. It was not possible to be rid of it root and branch and be left with anything of substance. The Hindu faith, its mythologies, its heroes and its rituals were shot through with caste. What was needed to make caste modern and appealing was to address untouchability and laud the rest. Golwalkar's attempt to do this is not touched by enthusiasm.

His solution to discrimination is for its victims, the Dalits, to hide their identity when they go to the local temple. Golwalkar's understanding of the motivation of the Dalit to go to the temple she is forbidden from entering is that she is burning with religious fervour. This fervour must and will be taken care of by the broader Hindu society, but for this the Dalit must not announce who she is and she must pray and leave.

The right to enter freely as an extension of the Dalit's desire for equality and for making a statement against discrimination and against tradition does not seem to occur to him. The temple entry movement he has a problem with was only marginally about religion: it was about equality and access to public spaces. It was about Dalits announcing their identity and not hiding it and it was not about increasing the volume of offerings at the temple coffers. Golwalkar's casual dismissal of violence against Dalits as being either done by Muslims or by a foreign nation reveals him to be either blinded by his prejudices or being ignorant. It is a phenomenon as ancient as Hinduism and widespread even today.

Golwalkar's argument that caste keeps tyranny at bay is original. If only Vaishyas were allowed to trade and if only Kshatriyas were allowed to rule and if only Brahmins were allowed to interpret and oversee ritual then there would be no tussle for power. Everyone would know their place by birth. He does not however attempt to sell this formulation to modern India because he cannot. His argument that caste kept Hinduism intact while Buddhism surrendered to Islam in Afghanistan is also original.

Golwalkar is the most openly enthusiastic Hindutva ideologue about the benefits of caste. The RSS today would not repeat what Golwalkar says openly because India has changed over the last few decades. It continues to promote his book, but few read it, including inside the RSS, and so the secret is safe. Golwalkar says that the identifiable characteristic of the society worthy of worship is that it is caste-based, which is a good thing. And that it is the Brahmin's right to determine the right and the good which kept the system intact for millennia. How many Hindus would agree with this? That would depend of course on what caste of Hindu one puts this question to. Golwalkar's interest in what the masses may think or feel on this is limited. The word 'Shudra' occurs twice in Golwalkar's text, while 'Brahmin' is referred to, twenty times. *Bunch of Thoughts* is the reimagining of caste as a utopia and it should not surprise anyone that this is the view of the Brahmin examining caste and finding only the good. The RSS is run as a monarchy and the next Sarsanghachalak is appointed by the current one. Golwalkar left the organisation in the safe Brahmin hands of M.D. (Balasaheb) Deoras.

If the issues of Hindu society were the concern of the RSS, as Golwalkar says they were, then the primary one should have been the elimination of discrimination in it, which continues. Golwalkar has absolutely no interest in this. If the RSS continues to get the BJP into trouble even today through its statements on and allusions to the elimination of reservations, it is because it is putting forward the view of Golwalkar and of the wider upper caste society. If we removed reservations, everyone would then be equal and society would not be divided. That reservations exist because society is hopelessly divided and discriminating is not to them sufficient cause.

Hindu society must be united. To what end? It was not to reform itself or even to modernise itself. It was to fix Muslims. Who is the RSS doing its martial training and lathi-twirling in tens of thousands of shakhas across India every morning for? Not the Chinese. It is for India's minorities. Golwalkar's opinion of Muslims has the virtue of honesty. His words do not need to be interpreted. They are unambiguous and would be classified as hate speech against a persecuted minority in a civilised nation. He sees Muslims as congenitally villainous. They have little or no individual agency, they are programmed for treason and must be countered. Scores had to be settled with them.

They existed only to spite the Hindus and that was what they did. Partition was not the result of a failure to arrive at a political settlement but the extension of a millennial war of civilisations. With Golwalkar, we begin to arrive at the real meaning of Hindutva, the word coined and popularised by Savarkar.

The third and last man in the list of Hindutva's twentieth century thinkers was Deendayal Upadhyaya. What Savarkar had defined, what Golwalkar had operationalised in society, Upadhyaya would attempt to politicise and introduce into government.

The BJP's constitution (Article 3) says, 'Integral Humanism shall be the philosophy of the party.' The party's membership form has a pledge which members are required to take. The first line of this pledge is: 'I believe in Integral Humanism which is the basic philosophy of the Bharatiya Janata Party.'

Integral Humanism is not a book but the text of four lectures in Bombay given by Upadhyaya between 22 and 25 April 1965. Upadhyaya held a bachelor's degree in arts and was a journalist at the RSS house publication, *Panchjanya*. He was about fifty when he gave these lectures and became president of the Jana Sangh a couple of years after he delivered them.

The lectures seek to explain the phrase 'integral humanism' that the Bharatiya Jana Sangh (the BJP's precursor) adopted in a statement of its principles and policies in January 1964. The following is a summary of the argument that Upadhyaya presents in the Bombay speeches.

The cause of the problems facing Bharat is a neglect of national identity. The nation is like an individual and becomes ill if its natural instincts are disregarded or suppressed. Seventeen years after independence, India was still undecided about the direction it would take to realise development. Independence is meaningful only it is the instrument to express culture.

The focus in India was on episodic problems: economic, social and political. This was because India adopted a Western way of looking at economic, social and political doctrines along with Western science.

Westernisation was synonymous with progress for Indians. However, the West was unable to reconcile nationalism, democracy and socialism. These were essentially Western ideals and they were all in conflict with one another. These ideologies were not universal and not free from the limitations of the particular people and cultures which gave birth to these isms. Ayurveda said that we need to find local cures to local diseases. Could Bharatiya culture provide a solution for the world?

For that we would have to consider our culture, which was holistic and integrated. Unity in diversity and expression of unity was the central thought of Bharatiya culture. If this truth is accepted by all nations, there will be no global conflict. There is another contribution India has made on the subject. It is thought that Bharatiya culture thinks of salvation of the soul and does not bother about body, mind and intellect but that is untrue.

Dharma is given foremost place in Bharatiya culture. Dharma is the natural law that is eternal and universally applicable.

Dharma is ethics teaching us not to lie, not to fight. When nature is channeled according to the principles of dharma, there is culture and civilisation.

Dharma is higher than the executive, legislative and the judiciary, and it is also higher than the people. If out of 450 million Indians, all except one voted for something it would still be wrong if it was against dharma. The people have no right to act against dharma. The words 'secularism' and 'dharmnirpeksh' (the Hindi phrase for secularism meaning 'that which is not dependent on dharma') used in the constitution are wrong and bad because dharma is a necessary condition for the State. That which is not based on dharma is unacceptable and therefore secularism was fatally flawed. National unity is India's dharma and so diversity was problematic. For this reason India's Constitution needs to be changed from federal to unitary with no legislative powers for the states, only for the Centre.

Conflict between individuals and institutions of society is a sign of decadence and perversion. The West was wrong to see the adversarial relationship between the individual and the state as the reason for progress. The individual was made up of body, mind, intelligence and soul. A human being is born with a soul. Personality, soul and character are different from one another. The person's soul is unaffected by personal history. Similarly, national culture is continuously modified by history. Culture includes all the things held as good and commendable, but they do not affect 'chiti', the national soul. India's national soul is fundamental and central. Chiti determines the direction of cultural advance. It filters out what is to be excluded from culture.

Societies are animate and a society has a body, mind, intellect and soul. Some Westerners were beginning to accept this truth. One of them, William McDougall said that a group had a mind and a psychology, its own methods of thinking and action just as an individual did. Societies have an inborn nature that is not based on its history. Events do not affect it. This group nature is like the soul in individuals, which was also unaffected by history. This group mentality is like mob mentality but developed over a longer period. The nation needs both an ideal and a motherland and only then is it a nation. And the State exists to protect this nation, which has an ideal and a motherland.

These four elements were integrated and could not be thought of separately. The difference between India and the West was that we regard the body only as an instrument to achieve dharma. Our efforts were for dharma, artha (money), kama (pleasure) and moksha (liberation).

The mistake of the West was to treat the four separately. You could get voting rights but then you didn't get food. The United States had both political freedom and wealth but it also topped the list in the number of suicides and mental patients. This was puzzling—there was bread and voting rights but no peace or happiness. Sound sleep was scarce in America because they had not thought of the integrated human being.

The Americans said 'honesty is the best business policy' and the Europeans said 'honesty is the best policy', but the Indians said 'honesty is not a policy but a principle'. Dharma was a regulator of both economics and pleasure. The stability of the State was essential for the spread of dharma and to do this, education, character-building, idealism and suitable economic structures were needed.

Capitalism was greed-based and incapable of helping the development of an integrated human being. Socialism is like capitalism run by the State. India should not import machines but develop Bharatiya technology. Education should be free and so should healthcare. The right to food is a birthright and there must be a right (guarantee) to work. Machines are good but not those which replace too many workers. The West had developed efficient machines because they were short of manpower, which India was not short of.

Through this integrated form of humanism, nationalism, democracy and socialism could be reconciled with the values of Bharatiya culture. All this is philosophy, but the members of the Bharatiya Jana Sangh are not mere philosophers or academicians and must carry out programmes of national reconstruction based on this foundation of Integral Humanism. The goal is not merely to protect culture but revitalise it so as to make it dynamic.

This was the message of the four lectures. It is not easy to figure out what the meaning of it all is. What, for instance, is the difference between mind and intelligence? What is a soul? How are these three separate from a body? What does the sentence that personality, soul and character are all distinct from one another mean? And what is the role of a political party and of government in any of this?

The national soul, chiti, and group mind are not scientific phenomena and the works of William McDougall are not science (he thought, like Upadhyaya did, that the mind influenced evolution). How would we know what India's chiti was telling us? Did it come to us through some individual messiahs or was it the case that whatever was popular at the current time was the expression of chiti? The group mind assumes a constant and unbroken unanimity and no real individual freedom. That is an absurdity. Even if possible, a nation thinking in unison and marching or being forced to march in lockstep is a dangerous thing for itself and for others. The justification is aimed at geographical unity at the expense of the rest.

Explaining the lectures on its website, the BJP says, 'The philosophy of Integral Humanism looks at the individual not merely as a material object but one who has a spiritual dimension. It talks of (an) integral approach to economic development that has (the) individual at its core that is linked to the family, the society and the nation.'

What do these words mean? What does a government and political party have to do with the spiritual dimension and even if this is possible how can this spiritual dimension be tapped into with the usual levers available to the state? How are these words reflected in the BJP's manifesto or in the BJP's budgets through actionable policies? If they are, in what way are they missing from the policies of other parties? We do not know.

The BJP also says on the first page of its constitution that 'the party shall bear true faith and allegiance to ... the principles of socialism, secularism and democracy', which appears to put it at odds with Upadhyaya's rejection of 'isms' as being Western and inappropriate for India. Upadhyaya nails socialism to the wall and specifically rejects secularism as opposed to the desired presence of dharma. He does say that Integral Humanism reconciles them but doesn't explain how it does so, because it really doesn't.

The word 'dharma' appears in *Integral Humanism* 167 times but what is this eternal and unchanging law? Who decides what it is and who interprets it when it is not clear? In what way does the Indian Constitution and its ideals oppose dharma? Upadhyaya says the people are not sovereign over dharma and this phrasing is the same as in the constitution of religion based states like Pakistan. Upadhyaya concedes no space for dissent against his absolutism even when the view expressed is that of a democratic majority. Sovereignty belongs to dharma, as it does to Allah in the preamble of Pakistan's Constitution. The one place where dharma is defined, it is tied to geographical unity of Bharat Mata which is considered sacrosanct.

Integral Humanism reads like a 'pravachana', a sermon by an Indian holy man. Intellectually, it is sophomoric. Its laying out of the problem, even if we were to disregard the factual errors (the United States does not lead the world in suicides or mental disorders, and in fact the suicide rate in India is higher than in the US) is generalised and folksy. Upadhyaya's analysis and dismissal of such things as socialism, capitalism and democracy are not especially sophisticated. It would be difficult to defend it against the accusation that the analysis is shallow. Integral Humanism's prescriptions are weak and inconsistent.

On economics, in the only place where Upadhyaya offers specifics, his understanding seems to be quite elementary. This may be one reason the BJP itself has rejected his swadeshi thrust where it has taken power, including at the Centre as it did and has done since the late 1990s. Upadhyaya's attitude to machines is quaint and belongs to another time. Industry does not calibrate its use of automation based on how many more people it can employ but on how many fewer. All in all, Integral Humanism is like a religious text in an ancient language. It is revered by some but it is not read by many and certainly its moral instruction is not followed, including by those who claim to own it, in this instance, the BJP.

The word 'culture' occurs in the text thirty-five times. Upadhyaya says the aim is not only to protect Indian culture but to revitalise it. Which Indian culture? That he does not say. What is Indian culture? He does not go there either in these speeches. However in a 1952 speech, Upadhayaya said: 'There exists only one culture here. There are no separate cultures here for Muslims and Christians. Culture is not related to mode of worship or sect; it is related to the country. Kabir, Jayasi and Rasakhan (a Pushtun poet who wrote about Krishna) should serve as models for Muslims. Today their centre of loyalty is outside Bharat. The Muslims must completely change their sentiment and view.'

In *Integral Humanism*, there is no reference to music, art, literature, food, astronomy, theatre, mathematics or science of any sort that is Indian. He tells us nothing about where these

aspects of culture stand in his scheme of things and how they
are to be protected and revitalised. Other Hindutva writers and
leaders share this lack of interest in the lived cultures of the
subcontinent. This they have in common with those in other
nations who push religion in the state.

Culture is both preserved and revitalised only through
practice and popular spread. Upadhyaya insists that the chiti or
national soul is the arbiter of what is to be included in culture and
that 'what is against chiti is discarded as perversion, undesirable
and to be avoided'. But this is not how popular culture, much of
which is at the edge of immorality and licentiousness, spreads.
Culture is not the product of piety. Popular music and art like
cinema are pluralist and not reflective of the devotional attitude
and sentiment Upadhyaya writes about. They integrate and
modernise and keep up with the times. Often culture moves
society along, shifting attitudes towards the weak and the
marginalised and dragging the reluctant orthodoxy along.

The texts quoted in *Integral Humanism* are religious and
the examples cited are mythological. The language of quotations
approvingly used is Sanskrit. Is the culture of India limited to the
collected Hindu texts and mythologies and religious practices? It
would appear so from *Integral Humanism*.

What specific changes should we make in our lives and
laws to align ourselves further with dharma and so be able to
reap rewards for 'body, mind, intelligence and soul'? There are
no details about this. Shouting 'Bharat Mata ki jai' (victory
to Mother India) in unison appears to be the one action that
Upadhyaya and also Hindutva today wants us to take. He ends
the lectures with this exhortation. What will shouting it achieve?
What does this victory look like and how will we know when we
have won?

Such questions are not answered in *Integral Humanism*.
Indeed, they are not even asked. One can sense a burning passion

felt by Upadhyaya as well as the Hindutva zealots of today and
it is true that many of them are driven and often motivated. But
towards what? What is Integral Humanism ultimately for and
to what end does it seek to reconcile nationalism, socialism and
democracy? It is not a specific goal that marks out the developed
from the underdeveloped.

India's problems are material. What is underdeveloped in
India is not religion and spiritualism—we may even be considered
world leaders in such things—it is the economy and the rule of
law.

The well-being of nations is measurable because it is the
well-being of its people. It lies in the rates of infant mortality
and in gender ratios, in the human development index and in
per capita GDP and median incomes, in Nobel Prizes awarded
and Olympics medals won, in inventions and philanthropic
contributions.

There is no road map in *Integral Humanism* to getting India
there. Nor is there even the expression of a desire to get there.
All of what could be seen as measurable progress of the nation
is either incidental or irrelevant. Upadhyaya's interest is in the
unity of the physical entity.

Upadhyaya's India is not a real nation with people and faiths
and sects and states and languages and dietary preferences and
music and dissent and disputes. It is a construct. Bharat Mata is
an anthropomorphic image of geographical lines, an imagined
map, an idea. What is desired to be made great is this abstraction.
The actual people and cultures it contains today are useful only
in so far as they help in achieving this undefined greatness.

There is mumbo jumbo about the existence of a soul and
group mind and group think which does not stand up to scrutiny.
It is difficult to take *Integral Humanism* seriously and that is why
it isn't in fact taken seriously, including by the BJP. When the BJP
member takes the pledge that he believes in Integral Humanism,

he isn't speaking the truth. He doesn't even know what it is. Nobody does. When the BJP claims Integral Humanism is its 'basic philosophy', it is lying. There is nothing that connects its actual programme of work at the central and provincial levels to the half-baked thoughts uttered by Upadhyaya in 1965.

The truth is that it is not in fact the philosophy of the BJP as the party claims it to be, because Integral Humanism is hardly philosophy of any sort at all.

Two years after the Integral Humanism lectures were given, India held a general election in 1967. The Jana Sangh contested under Upadhyaya. There was no reference to Integral Humanism in the party manifesto. And there is little or nothing in it that appears to connect to the things said by Upadhyaya. The election was the first one after the China war of 1962, the death of Jawaharlal Nehru in 1964, the Pakistan war in 1965 and the death of Lal Bahadur Shastri in 1966. India was still under wartime emergency, the Congress was adrift, the economy was shot and confidence in government low.

Clearly there was the space for the Jana Sangh to push for the radical shift that Upadhyaya appears to aim for, and unleash the natural instincts of the nation. This did not happen. The manifesto asks for the weaponisation of India's nuclear programme (as the Congress would do under Indira Gandhi soon after), without considering what it would do to India's access to technology or reputation, and referred to the peace talks with China and Pakistan as 'needless prattle'. There are dark references to unnamed anti-national forces which the Sangh would put down through force.

There is a reference to amending the Constitution and making India a unitary State, to deletion of Article 370, to politically reorganising the Northeast and to restricting the activity of missionaries there. There is a demand for an uniform civil code and for a ban on cow slaughter and for enforcing prohibition because drinking is a 'social evil'. The Jana Sangh agrees with the Congress that India needs a planned economy but it will tweak it 'to be based on our own resources and capacities'. The aim is to spend more on defence and raise the standards of living.

Trade with non-communist nations will be privatised but the insurance of foreign trade will be nationalised. Foreign capital will be discouraged and the Indianisation of tobacco, jute, rubber, soap, tea and biscuits encouraged. The document then surrenders to the banal business of pay scales and dearness allowances and teachers' salaries. The manifesto ends with the words: 'Let us exert to bring about a democratic revolution through this Fourth general elections and give the country a new direction.'

However what this revolution is, that unifies socialism and democracy and individualism or anything else, and how the programme of work laid out fits into a larger plan that seeks radical change is difficult to discern.

There was no opportunity to find out how it worked in practice. The Congress under Indira won the election and Upadhyaya passed away the following year, being murdered in a train robbery. Upadhyaya never had the political power to be able to enforce his Integral Humanism in government because in his time with the Jana Sangh it did not win a single election, whether in the state assemblies or at the centre.

After his passing, Integral Humanism as an ideology or a philosophy was not worked on, improved upon, expanded or interpreted. It has also become, like *Essentials of Hindutva*, an ossified text. The words in it, including the spelling errors, were passed on when the Jana Sangh renamed itself as the Bharatiya Janata Party and copy-pasted the text of the lectures on its website.

The BJP used to carry the full text of the four Integral Humanism speeches on its website. Now, it only has a brief précis of the material. Earlier, it excised from Upadhyaya's speech the casual bigotry it contains. For instance, this paragraph from the third speech on 23 April in which Upadhyaya gives an example of his group mind theory:

'Let me give you an illustration. Once during a conversation between Shri Vinobaji and the Sar Sanghachalak of Rashtriya Swayamsevak Sangh, Shri Guruji, a question arose as to where the modes of thinking of Hindus and Muslims differ. Guruji said to Vinobaji that there are good and bad people in every society. There can be found honest and good people in Hindus as well as in Muslims. Similarly, rascals can be seen in both the societies. No particular society has a monopoly of goodness. However, it is observed that Hindus even if they are rascals in individual life, when they come together in a group, they always think of good things. On the other hand when two Muslims come together, they propose and approve of things which they themselves in their individual capacity would not even think of. They start thinking in an altogether different way. This is an everyday experience. Vinobaji admitted that there was truth in this observation but had no reasons to explain it.'[7]

This sort of crude reduction is unacceptable in our time and this is why the BJP hides it though it is perfectly representative of what they say and feel. Integral Humanism is just a phrase and has become a cover. Under its guise, there operates in the BJP another philosophy, assuming the word 'philosophy' can be used for old-fashioned majoritarianism. In the 1952 speech referred to above, Upadhyaya explained that the Jana Sangh principle was that 'there is only one nation in this country. There is no minority in this nation.'

It is the exclusionary Hindutva of Savarkar and Golwalkar. Inside the BJP, the word 'Hindutva' is not ignored and is not inert

---

7. These paragraphs are still to be found in the Integral Humanism text published on the official website of the party in Gujarat at https://bjpgujarat.org/philosophy/.

like Integral Humanism. It is in fact deployed quite actively and enthusiastically. And its meaning is understood umambiguously: putting India's Muslims in their place.

Speaking in Pune in 1965, the same year as the Integral Humanism lectures, Upadhyaya says why Muslims cannot be considered Indian: 'Some argue that Muslims are our brothers and should not be called foreigners. Arguing the same way, why is Aurangzeb, who lived and utilised the wealth here, regarded a foreign ruler? Are not Mughal kings to be treated as foreigners? If not, Shivaji, who fought against Mughal power, must be regarded a traitor to this country. If Akbar is our man, Rana Pratap, who fought with him, will no more be a patriot. If Rana Pratap, Chhatrapati Shivaji, Chhatrasal, Durgavati are patriots, then those against whom they fought must be regarded as foreigners. Akbar may have been great but he was not ours. We speak of having become free after a thousand years of slavery. This simply means that during Akbar's reign we were in bondage.'

Upadhyaya then explains what the political aim his party seeks to achieve is: 'Our quarrel is not with Mohammed, nor with Mullas and Maulavis. Our quarrel is with the way Muslims behave, coupling political ambition with religious zeal. This is why this war is not religious but political ... There is only one way to defeat Muslim bigotry, and it is to politically defeat them. That is the real solution of the Muslim problem. So long as they are not politically defeated, the rot will continue to grow. Only such a defeat will make them have second thoughts and the process of Hindu-Muslim cooperation will begin. It is a general rule that defeat makes men introspective. So far as Hindus are concerned, their tradition is that of accommodation of any sect. Our policy should be aggressive on the national plane, tolerant on the religious plane and accommodative on the social plane.'

Stripped of the gobbledygook of group mind and science of spirit, what remained in the texts of the so-called Hindu right was first a defence of caste and second, a hatred of Muslims. These two are what really underpin Hindutva. The first was not a good political platform. That is why it fell away between Golwalkar and Upadhyaya. India's Hindu population is overwhelmingly Shudra as the strength of the Mandal agitation showed. Dalits and Adivasis could hardly be expected to be enthusiastic about Golwalkar's full-throated support of caste-based discrimination either. This part of the Hindutva ideology was kept muted and became secondary. The campaign against Indian Muslims would dominate and would also accommodate the elements of discrimination that are important to Golwalkar's Hindu sentiment. Golwalkar's and the RSS's despising of Indian Muslims would manifest itself in the political party the Sangh would form, and in time, form the core of its three policy thrusts. Upadhyaya said in Pune: 'There need not be any doubt as to whether this political problem should be solved or not. It will have to be solved and there is only one way in which it can be solved. It can't be solved unless and until Muslims are politically defeated. It is only after such a defeat that it will be possible to assimilate the Muslims. It was this basic ignorance of the Hindu-Muslim problem that led to the appeasement methods or hollow appeals. It is not a surprise that they failed. The inferiority complex in the Hindus that has resulted from these wrong policies will also disappear with the defeat of the secessionists. The national sense of achievement will find free scope. Defeat often makes a person prone to self-analysis. When Muslims make a candid self-analysis, they will awaken to the truth that their traditions are Indian traditions, they have common ancestors and Bharat Mata is their Motherland.'

This political defeat of Muslims was the task with which the BJP was charged by the RSS.

5

AND THEN CAME ADVANI

Why was the Jana Sangh formed by the RSS and for what reason? In 2006, the BJP published a set of six books on its predecessor, the Bharatiya Jana Sangh. The set of party documents includes volumes on the Jana Sangh's manifestos, policies and statements made from the year of its founding till it was folded up into the BJP in 1980. Volume six is the history of the Jana Sangh which explains why the RSS itself was founded and the background to its entry into politics.

The following is a summary of the text.

In order to understand the principles and policies of the Jana Sangh it was important to know the past. The animosity between Hindus and Muslims was ascribed to the British policy of 'divide and rule'. However, it was actually a divide that was created by the Muslims. The British merely widened it.

Muslims had ruled large parts of India for more than six centuries before British rule. In this period there was little animosity between the masses of Hindus and Muslims. This was primarily because Muslims had been recently converted and participated in Hindu celebrations and festivals. They retained Hindu first names.

However the Muslim elite stood apart. They refused to accept Indian heroes like Kalidas and Panini, or Chandragupta

Maurya and Harshavardhana as their own. Buddha and Mahavir were not figures of reverence for them and they felt the need to purge themselves of what was Hindu. They were encouraged to give up vegetarianism, consultation with astrologers and the visiting of shrines and tombs.

The Muslims made up the myth that they were the instigators of the Mutiny and the primary victims of the 1857 violence. They also made up the myth that Muslims were backward in civil service employment (in the government) and in education. Muslim leaders like Sir Syed Ahmed Khan, the founder of Aligarh Muslim University, urged the community to be quietist and acquiesce to British rule. This collaboration was preferred also because both Muslims and the British (who were Christian) were people of the book, and didn't have the dietary taboos that Hindus did.

Sir Syed was therefore the real source of separatism and the father of Pakistan, being acknowledged as being so even by Pakistani scholars. A few years after the death of Sir Syed in 1898, the Muslim League was formed in 1906 to promote the interests of the community. This was encouraged by the British, who gave them concessions, including separate electorates. From then till 1947, the British found in India's Muslims their allies and a handle with which to beat Hindus.

Gandhi's attempt to unify Hindus and Muslims under the non-cooperation movement failed because of his appeasement of Muslims. The Khilafat movement fired up fanatical sentiments and was the cause of the Mappila rebellion in Kerala which began as an anti-colonial movement but degenerated into communal riots. In these, the Hindus were at the receiving end of massacres, rape and forced conversions by the Muslim population.

In a parallel development, the Hindus in what is now Maharashtra felt that they needed to act to secure their own interests. The Hindu Mahasabha leader, B.S. Moonje wrote that communal violence frequently happened in Nagpur because though only numbering 20,000 of the population of the city, 'We (Hindus) felt insecure because the Muslims were never afraid of 1.3 lakh Hindus.'

Moonje felt this was because Hindus were divided into water-tight compartments, 'each having a special and cultural life of its own that there is hardly any association between them'. This was in contrast to the Muslims who 'form one organic community, religiously well organised and disciplined'. And because of this 'any injury done to any part of the community anywhere is felt as keenly all throughout'.

The formation of the RSS was to address this problem of disunity of Hindus in relation to taking on Muslims. It would work towards the cause of Hindu unity and solidarity and cultural nationalism. Its founder K.B. Hedgewar went about organising Hindu society and addressing its two problems of disunity and the caste system. He did both of these through the mechanism of the shakha, where Hindus of all castes would gather for an hour daily. They would play games, exercise, learn to march and do some drills. They would also sing songs together addressed to Bharat Mata.

The problem of caste would be addressed through their playing and eating together. M.D. Deoras, the third head of the RSS described it thus: 'I was present in the first Sangh camp. In that there were quite a number of Mahaar brethren. At the time of meals, some began hesitating to sit with them. They had never before in their lives sat for meals with Mahaars, They placed their problem before Doctorji (Hedgewar). But he did not enforce the discipline of the camp and ask them to get out. Doctorji simply said: "Our practice is to sit together. We shall sit accordingly." All of us sat together for meals. Those few that were hesitant sat in a separate line. But for the next meals those very people came to Doctorji and apologised and sat with us of their own accord.'

Hedgewar died in 1940, by when the RSS had spread beyond Nagpur and had 100,000 members. His successor was Golwalkar, under whom the RSS continued to grow and spread. Golwalkar was pragmatic and felt the RSS had to operate within the law. When the British forbade Indians in 1943 from military dress and drill, the RSS gave it up immediately.

During Partition, the RSS became the defence force of the Hindus and put their lives at risk to save Hindus and Sikhs from murder, rape, loot and conversion. It became popular for this reason among the displaced communities and refugees. Sangh workers saved millions of Hindus in Pakistan areas from annihilation. The RSS also blocked the Muslim conspiracies in East Punjab and Delhi. Additionally it threw itself into relief work.

An RSS rally in Delhi in December 1947 drew a large crowd and also attracted Hindu princes, businessmen and leaders of other Hindu organisations. This popularity was something that alarmed the Congress, especially Nehru. The assassination of Gandhi on 30 January 1948 gave the Congress the opportunity to act. It decided to ban the RSS on 2 February, three days after Gandhi's murder.

Golwalkar had sensed that the RSS would get into trouble once the details of Gandhi's assassination were out. He acted immediately. On the day of the killing, 30 January 1948, he sent telegrams to RSS branches suspending operations for thirteen days. The same day he also telegrammed Nehru, Patel and Devdas Gandhi with a message of condolence: 'Shocked at this cruel fatal attack and tragic loss of greatest personality.'

The next day he again wrote to Nehru expressing his shock and referring to Godse as 'some thoughtless perverted soul' who had 'committed the heinous act of putting a sudden and ghastly end to the life of poojya Mahatmaji by the bullet'. He called the killing unpardonable and an act of treason.

That day he wrote also to Patel: 'My heart is wrung with extreme agony. It is difficult to find words to condemn the person who committed this crime...'

The government notification declaring the RSS unlawful said: 'The professed aims and objects of the RSS are to promote the physical, intellectual and moral well-being of the Hindus and also to foster feelings of brotherhood, love and service amongst them ... the Government have, however, noticed with regret that in practice members of the RSS have not adhered to their professed ideals.

'Undesirable and even dangerous activities have been carried on by members of the Sangh (who) have indulged in acts of violence involving arson, robbery, dacoity, and murder and have collected illicit arms and ammunitions. They have been found circulating leaflets exhorting people to resort to terrorist methods to collect firearms ... rendering it incumbent on the government to deal with the Sangh in its corporate capacity.'

Golwalkar was arrested on 3 February along with 20,000 swayamsevaks. The RSS was shocked that no political party and no political leader spoke up for it or stood in its defence. The ban remained for a little under a year and a half. It was lifted after the RSS was asked to produce a constitution. This was written up and submitted. The ban was lifted on 11 July 1949.

Immediately following this, the RSS began debating entering politics in the pages of its house organ, *The Organiser*. It published articles from RSS workers including K.R. Malkani who wrote that the Sangh 'must take part in politics not only to protect itself' but also 'to stop un-Bharatiya and anti-Bharatiya politics' and to 'advance the cause of Bharatiyata through state machinery'. For these reasons, the Sangh must 'continue as an ashram for the national cultural education of the entire citizenry, but it must develop a political wing for the more effective and early achievement of its ideals'.

Malkani said the new party 'will be revivalist of ancient values as it will be futuristic in its targets' and it would be told 'not to depend on foreign values, attitude and manners' and that 'the principle of this re-organisation in Hindustan can only be Hindutva'.

RSS worker from the Arya Samaj Balraj Madhok wrote that the Sangh 'must give the lead to the country in regard to the political and economic problems of the country' because this was 'vital to the very existence of the Sangh itself'.

There was little or no opposition from inside the RSS to forming a political party. Three other things catalysed the decision. Firstly, the resignation in April 1950 of S.P. Mookerjee, a former Hindu Mahasabha leader, from the Nehru Cabinet, over the issue of Muslim appeasement by Nehru. Secondly, the death of Patel in December of that year. Thirdly, the election the same year of P.D. Tandon as Congress president and his being forced to resign by Nehru. Tandon was a Hindu conservative who Nehru felt was being supported by RSS elements.

Mookerjee in his statement to Parliament on 19 April 1950 said that he had 'played a very large part in creating public opinion in favour of a Partition of Bengal". As part of this he 'gave assurances to the Hindus of East Bengal (later, Bangladesh) stating that if they suffered at the hands of the future Pakistan Government ... free India would not remain an idle spectator'.

The same evening he met a group of people, including RSS members and businessmen in Delhi, who told him that his resignation 'represented the other unexpressed feelings of the people' and that the new politics he would now pursue 'will not be based on lack of hope and abject appeasement of the enemy'.

In the months before this, in the period immediately after Golwalkar's release from jail, Mookerjee had met the RSS head several times. It was decided that instead of the RSS itself becoming a political party it would permit RSS 'workers to cooperate and collaborate with Mookerjee for the formation of a party which might reflect their viewpoint on national questions'.

On 5 May 1950, Mookerjee announced the agenda of the party which had an eight-point programme. These were: 1) United Bharat; 2) reciprocity instead of appeasement towards Pakistan; 3) an independent foreign policy; 4) rehabilitation of refugees; 5) increased production of goods and decentralisation of industry; 6) development of a single Bharatiya culture; 7) equal rights to all citizens and improvement of the backward classes; 8) readjustment of the boundaries of West Bengal and Bihar.

Golwalkar provided the nationwide framework for the party and deputed pracharaks to it, including Deendayal Upadhyaya from Uttar Pradesh. At the launch of the party on 21 October 1951, Mookerjee spoke of the reasons why it was formed. He said four years after Independence India was in worse shape than before. Black-marketing, profiteering and corruption had demoralised society.

The party would be inclusive, and it would assure those minorities who were truly loyal to their motherland full protection under the law and complete equality. However, it would reverse the Congress policy of appeasement of Muslims. Pakistan had violated the agreement on treatment of minorities and Congress had ignored that. It had also allowed the capture of a third of Kashmir without resistance. The Jana Sangh would work to correct this.

This, according to the Jana Sangh's official history, is the background to its formation and that of the RSS. It is a simple and straight enough explanation for the existence of both the RSS and the Jana Sangh. It was for one reason that the RSS was formed: to sort out the Muslims of Nagpur and then later of India, and impose an idealised and uniform culture on Hindus. The Jana Sangh was formed to allow the RSS to carry out its activities, and to expand its ideals through the political space. The RSS needed a political shield for its activities and its objectives and vision, according to the Jana Sangh. The Jana Sangh would do this and it would insert into the state its idea of Bharatiyata (Indianness) which it thought of as being above politics.

It would ensure that future governments would not try and shut the RSS's activities down. The other point, the bit about Bharatiyata, is purely about rejecting secularism. It is not articulated otherwise in any meaningful way. Like Savarkar's Hindutva, Bharatiyata is coined and is offered as a complete, monolithic and real thing which cannot be debated.

The accusations against the Indian Muslims as being alien to the land and unmoved by 'Indian heroes' like Kalidas, Panini, Harshavardhan and Mahavir is a repeat of the one made by Savarkar in *Essentials of Hindutva*. But this time there is a plan of action included, in the form of the eight points.

United Bharat meant fighting Pakistan over land. Reciprocity towards Pakistan meant the bullying and harassment of India's Muslims. As may be expected, the refugee problem is seen through the lens of religion and the rehabilitation of the inbound. No reference is made to those Indian Muslims who might face difficulty or danger in reaching Pakistan even if they were forced out of India. There is no mention of or reference to China or its threat, even in passing and it is unclear what 'independent foreign policy' really means or seeks to achieve.

The single Bharatiya culture was of course Hindutva as defined by the Sangh and Savarkar. There is no mention, again we must note this, of the development of music, language, food, the arts, architecture or anything else that one might actually think of as being culture. This lack of interest in the actual culture of India would remain with the Sangh and its political arm as we shall see later as well.

The mention of equal rights and improvement of the backward classes and of increasing production come with no details. For the RSS the problem of Hindu society was not caste but untouchability. Lack of diversity was not really an issue and as long as everyone ate together, the matter stood resolved. There is no real economic thrust and the confusion about whether India must have state intervention, and to what extent, and whether it should attract foreign investment or not and to what extent, remained a problem with the Jana Sangh and the BJP throughout, and remains today. The reason is that the party wasn't really invested in anything much other than communalism.

The final point, a minor one, on the transfer of some territories from Bihar to Bengal, shows that the appeal of Mookerjee was quite provincial. That something so banal (the issue was resolved by Congress a few years later and was dropped) should find space on par with the unity of the nation and the upliftment of the backward classes proves that.

The RSS was apolitical, in the sense that it was not registered as a political party. It was a membership organisation which any Hindu male eighteen or older could sign up for.

The Jana Sangh analysis of why the RSS was required to be formed is reductive. Its analysis of Muslim political aspiration is cast in adversarial terms. The matter of the Mappila rebellion in Kerala allows no discussion of the complexity of land ownership or the issue of British changes that alienated the Muslim peasantry of the area from their rights.

The most striking feature of the Jana Sangh perspective is its rejection of the individual. Everyone must be seen as part of their community, which is monolithic, and individuals have no agency. How many Hindus are familiar with Panini or Harshavardhana and know the first thing about them? Is their ignorance of these figures treason and a lack of national love or is that accusation only reserved for Muslims?

There is no evidence and no data presented to show how Muslims were being led away from a vegetarian diet or why if this was true it was a bad thing. The majority of Hindus are not vegetarian, as the evidence shows. Meat eating is linked to economics more than it is to anything else. The amount of flesh actually consumed by non-veg (a word only Indians use) eaters of the subcontinent is insignificant compared to amount of grain and vegetables they consume. For most meat is a luxury.

Even if it is true, it is hard to see why anyone being drawn away from the consultation of astrologers is a bad thing. And enough evidence exists to show that shrine worship is actually one of the primary ways in which Muslims of the entire subcontinent engage with their faith. Both the pious, victim Hindu and the barbaric, oppressive Muslim are creations of the RSS imagination.

The terror of this imagined Muslim showed itself in the justification for the RSS's creation. Hindu unity was desired for offensive reasons: because Muslims were united and were able to resist rioters. It is astonishing that this should have been the hard basis for the formation of the RSS in Nagpur, but it is so according to its own people and acknowledged in its official texts.

So how did the policies and demands of the Bharatiya Jana Sangh connect in reality to the goals that were set out for it in the eight-point agenda?

The party's constitution said its aim 'is to make India a political, social and economic democracy on the basis of Bharatiya Sanskriti and Maryada. In this democracy every individual shall have equal opportunity and freedom. This democracy shall be oriented towards making India prosperous, powerful, organised, progressive, modern and alert nation, which may successfully contain the aggressive tendency of other countries and play an effective role in the international sphere in establishing world peace.'

The party had the opportunity to express how it would go about its eight-point agenda soon, when elections were announced in 1951. The Jana Sangh manifesto has three pages devoted to the points about a United Bharat and the development of a single Bharatiya culture.

It says the Congress approach was 'Abharatiya' (un-Indian) and therefore unrealistic. In trying to imitate the West, Nehru had ignored and neglected Bharatiya life and ideals. A new direction was needed, and the Bharatiya Jana Sangh would provide this.

The fundamental reality was that Bharatvarsha from the Himalayas to Kanyakumari was a living and organic entity. It was necessary therefore for it to be culturally, economically and politically united. Bharatiya nationalism was based on undivided allegiance to Bharat as a whole and its ancient culture, which is what separated it from other nations.

Bharatiya culture flowed from the Vedas down to the present times and for this reason was indivisible. Any talk of composite or mixed culture was wrong, illogical, dangerous and would not be permitted because it weakened national unity and encouraged secession.

The Bharatiya State that the Jana Sangh would introduce would draw inspiration and sustenance from the ancient Bharatiya culture because this State has always been separate from religion and gave equal protection to all. It would not be a theocratic State because such a thing was alien to Bharat and its people.

However, it would not be a secular State because what was passing for secularism was appeasement of Muslims which would be stopped. Composite nationalism attempting to unite Hindus and Muslims was not nationalism and was a compromise with communalism.

The Jana Sangh would establish 'Dharma Rajya', where all would live in unity and freedom, and pursue a common culture and serve a common motherland. The party would revive Bharatiya culture and real Bharatiya nationalism but if some adjustments were to be made to make the country modern, it would make these adjustments. What would be achieved would be an ideal Bharatiya model of progress which would be spiritual as well as national.

To this end, the object of Jana Sangh was to rebuild Bharat on the basis of 'Bharatiya Sanskriti' and 'Maryada'. This would happen by granting equality of opportunity and individual liberty which would in turn make India united, prosperous, progressive, modern and enlightened. This object would be achieved democratically and peacefully and in constitutional ways.

In these three pages, it is hard to make sense of what the Jana Sangh is saying and what it means. It makes no reference to the Constitution and the existing framework to show what it plans to do differently. It is clear that it feels strongly about 'Bharatiyata', 'Sanskriti', 'Maryada' and 'national rejuvenation Yajna' but is unable to say what they are. It doesn't set out to explain how these words and concepts will look as law or policy.

It appears that the Jana Sangh does not have any ideology. The party says it is 'not wedded to any "ism" but it will not hesitate to take any action, however drastic, to provide for food, clothing and shelter. Sacrifices will have to be made by all in the interest of all.' In a later document, written in 1973, Vajpayee would claim that the Jana Sangh was actually a 'centrist party' which was 'subjected to attacks both from the extreme right as well as the extreme left'.

Jana Sangh manifestos move effortlessly back and forth from grand and formless expression directly to things like running more trains with third-class compartments as opposed to air-conditioned ones, pushing the benefits of cow manure and asking linguists to introduce technical and scientific terms based on Sanskrit to replace English.

There is no comment whether positive or negative on the Constitution, which was adopted months before the first manifesto, or even about the ideals it represents. It takes objection to the use of the word 'states' to describe the component unit of the Indian federal structure and says it wants a unitary government and no individual states. It wants a strong Centre and at the same time it says it wants decentralisation with the village as the primary economic and social unit without saying what comes between the Centre and the village and how governance will be done. It opposes linguistic states, because of its constant fear of 'fissiparousness' but does not consider why these states, the product of demand from citizens, came to be.

In the first manifesto the party identifies black-marketing, profiteering and nepotism as key problems. These seemed to be the catch phrases of the time, used by all, perhaps because aspects of the difference between Raj and self-rule began to become apparent. Jinnah also used them in his most important speech before the Pakistan Constituent Assembly. Over time, the Jana Sangh drops reference to these problems without saying whether they had been solved or had become less relevant to the party. There is a casualness and lack of seriousness that is apparent from the text.

Its attitude to other issues can also be gleaned from its manifestos over the years. Here is where it stands on some of the major ones.

SOCIAL REFORM

Ambedkar had proposed modest changes to Hindu personal law, especially on the question of inheritance for women. He identified the two dominant forms of traditional inheritance law and modified one of them to make inheritance fairer for women.

In its 1951 manifesto the Jana Sangh opposed this in the Hindu Code Bill, saying social reform should not come from above but from society. In 1957, it said that such changes were not acceptable unless rooted in ancient culture. 'Riotous individualism' would ensue as a result.

The party said it would create a 'feeling of equality and oneness in Hindu society by liquidating untouchability and casteism'. But it did not speak of how. Jana Sangh did not add to the Congress policy of reservations for the Scheduled Castes and Scheduled Tribes, for example by pushing for it in the private sector or expanding it. The support to the Dalits comes from such ideas as 'arranging for extra training classes, refresher courses and in-service training for their benefit'.

Culturally, the party stood firmly against alcohol and sought nationwide prohibition. And it wanted English to be replaced in all spheres by local languages and especially, Hindi.

AGRICULTURE

Here the Jana Sangh showed itself to be a party of the urban middle class. The first point on agriculture of its first manifesto calls for 'a country-wide campaign to educate and enthuse the cultivator about the necessity of harder work for more production'. Later it is for 'encouragement of the use of mechanical appliances in agriculture'. However, still later it says that 'tractors will be used only to break virgin soil. Their use for normal ploughing purposes will be discouraged'. (1954)

This was of course because it was trying to protect the bull and the ox from slaughter. In 1951, prohibition of cow slaughter was explained as something needed 'to make the cow an economic unit of agricultural life'. In 1954, the text was more religious and called cow protection a 'pious duty'.

ECONOMY

There is no particular thrust that the Jana Sangh favoured when it came to the economy. The party manifestos say it would develop an economic system that would not undo state enterprises but would give private enterprises their proper place.

Swadeshi meant giving subsidies to local industries and also tariff protection. Import of consumer goods and luxury goods would be discouraged. Labour rights including strikes and lock-outs would be discouraged.

In 1957, the party announced it would introduce 'revolutionary changes' to the economic order, which 'will be in keeping with Bharatiya values of life'. However, these were not elaborated on nor was this theme of revolutionary change picked up again in any future manifesto.

In 1967, the party said it backed the idea of a planned economy, but would tweak the plan and 'adopt the system of microeconomic planning region-wise and project-wise'. It sought State intervention, but not everywhere. It encouraged private investment but definitely not in the defence sector. The party said that 'laissez-faire belonged only to the Krita Yuga' (also called Sat Yuga, the first ideal era when the gods themselves governed the earth). The State thus must accept responsibility of ownership and management in certain spheres of the economy.

In 1954, and again in 1971, the Jana Sangh resolved to limit the maximum income of all Indian citizens to Rs 2,000 per month and the minimum to Rs 100, maintaining a 20:1 ratio. It would continue working on reducing this gap till it reached 10:1 which was the ideal gap and all Indians could only have incomes inside this range based on their position. Additional income earned by individuals over this limit would be procured by the State for development needs 'through contribution, taxation, compulsory loans and investment'.

The party would also limit the size of residential houses in cities and not allow plots of more than 1000 square yards.

FOREIGN POLICY

The Jana Sangh did not have any particular strategic view of the world and India's place in it besides stating that India should be friends with all who were friendly and tough on those who were not. India should seek a place in the Security Council but there was no reference to why or what India's role would be, or how its influence and options could be increased. It offered no path for getting to the Security Council.

There appears to be no continuity in the way the Jana Sangh thought about such things. The 1957 manifesto opened with a grim warning of a threat emanating from a Pakistan-Portuguese alliance. The 1962 manifesto made no reference to this but opened with an admonition against Nehru for losing the war to China. The 1972 manifesto made no reference to the war in Bangladesh which had been created out of Pakistan only weeks earlier.

Its idea of defence policy came through such demands as compulsory military training for all boys and girls, removal of licences for possessing muzzle-loading guns (an eighteenth century weapon), expansion of the National Cadet Corps and the manufacture of nuclear weapons. In case of border violations, the Jana Sangh says its policy would be 'one of retaliation rather than of issuing protest notes'.

CIVIL LIBERTIES

In 1954 the party said it would repeal the first amendment to the Constitution that curbed freedom of speech by imposing 'reasonable restrictions'. This amendment essentially took away freedom of expression because the list of what is seen as a reasonable restriction was far too wide and broad. The Jana Sangh sensed that it was not something that could be allowed to go unchallenged. However, after 1954, this demand that the first amendment be repealed and freedom of speech, association and assembly be restored to Indians disappeared from the Jana Sangh manifestos.

Interestingly, the Jana Sangh said it would also repeal preventive detention laws which it said were absolutely in contradiction to individual liberty. This promise was made repeatedly in the 1950s. However by 1967 it began to qualify the demand and said that 'care will be taken to ensure that fifth columnists and disruptionist elements are not allowed to exploit fundamental rights'. In time, the Sangh and BJP became the most enthusiastic champions of preventive detention.

The Jana Sangh manifestos appear often to be in response to what was going on in India under the Congress. If Nehru initiated land reform, the Jana Sangh added a paragraph or two on how their land reform would be better. When Indira spoke of a land ceiling, the Jana Sangh defined what their land ceiling would be. A planned economy was fine, but the Jana Sangh would plan it deeper to the micro level but would also be project-focused. Mechanisation was good but not too much mechanisation because it led to unemployment so it must be a Bharatiya modernisation.

On what would presumably have been one of the most vital element of its programme, Hindu social reform leading to greater unity, there is little to write home about. The real problem of the Scheduled Castes is that of their lack of inclusion. The Jana Sangh puts forward no programme deepening the Congress's reservation policies. The Jana Sangh's 1973 analysis of caste violence 'reveals that in most cases the conflict is not between Harijans and caste Hindus as such, but it is between Harijans and a set of people who are in power and who also happen to belong to upper castes'. Meaning that caste itself is not the source of the conflict.

The Jana Sangh was itself not an inclusive party. On its fifty-one member national executive, it gave two reserved positions each to the Scheduled Castes and the Scheduled Tribes. Its parliamentary board before it merged with the Janata Party comprised Vajpayee, Advani, Scindia, Nana Deshmukh, Bhai Mahavir, Sunder Singh Bhandari and J.R. Joshi, all upper caste and most of them Brahmin. From its first president, the Brahmin Mookerjee, to its last one, the Brahmin Vajpayee, the Jana Sangh itself was reflective of all the iniquities, prejudices and bigotry of the wider Hindu society it sought to champion but whose diversity it did not represent.

The Bharatiya Jana Sangh pushes Hindutva but it is an amorphous and elusive Hindutva. The tone of the Jana Sangh towards the minorities was certainly adversarial but it was what can be called passive-aggressive. It said it would 'nationalise all non-Hindus by inculcating in them the ideal of Bharatiya culture' (1957). The party referred to Congress policy as pseudo-secularism which is unacceptable. It calls on the followers of all religions to 'accept the Indian ideal of Sarvadharma Samabhava and cherish a feeling of not merely tolerance, but equal respect for all faiths'.

It said it was open to promoting Urdu but was opposed to Urdu being made the second official language in Uttar Pradesh and Bihar (1971). It pushed a uniform civil code that was aimed essentially at stopping polygamy. It spoke in dark terms of 'fifth columnists of the enemy threatening India's integrity and sovereignty' who would have to be 'put down with a firm hand'. The party would 'enact a law of treason and deal with these anti-national elements' (1967 manifesto).

But while it signals anti-Muslim intent, the Jana Sangh did not have the transparency of the Bharatiya Janata Party and its open dislike of Muslims. The Jana Sangh was unable to express its majoritarianism as clearly and in as full-throated a fashion as the BJP was later able to.

This was because it lacked a specific programme on the back of which to mobilise anti-Muslim sentiment, such as the campaign against the Babri Masjid. Even though the idols were smuggled into the mosque a few months before the Jana Sangh was formed, there was no reference to Ayodhya or a Ram temple there in any of the Jana Sangh manifestos from 1951 to 1980. It was not important as an issue all this time. The lack of a mass-mobilisation issue nationally meant that the Jana Sangh remained a minor political player, getting only a few seats in each election. In the last election it contested under its own name, in 1971, the Jana Sangh won 22 seats and 7 per cent of the vote, making it only the fourth largest party.

With the Emergency, the Jana Sangh merged electorally with the Janata Party, the umbrella opposition alliance, and this united force defeated the Congress. It is only now, in the Janata Party manifesto of 1977, that we find the first positive reference to minority rights. The Janata Party says it is 'committed to the secular and richly diverse character of our State. It will accord the highest respect to the rights and legitimate needs of the minorities.' The RSS members now inside the Janata Party had apparently no problem endorsing this. The joint manifesto pledges to prevent any discrimination against the minorities, and offers protection against this.

The Janata Party experiment did not last long and the government fell after a couple of years. Its next manifesto of 1979 spoke of its achievements while in office, including the setting up a Minorities Commission, enabling easier access to Pakistan for Indian Muslims, restoring the autonomy of Aligarh Muslim University, giving financial aid for Haj. Here it sounds like the Congress and once power was gone it was not easy for the Sangh's instincts to remain subdued.

Soon after the collapse of the Janata Party government, the experiment of a joint opposition to the Congress ended. The Jana Sangh members were asked to choose between their membership of the Janata Party and membership of the RSS.

They chose to remain true to the RSS and left the Janata Party to return to the Jana Sangh.

Atal Bihari Vajpayee however decided not to go back to the original name, saying the Jana Sangh had learned from the experience of being in the Janata Party. He renamed it the Bharatiya Janata Party, and gave it a constitution that swore by secularism. Under Vajpayee the party also said the BJP's guiding philosophy would be 'Gandhian Socialism', in continuation with the Janata Party, whose manifesto said it was 'firmly dedicated to the political philosophy of Mahatma Gandhi'. This move to retain the Gandhian thrust was resisted internally by some in the BJP including Vijayaraje Scindia, but was adopted nonetheless.

In 1989, the Rajiv Gandhi government amended the Representation of the People Act, requiring all parties to 'bear true faith and allegiance to the Constitution of India as by law established, and to the principles of socialism, secularism and democracy'.

But the BJP under Vajpayee had already done this nine years before, voluntarily and without external coercion. As a compromise to those resisting it internally, Deendayal Upadhyaya's Integral Humanism speeches were made the party's 'basic philosophy' while retaining Gandhian socialism as its 'guiding philosophy'. In keeping with the abandoning of the word Sangh in its name, the party would also be welcoming of non-RSS individuals as members and office-bearers. However, the party's leadership remained the same and the state units remained the same and the policies, such as they were, also remained the same. It was essentially just a renaming and in that sense, cosmetic. The Bharatiya Jana Sangh was now the Bharatiya Janata Party.

Vajpayee's new BJP was able to win only two seats in the election following Indira Gandhi's murder in 1984 when the Congress, under Rajiv Gandhi, swept up more than 400 seats.

Vajpayee stepped down as leader soon after and in May 1986, L.K. Advani became BJP president. Under Advani, the BJP would transform from being a cadre-based party to a mass-based one. This happened after Advani hitched the BJP to a movement that was launched by the Vishwa Hindu Parishad in 1984. The movement was headed by a body called the Ramjanmabhoomi Muktiyajna Samiti (Ramjanmabhoomi Liberation Committee).

The Jana Sangh's performance electorally before Advani became its leader for a second time (he was president of the Jana Sangh once) had always been mediocre. RSS men who were in politics like Bhairon Singh Shekhawat in Rajasthan, Shanta Kumar in Himachal Pradesh and Kailash Joshi in Madhya Pradesh had become chief ministers after the Emergency but this was as part of the Janata Party coalition. The Jana Sangh/BJP had never won a single state on its own from 1951 to 1990, a few years after Advani became its leader.

We noted that in the last general election before it merged into the Janata Party, the Jana Sangh under Vajpayee, contesting in an alliance with a couple of other parties, won 22 seats. In the four preceding general elections it had won only 3, 4, 14 and 35 seats and never had a national vote share of more than 9 per cent.

In its official history, the party describes the last state assembly elections it contested on its own: 'In the 1972 Assembly Elections (for various states across India), Jana Sangh went to poll largely on its own. It fielded 1233 candidates and won 104 seats with an overall 8 per cent of the votes. In almost all the states it suffered losses... For the first time since its founding, Jana Sangh could not improve upon its earlier performance.'

The party had plateaued and this became clear when it again contested the 1984 general elections on its own, winning 7 per cent of the vote and only two Lok Sabha seats. When Advani took charge of the party in 1986, he had never been a participant in electoral politics. His entry into politics came after time spent as a journalist in the RSS magazine, where he wrote film reviews.

As a politician, Advani had always been a nominated member, whether in the Delhi Council or in the Rajya Sabha. He had no experience of political mass mobilisation and, going by his autobiography (*My Country, My Life*, published in 2008) does not appear to know how it worked.

The Ayodhya issue had actually been launched by the non-political groups inside the RSS, led by the Vishwa Hindu Parishad. At a meeting in UP in 1983, Rajendra Singh, who would later become RSS chief, demanded that the Babri Masjid be opened to Hindu devotees. In September 1984, the VHP began a campaign against the mosque. This received sufficient public response for the group to claim in 1986 that they would forcibly break the locks open. Rajiv Gandhi succumbed to the pressure and the government told the courts there would be no law and order problem if this happened. The locks were thus opened and Hindus allowed into the mosque.

But the VHP did not stop with being given access to worship at the site: its target was the destruction of the mosque. In February 1989, at the Kumbh Mela in Allahabad, the VHP said it would lay the foundation stone for the temple in November. This would involve the making of bricks across the country with Ram's name embossed on them and their being carried in processions through towns and villages to Ayodhya in November.

Till this time, Advani writes in his autobiography, a few members of the BJP like Vijayaraje Scindia and Vinay Katiyar had participated in the Ayodhya movement in their individual capacity. It was not an issue in mainstream politics. In June, at the BJP's national executive meeting in Himachal Pradesh, Advani threw the party behind the issue. The BJP resolution demanded that the site 'should be handed over to the Hindus' and 'the mosque built at some other suitable place'. The whole thing was now coloured with religious sentiment.

Elections came a few months later, in November 1989. The BJP's manifesto now made its first reference to Ayodhya: 'By not allowing the rebuilding of the Ram Janma Mandir in Ayodhya, on the lines of Somnath Mandir built by the government of India in 1948, it has allowed tensions to rise, and gravely strained social harmony.' It was a violation of the BJP's own constitution, which on its first page and opening articles pledged it would bear true faith and allegiance to the principle of secularism.

A few days before voting, the VHP brought all its processions from across India to Ayodhya and laid the foundation stone next to the mosque.

Powered by its divisive, anti-Muslim demand, Advani's BJP won 85 seats, four times as many as the Jana Sangh in the last election it contested alone and more than forty times as many as Vajpayee had delivered in his reformed and renamed party. Advani had become the most successful political leader from the RSS and had found the recipe for electoral success. He began to invest more in the issue that had brought the dividend.

The Congress lost its majority in the election, and a coalition led by V.P. Singh took power with support from Advani, though for only a short period. Three months after the election, in February 1990, the VHP resumed its mobilisation against the mosque and said it would continue the process of what it called kar seva from October.

The political escalation, according to Advani, happened by accident. Advani writes in his autobiography that in June he was to visit London, and just before he left he was interviewed by the editor of the RSS journal *Panchajanya* who asked him what would happen if the government failed to resolve the Ayodhya matter. Advani told him that the BJP supported the decision to begin kar seva on 30 October, and if it was stopped there would be a mass movement led by the BJP.

'Frankly, I had forgotten about this interview,' Advani writes, when his wife telephoned him and asked, 'What have you said? The papers here have reported it with blaring headlines: "On Ayodhya, Advani threatens the biggest mass movement in the history of independent India".' Advani adds: 'The die had been cast.'

After this, Advani says he offered the Muslims a deal. If they would hand over the Babri Masjid, he would 'personally request' the VHP to not campaign against two other mosques in Mathura and Varanasi. He writes that he was 'deeply disappointed' and 'annoyed' that this was not considered to be satisfactory by the Muslims. He announced he would begin his campaign against the mosque on Deendayal Upadhyaya's birthday, 25 September, in Gujarat, and ride a 'chariot' (actually a truck) to Ayodhya on 30 October 1990.

Advani writes that he was astonished by the frenzied response his campaign received. 'I had never realised that religiosity was so deep-rooted in the lives of the Indian people,' he said, adding that it was the 'first time he understood the truth of Swami Vivekananda's statement that "religion is the soul of India and if you want to teach any subject to Indians, they understand it better in the language of religion".'

At each stop along the way Advani went about talking about why the Babri Masjid had to be taken down, using the vocabulary and metaphors of religion, in basic speeches that he says were no more than five minutes long. The reduction can only be imagined; the consequence was predictable. The scale of the violence unleashed by Advani's decision to politicise a communal issue and mobilise on it was staggering in both the numbers killed and the geographical spread.

B. Rajeshwari of the Institute of Peace and Conflict Studies in her work, *Communal Riots in India: A Chronology 1947-2003*, writes: 'The mobilisation campaign for kar sevaks to construct the proposed Ram Janma Bhoomi Temple at Ayodhya on 30 October 1990 aggravated the communal atmosphere in the country. Communal riots occurred in the wake of L.K. Advani's Rath Yatra wherever it went. These riots were led by RSS-BJP men to consolidate the "Hindu" vote bank. They were widespread over almost all the states from Assam to West Bengal, Bihar, Orissa, Uttar Pradesh, Madhya Pradesh, Rajasthan, Andhra Pradesh, Karnataka, Gujarat, Maharashtra and Delhi.'

Between April 1989 and April 1990, Gujarat recorded 262 dead, mostly Muslim. In October 1990, days after Advani's yatra began, 41 were killed in Ahmedabad. The same month, 52 were killed in Jaipur, 20 in Jodhpur, 33 in Lucknow, over 100 in Delhi, 37 in Assam, 18 in Patna and 165 in Hyderabad. Also in October, a pogrom against Muslims in Bhagalpur, Bihar, saw 960 killed of whom about 900 were Muslim, In November, 31 were killed in Agra, again mostly Muslim and 13 in Indore. In December, 60 were killed in Karnataka and 134 in Hyderabad.

Many parts of India remained tense for long periods of time. Between April and May 1990, three riots in Kanpur killed 30; between May and November 1991 more than 50 were killed in Varanasi. In May 1991, 26 including 24 Muslims were killed in Vadodara.

In October 1992, 44 were killed in Sitamarhi. On 6 December that year, immediately after the Babri Masjid was destroyed, pogroms against Muslims broke out in Surat where 200 died, of whom some 95 per cent were Muslim. In Bhopal in December, 143 were killed. The Bombay riots that broke out at the same time saw more than 1,000 killed, mostly Muslim.

Advani absolves himself of any responsibility here. He accepts there was violence around India but acquits himself by saying, 'There were indeed riots in several parts of the country, but none at all along the yatra trail.'

He asks: 'Was my campaign anti-Muslim?' and answers himself: 'Not in the least.' When the mobs he gathered began to shout, *'Jo Hindu hit ki baat karega wohi desh pe raj karega'* (only those speaking of Hindu interest will rule India), Advani says he requested them to replace the phrase Hindu hit with rashtra hit. He adds: 'I was, therefore, pained to see a section of the media carry reports that had sensational titles like "Advani's blood yatra".' Other than this sympathy for himself, Advani has no comment on the killings in his book written fifteen years later.

Many of the riots broke out after calculated provocation. Rath Yatras and associated processions were deliberately taken through Muslim neighbourhoods. Violence was good because it led to polarisation and that made voter choice easy. Advani successfully polarised India from north to south and east to west, pitting Indians against their fellow countrymen and women and children.

The reward was a doubling of the BJP's vote share. In the general elections held in mid-1991, the BJP got 20 per cent of the total vote and won 120 seats. In the first election held after the demolition, in 1996, the BJP won 161 seats.

Over 3,400 Indians were killed in the violence triggered by Advani's anti-Babri Masjid campaign and it brought the BJP to the doorstep of power. Advani's success was built on the corpses of Indians and cemented with their blood.

He writes the day the mosque was demolished was 'the saddest day of my life'. Having assembled a mob and fired it up against the mosque, he says he was surprised that they immediately tore it down. As a mark of sacrifice, he says that when celebrations broke out on the dais he was sitting in he refused refreshment saying: 'No, I will not have sweets today.'

The blood profits were not limited to the general elections. Northern states going to Assembly elections after the beginning of the anti-Babri Masjid campaign fell to the BJP for the first time in the party's history as it won majorities on the back of anti-Muslim mobilisation.

There were BJP chief ministers in Rajasthan, Madhya Pradesh and Himachal Pradesh in 1990, Uttar Pradesh in 1991, Gujarat in 1995 and Maharashtra in coalition with the Shiv Sena the same year.

Advani made the BJP India's dominant political force. The Babri demolition and the communal violence in its wake also gave the party the template to further expansion. It would abandon or disregard everything that its manifestos claimed, from mechanisation in the economy to limiting private property to prohibition to Swadeshi to throwing English out to Integral Humanism and the other mumbo-jumbo. The BJP would concentrate its politics on India's Muslims and focus on those issues alone on which Indian society could be divided and kept on the boil.

Advani discovered through the Babri campaign what the rest of the subcontinent knew. That majoritarianism was politically rewarding and that it worked essentially by mobilising against the minorities. Hindutva politics shed its passive aggressive majoritarianism under Advani with the Babri campaign, but Advani's overt bigotry was still in some ways apologetic. His urging the mobs he had gathered to talk of 'rashtra hit' (national welfare) and not 'Hindu hit' (Hindu welfare), his sadness at the demolition was not representative of the emotion the RSS cadre or the BJP felt at their vandalism, which was for them a moment of triumph over India's Muslims.

This separation between what Hindutva was and wanted to be, and what it pretended to be, was reflected in the first BJP-led Union government, which came in the next general election, four years after the demolition and the massacres. The Congress lost its majority, but the BJP did not secure one on its own. Advani had led the party to the cusp of victory and the credit was his alone, but the allies whose support the BJP needed could not endorse the man behind the Babri demolition.

In Advani's stead, Atal Bihari Vajpayee became the BJP leader and prime minister for three terms, the shortest being his first of a few days and the longest his last, ending just six months shy of a full term. His leadership and general sobriety allowed allies to pretend they were not in bed with the RSS. Some of Vajpayee's policies were unhinged, such as the overt weaponisation of India's nuclear programme. This was an act that brought no particular strategic benefit, goaded Pakistan immediately into weaponising its own programme a few days later and lost India billions in foreign direct investment, which fled from the uncertainty. Vajpayee also fought a defensive war against Pakistani intrusion in Kashmir. This and the nuclear explosion, which Advani said was aimed against Pakistan, brought some joy to the cadre.

However, under Vajpayee the BJP was unable to express the confident majoritarianism that had actually brought it success. The BJP's national vote share fell from over 25 per cent in 1998 to 23 per cent in 1999 and then 22 per cent in 2004, when it ran out of steam and Vajpayee was defeated in the general election. Instead of an angry and hostile campaign against Indian Muslims, Vajpayee chose an economy-focussed message captioned 'India Shining' that was firmly rejected.

The post-Ayodhya Advani was also a shadow of his former self. There was no second Babri that he could conjure up and his mobilisation days were over. As home minister in 1999, he presided over an act that the BJP would have hauled another party over the coals for: releasing terrorists in exchange for hostages, and then witnessing the released individuals play havoc. One of them immediately founded the Jaish-e-Muhammad and another beheaded a *Wall Street Journal* reporter.

After the general election defeat, on a visit to Karachi in 2005, Advani visited the mausoleum of Jinnah. 'There are many people who leave an inerasable stamp on history,' he wrote in the register. 'But there are very few who actually create history. Quaid-e-Azam Mohammed Ali Jinnah was one such rare individual.' Advani also quoted Sarojini Naidu's famous line about Jinnah being an 'ambassador of Hindu-Muslim unity'. Advani said Jinnah's address to the Constituent Assembly of Pakistan on 11 August 1947, 'is really a classic, a forceful espousal of a secular state in which, while every citizen would be free to practise his own religion, the state shall make no distinction between one citizen and another on grounds of faith. My respectful homage to this great man.'

This was the end of Advani. The RSS distanced itself from him. In any case, he was now approaching his eighties and the BJP vote had plateaued again under Vajpayee. The party's cadre had gravitated towards the chief minister of Gujarat who was expressing anti-Muslim sentiment more cleanly. In Modi and his Gujarat, the full hard face of prejudice as directly expressed as it was by the RSS and the VHP was shown to the Indian Muslim.

In history, no leader of an Indian state has returned to power after presiding over a full riot. The 1992 violence cost Sudhakarrao Naik his job in Bombay. In Gujarat, in the same period, chief minister Chimanbhai Patel died before the next election. After Bhagalpur in 1989, the Congress lost power. Vasantdada Patil lost his job after the Bhiwandi riots in 1984, Hiteshwar Saikia lost his after Nellie in 1983. Rajiv Gandhi won a majority at the Centre amid the massacre of Sikhs in 1984 but never again returned to power. Going back to Hitendra Desai, who lost his job after the first major riot of independent India in 1969 in Gujarat, there has been a tradition or at least a history of replacing the individual under whom mass murder happened, perhaps as a way of moving on. Rajiv Gandhi was perhaps the only exception, but that was in the immediate aftermath of Indira Gandhi's death, when he had arguably not yet assumed complete control.

In Gujarat, after the pogrom of 2002, such an individual, for the first time in India, not only remained in power but kept returning to it till he left for Delhi in 2014. All this time he was endorsed and glorified for enabling violence in which ministers participated and actually got convicted before being subsequently acquitted. He was unapologetic about the fact that he had not been able to control the massacre and about the persecution of those who had tried to stop it.

Senior Indian Police Service (IPS) officers who prevented violence were openly punished and even jailed, with no resistance, and indeed silence, from the IPS Association. Narendra Modi was able to build a nationwide and really a global notoriety and fame because of the BJP's refusal or inability to change its leadership in Gujarat. Here was the man to take over from Advani. The apologetic Hindutva of the decade following the fall of the Babri Masjid was about to end. The BJP cadre and the Sangh had a real hero who spoke and felt and did as they really wanted their leaders to.

In April 2002, only a month after the violence after Godhra had led to the death of about 1,000 Gujaratis, mostly Muslim, the BJP National Executive met in Goa. There was talk in the media that Vajpayee was going to get Modi to step down.

India Today ('How Vajpayee ended up as the Hindutva choir boy', 29 April 2002) reported what happened next: 'No sooner had party President Jana Krishnamurthy completed his "taken as read" presidential address than Modi got up and said in his sombre, chaste Hindi: "Adhyakshji, I want to speak on Gujarat ... From the party's point of view, this is a grave issue. There is a need for a free and frank discussion. To enable this I wish to place my resignation before this body. It is time we decided what direction the party and the country should take from this point onwards."

'He didn't need to say more. With one stroke, the Gujarat chief minister had seized the initiative. He galvanised his supporters who now stood up to be counted. Food Minister Shanta Kumar, who had spoken out against Modi and the VHP's extremes, found himself being rebuked and facing a disciplinary committee. He was forced to apologise.

'Even if the prime minister may have thought Modi's resignation prudent for the sake of both his personal image and the unity of the coalition, there was absolutely no way he could go against the ferocity of the pro-Modi sentiment. He tried shelving the issue for a day but even this was resisted.'

Vajpayee's inability to wrestle Modi down was predictable. Leaders in extremist parties are always vulnerable to charismatic persons on their right, who are willing and eager to push harder and risk more and are better able to express the cadre's zealotry. What had happened in the Hindutva party had followed an arc probably prophesied by Golwalkar.

Vajpayee's Jana Sangh was more extreme than Upadhyaya's, Advani's BJP more than Vajpayee's. And under Modi we have been given the leader Hindutva has always ached for. He is unafraid, and indeed he is enthusiastic, about taking the party and the nation down the road the Rashtriya Swayamsevak Sangh had outlined for it, by brutalising and marginalising India's minorities and especially its Muslims.

6

THE MYTH OF APPEASEMENT

'Muslims are being appeased' is a complaint Hindutva has been muttering since before Independence.

The Jana Sangh's first manifesto of 1951 says, 'Secularism as currently interpreted in this is country is only a euphemism for the policy of Muslim appeasement.'

This has been a consistent lament from the party across the decades and appears in every BJP manifesto. In 2019, after five years in power, the party still spoke of 'what is happening today; appeasement of one, at the cost of the other'.

In 2016, Modi repeated a remarkable statement by a previous party leader: 'Fifty years ago Pandit Upadhyaya said, "Do not appease Muslims, do not shun them but purify them."' The word 'purify' got so many headlines including those globally, that the word appease was not remarked on. It is so frequently used by Hindutva across its platforms as to have become acceptable. The RSS's website also speaks about 'the Congress leaders' policy of appeasement of the Muslims'.

The BJP, the RSS and the prime minister offer no material, no data and no evidence to show how or whether Muslims are being appeased. Like all mantras, 'Muslim appeasement' is muttered and assumed to be the truth.*

The dictionary defines appeasement as 'to pacify or placate someone by acceding to their demands'. Let us examine how appeased Muslims are in India.

No Hindu can become prime minister or president of Pakistan by law. India has no legal restriction by religion, but it has not been possible for a Muslim to aspire or get anywhere close to the position. What the law does not restrict, majoritarianism does. In theory, it is possible, but practically it is impossible. The very idea of a Muslim prime minister in India may sound ridiculous to most.

---

*The things cited to illustrate appeasement are such things as iftar parties (dusk meals organised by political figures to mark the breaking of the Ramzan fast), the Haj Committee Act of 1959 (to assist Muslim pilgrims to Saudi Arabia, Iraq, Syria, Jordan and Iran) and a law overturning a judgment on alimony for Muslim women (the Shah Bano case). The Haj 'subsidy', which was terminated in 2018, was in essence a kickback by the State to Air India, which inflated the airfare for fliers going to Jeddah ('Is Haj Subsidy a sleight of hand to keep Air India afloat', *Outlook*, 16 January 2017). It is a view commonly held that Muslims were the only recipients of State aid in pilgrimage. This is untrue. The Uttar Pradesh chief minister Yogi Adityanath announced in his first speech on taking office that he would subsidise pilgrimage for Hindus ('Kailash Mansarovar pilgrims to get Rs 1 lakh', *Hindustan Times*, 25 March 2017). The Modi government's Pilgrimage Rejuvenation and Spirituality Drive had a budget for Rs 800 crore just for Kashi, Mathura and Ayodhya ('Cancelling Haj Subsidy Is a Good Step, Now the Government Should Stop Spending on All Religions', *www.thewire.in*, 17 January 2018). Madhya Pradesh, Rajasthan, Karnataka, Bihar, Kerala and Tamil Nadu are among the states which spend money on pilgrimages and on state support to temples, religious institutions and infrastructure. The Muslim personal law's allowance of polygamy is possibly the most cited reason for assuming appeasement. The last Census that recorded polygamy, in 1961, found that the incidence of polygamy among Muslims (5.7%) was lower than it was among Hindus (5.8%), Jains (6.7%), Buddhists (7.8%) and Adivasis (15.25%). A 1974 survey put the figure at 5.6% for Muslims and 5.8% for Hindus ('Muslim women and the surprising facts about polygamy in India', *www.scroll.in*, 8 July 2014). The strongest opposition to polygamy in recent times has come from organised groups of Muslim women. The worry from this fear of polygamy, that Muslims will overrun Hindus in terms of population, is overblown and illogical. Fertility rates are declining across all communities in India and 'population explosion' is no longer a serious concern.

To preserve its façade of secularism, India allows Muslims to assume the ceremonial offices of president and vice-president, but they have no access to offices with real power. If the Indian president, like the Pakistani one, had the authority to dismiss Parliament, there is no chance that a Muslim would be given the office in India.

There was not a single Muslim chief minister in India in 2020: the last one having lost her office with the dismissal of the Jammu and Kashmir government and the state's subsequent dismemberment and demotion to Union territory. It is not easy to see when and where India will see its next Muslim CM. The list of Muslims individuals who have ever became CM is quite sorry and their tenures revealing.

Outside Kashmir, no Muslim chief minister of a state has even completed a full term since independence. India's 200 million Muslims have been kept marginalised in politics.

The most famous example of a Muslim CM was A.R. Antulay in Maharashtra, who served only two years and resigned on account of a corruption scandal. The most successful one was someone who led not a state but a Union territory: M.O.H. Farook, who headed Pondicherry three times (April 1967 to March 1968, March 1969 to January 1974 and from 1985 to 1990).

Theprint.in published a report on 2 January 2020 headlined: 'No Muslim minister in fifteen of India's twenty-eight states.' In the cabinets of ten of the remaining thirteen states, there was a single Muslim minister, which is the normal pattern even under so-called secular governments which usually include only the minimum required to counter the accusation of total discrimination.

Muslims are not the only marginalised community in India nor the only one discriminated against, this is true. But the others have had political access given to them to overturn the prejudices, specifically through reserved seats. India's Scheduled Castes are about 16 per cent of the population, and are given 84 reserved seats in the Lok Sabha. The Scheduled Tribes, which are 8 per cent of the population, get 47 reserved seats. Muslims have none and are the most under-represented section of India in Parliament. There were 27 Muslims elected to the Lok Sabha in 2019. Through reserved seats for Dalits and Adivasis, India has acknowledged its discrimination against them but has refused to do so when it comes to Muslims.

By their share of the population Muslims should have 74 seats in the Lok Sabha. They have never got more than 49 (in 1980). Their average is 28 seats, about a third of what they should be getting. Most parties give Muslims tickets as a token share and that too usually in constituencies where they are a majority or close to a majority. This is not how tickets for Hindus are distributed, because one caste can never approach majority levels in a constituency. Candidates chosen for their caste are expected to be able to appeal to other castes also. Muslim candidates are however treated differently and face prejudice: the secularism of most parties is merely pretense when it comes to actual distribution of tickets, ministries and sharing of power. This is a demonstrable fact and even the State is officially aware of it.

In February 2000, the Atal Bihari Vajpayee government set up the National Commission to Review the Working of the Constitution. The eleven-member committee under former Supreme Court Chief Justice M.N. Venkatachaliah submitted its report two years later in March 2002. In its chapter on the pace of socio-economic change and development the committee observed: 'At present, the political representation of minority communities in legislatures, especially Muslims, has fallen well below their proportion of population ... This can lead to a sense of alienation ... It is incumbent for political parties to build up leadership potential in the minority communities. The role of the state for strengthening the pluralism of Indian polity has to be emphasised.'

The findings of the committee were not taken up. Today, the BJP does not even pretend to want Muslims or to be inclusive in any way. As we have noted, of its 303 Lok Sabha members of parliament, not one is a Muslim as was the case with its previous 282 Lok Sabha MPs. Where Muslims are given space, such as in the Union Cabinet, it is as minister for minority affairs. In UP, a Hindu holds the cabinet portfolio even for minority affairs and Waqf, overseeing Muslim charitable endowments, while his deputy is a Muslim.

On 24 December 2014, *The Hindu* published a report with the headline: 'Just the fourth Muslim MLA for BJP'. The report said that the party had 1,016 members of legislative assembly across India and of these four were Muslim: two from Rajasthan, one from Bihar and one from Jammu. In Assam after the 2016 election, the BJP had one Muslim MLA who was made deputy speaker, a post with no power.

Things have changed for the worse in terms of numbers since the report was published. The Jammu and Kashmir assembly has been permanently dissolved, of course. In Bihar, an election came the following year and the number of Muslims from the BJP has gone down to zero. Rajasthan had an election in 2018 and the number of Muslims from the BJP there also went down to zero. In Uttar Pradesh, which went to the polls in 2017, the BJP has 307 MLAs and no Muslims. There are over 40 million Muslims in Uttar Pradesh, the largest unrepresented group in the democratic world.

The *Times of India* published a report on 1 March 2017 with the headline: 'No tickets for Muslims in UP polls'. It quoted some party leaders who accepted that it may have been appropriate if the BJP had given a ticket to a Muslim but no explanation was offered for why it was not. The fact is that the BJP does not want Muslims and wants them to know that.

In Gujarat, where the party has run the government since 1998, there has been no Muslim BJP MLA for twenty-two years. There has been no Muslim representative of any party from Gujarat in the Lok Sabha since 1985. In the entire Hindi belt, there is no Muslim MLA in 2020 belonging to the BJP.

There is no material difference between the overt exclusion of minorities from high office and power in Pakistan and the covert exclusion in India. In both cases the exclusion is real. And yet Muslims are accused of being the recipients of 'appeasement'. If it does not show in politics and in the sharing of power, and as demonstrated, it clearly does not, then where does this appeasement show and how is it reflected in their lives? On this matter it is important to examine the data and see how true it is that Muslims are being mollycoddled by India.

The first and only comprehensive government paper on the status of Muslims in India was published in 2006. It was written by the Prime Minister's High-Level Committee on the Social, Economic and Educational Status of Muslims in India. Commissioned by Manmohan Singh in March 2005, the report was put out in a year, which was unusual in India where commissions, and especially 'high-level' ones, are a sinecure for officials who rarely finish their work and are usually associated with the word 'extension'. The urgency showed the seriousness.

This report was put together by seven individuals, all men, of whom four had PhDs. It was chaired by a retired judge, Rajinder Sachar, and the work is commonly known as the Sachar Committee report. It was this research that was behind a famous statement Singh made in November 2006: 'We will have to devise innovative plans to ensure that minorities, particularly the Muslim minority, are empowered to share equitably in the fruits of development. They must have the first claim on resources. The Centre has a myriad other responsibilities whose demands will have to be fitted within the over-all resource availability.'

This story was reported by PTI with the headline 'Minorities must have first claim on resources: PM', and then published and broadcast around the country to great outrage, including from the RSS, which immediately marked it down as an instance of 'appeasement'. Singh's statement is not scandalous except if one is totally unfamiliar with the data and even the anecdotal evidence on the condition of India's 200 million Muslims and, more precisely, the findings of the high-level committee.

The report, again unusually for India, was both commissioned in very brief and direct terms and was written and produced in elegant and simple prose. The terms of reference were for the committee to find out in which parts of the country did most Muslims live, the geographical pattern of their economic activity, their asset base and income levels, their education, their share of employment in the private and public sectors, the proportion of Other Backward Classes among them, and their access to health and other services.

The group writing the report looked at the available government data, but also met academics, individuals and groups from the community and non-governmental organisations, including some linked to foreign governments (the report thanks UNICEF, DFID, World Bank, CAPART, Agha Khan Foundation, OXFAM, Care India, Ford Foundation, CSDS, CRY, Indian Social Institute, Action Aid, Pratham, SEWA and UNDP) and multilateral bodies. This was not a report put together casually. Its findings were startling enough for Singh to have said what he did regarding the priority of their claim on resources.

The report identified discrimination against Indian Muslims that occurred at institutional levels. For example: 'Some banks have identified a number of Muslim concentration areas as "negative geographical zones" where bank credit and other facilities are not easily provided.' The data proved this and

Muslims received only a third of the advances they should have, including priority sector advances.

Half of all of India's villages where Muslims were 40 per cent or more of the population were less likely to have access to a road. Such places were also less likely to have educational institutions, medical facilities, post and telegraph offices or a bus stop. Where there is a concentration of Muslims, the Indian State is more likely to become delinquent and reduce its delivery.

Muslim children in north India were the only ones to have no access to pre-school unless they give up their mother tongue, there being no anganwadis with Urdu instruction. Article 29 gives all Indians 'having a distinct language, script or culture of its own... the right to conserve the same'. But often, Urdu schools had teachers who had no knowledge of Urdu. The problem was compounded by the fact that these posts were reserved for Scheduled Caste and Scheduled Tribes and such candidates were not available. Muslims from the Scheduled Castes have no access to SC reservation.

This was another serious problem of Muslim exclusion, the Committee revealed. The first Backward Classes Commission submitted its report in 1955. It identified 2399 castes and communities as being backward and of these 837 were considered 'most backward' and deserving of special focus and attention. This list contained Hindu as well as Muslim groups. However, as the Sachar report says, this 'did not find approval from the chairperson of the Commission and one of the reasons cited was the assumed castelessness of Muslims and Christians'.

The exclusion of Muslims from the Scheduled Caste list goes back to 1936, when the Imperial (Scheduled Caste) Order which said, 'No Indian Christian shall be deemed to be a member of the Scheduled Caste', also excluding Buddhists. Muslim groups were included in this SC list, because they were clearly identifiable, but were barred from availing benefits, making their inclusion meaningless. This imperial decree was the basis on which independent India has continued to deny Muslims inclusion in the SC category, though it chose to include Buddhists later.

This view that Muslims and Christians do not need reservations because they are casteless is commonly held but is incorrect in two ways. For one thing, even caste among Hindus is not sanctified by the Constitution which forbids Hindu practices such as untouchability. If its existence in one part of society is taken for granted, it must be assumed to be present elsewhere. In that sense, caste is a social and cultural phenomenon and not a legal one. For another, the documentation of disadvantaged and marginalised Muslim caste groups is thorough and the phenomenon is not disputed.

Arzal Muslims are Dalits from communities like Halalkhor, Bhangi, Lalbegi, Bediya, Hajam (barber), Chik (butcher), Faqir and Dhobi (washermen). Change in religion did not bring any change in status for them and they suffer social exclusion because of the stigma attached to their profession just as Hindus in the same professions do.

Ajlaf Muslims are converts from OBC communities and include Julaha (weaver), Idris or Darzi (tailor), Rayeen or Kunjara (vegetable vendors) who have 'clean' occupations. The Sachar report said that the Constitutional (Scheduled Caste) Order of 1950 gives the status of Scheduled Caste only to Hindu groups having 'unclean occupations', while the Muslims who are Dalit have been classified with the Other Backward Classes. Thus, Dalit Muslims and OBC Muslims are in the same reservation category and Dalit Muslims cannot access SC reservations in employment and education. The 1950 order has been amended twice to include first, Dalit Sikhs in 1956 and then Dalit Buddhists in 1990, leaving only Dalit Muslims and Dalit Christians out of the SC list. Puzzlingly, Sikhs and Buddhists are notified as religious minorities by the National Commission for Minorities along with Muslims and Christians (and also Parsis and Jains). So clearly it is not just their official status as religious minorities that is the reason India has denied its Dalit Christians and Dalit Muslims their rights.

Similarly, Muslims drawn from the Scheduled Tribes are usually denied reservation under the ST category, something that has attracted the attention of the judiciary ('Christian, Muslims' exclusion from SC/ST category needs review: CJI', *Hindustan Times*, 9 January 2020) though nothing has been done about it. The Sachar report refers to Uttar Pradesh's Banjara tribals whose Hindu members are included in the ST list but not its Muslim members. The Mandal Commission clubbed arzal and ajlaf together in an all-encompassing OBC category, 'overlooking the disparity in the nature of the deprivations they faced'. According to the Sachar report, 'being at the bottom of the social hierarchy, the arzals are the worst off and need to be handled separately. It would be most appropriate if they were absorbed in the SC list.'

Though about two million Muslims identify as Scheduled Caste or Scheduled Tribe, they have no access to reservations as SCs. The problem of Muslim exclusion extended to the OBC Muslims also. The report said the list of OBCs prepared by many states missed out many underprivileged castes and communities. Other groups had missed out because they had been identified in only the Central list but not on the state list and vice-versa. Kalwar in Bihar, Mansoori in Rajasthan, Atishbaz in UP and Churihars in West Bengal were examples of these.

In Gujarat, the Anthropological Survey of India had identified a total of eighty-five Muslim communities of whom seventy-six were not Ashraf (elite) meaning they were either from the Scheduled Castes or OBC. However, only twenty-two of these were on the Central OBC list and only twenty-seven on the state list. In UP, sixty-one out of the sixty-seven Muslim communities came from occupational castes but the central and state lists contained only thirty-two of them. Madhya Pradesh identified thirty-seven communities but the central list features only twenty-seven of them. A further obstacle was that Muslims were often not issued the requisite OBC caste certificates by officials, the Sachar report said.

Because of the nature and history of caste and conversions, the majority of the sub-continent's Muslims come from underprivileged communities who chose to convert en masse. The 1911 census identified 102 Muslim caste groups of whom 97 were not Ashraf. Many of them including Kumhar, Mali, Mochi, Rajput, Kayastha and Koli were common to Hindus and Muslims.

Only a few states have acted to partially correct this exclusion. Of the 40 per cent reservations for Backward Classes in Kerala, 12 per cent was for Muslims, 4 per cent for Latin Catholics and 1 per cent for Scheduled Caste converts to Christianity. Karnataka had 4 per cent reservations for poor Muslims. Tamil Nadu has included Muslim groups like Labbais and Deccanis in its Backwards list. Bihar had included some Muslim groups in its Most Backward Classes which as a whole has 18 per cent of the reservations. In February 2020, a minister in Maharashtra's coalition government announced that it was giving 5 per cent reservations to Muslims, however no progress on this had been made.

Again, this exclusion has been noted and acknowledged by the State. The 2002 Venkatachaliah report referred to earlier on the issue of Muslim political representation told the Vajpayee government: 'Backward classes belonging to religious minorities who have been identified and included in the list of backward classes and who, in fact, constitute the bulk of the population of religious minorities should be taken up with special care along with their Hindu counterparts in the developmental efforts for the backward classes.' This was ignored by the Vajpayee government.

The Sachar committee also looked at the data on employment of Muslims in government and found that their representation compared to their share of population was about a third of what it should be and preponderantly in the lower ranks. Muslims were only 4.9 per cent of the total 88 lakh state and central government employees, according to data submitted by various departments.

The Railways had 4.5 per cent Muslims while state banks and the Reserve Bank of India had 2.2 per cent. The share of Muslim employment in central public sector units was 3.3 per cent. It was better in state PSUs at 10.8 per cent.

The absolute number did not reveal the whole picture. In the Railways, 98.7 per cent of the Muslims employed were at lower levels, with only 1.3 per cent as Group A or Group B officers. SC and ST composition in contrast was 18 per cent in this set.

Government employment was desirable for two reasons. Firstly, because the government remains the largest employer of the organised sector in India. Of all organised sector jobs in 2004, when the data was gathered by the committee, 70 per cent were in government and only 30 per cent in the private corporate sector. And therefore it is crucial that Muslims and other marginalised groups find representation here.

Secondly, government employment gave individuals a privileged position through 'ascribed and sometimes assumed status' as a result of which they were accorded status and protocol privileges as representatives of the government. In a pluralistic society, the report added, reasonable representation was necessary to enhance participatory governance.

Among the elite bureaucrats, belonging to the Indian Administrative Service, the Indian Police Service and the Indian Foreign Service, Muslim representation was 3.2 per cent. Here, the committee accepted that the share of Muslims appearing for the examination was also low (4.9 per cent) and their success rate in clearing the exam appeared to be on par with the rest. In the judiciary, Muslims were 7.8 per cent, compared to 23 per cent OBCs, and 20 per cent SC/STs.

In the security agencies, India's Muslims faced open discrimination. They are assumed to be treasonous by birth and for this reason not hired. The Research and Analysis Wing (RAW), tasked with foreign intelligence, does not recruit Muslims by way of unwritten policy. *Outlook* magazine reported on this in its 13 November 2006 issue.

The report ('Muslims And Sikhs Need Not Apply') opened with this story: 'The year was 2000. The NDA government was restructuring the Indian security apparatus following the Kargil war. Kabir's grandson had been cleared for induction into the RAW's air wing, the Aviation Research Centre (ARC). He was found to be competent for the job and met all the required parameters. His interviewers were very impressed with him. They had no doubt that they had found their man.

'But hours later the decision was reversed. The members of the selection board came to the view that there was a question mark on Kabir's suitability for the job. He was a Muslim and the unwritten code within the agency was that Muslims could not be inducted. That code vis-a-vis Muslims is still followed. From 1969 till today—RAW's current staff strength is about 10,000—it has avoided recruiting any Muslim officer. Neither has the National Technical Research Organisation (NTRO), a crucial arm of external intelligence.'[8]

This discrimination was happening despite there being resistance to it from inside the force itself. The former RAW chief A.S. Dulat was quoted in the report as saying that appointing Muslims was not only necessary but also critical. He said: 'The Muslim psyche can be baffling to non-Muslims. However much

8. https://magazine.outlookindia.com/story/muslims-and-sikhs-need-not-apply/233087

a person claims to be in tune with what the community feels, he can never really know all the nuances. A Muslim, on the other hand, would have the feel for the language, the metaphor and the culture. If you have to know what is happening in Aligarh Muslim University or Students Islamic Movement of India, a Muslim will be much better informed. And you cannot wish away the feeling of neglect, the hurt and the discrimination that the community feels. That too is something a Muslim would be able to understand better.'

After a task force submitted its report to the NDA government, it began an exercise to revamp intelligence agencies. 'While new organisations were being set up, a senior bureaucrat approached the then national security advisor (NSA), Brajesh Mishra for guidance. "I asked him if we could induct Muslims into the organisations that were being set up. He promised us that he would look into it. I never heard from him after that," the bureaucrat said.'

The matter was taken up once again when J.N. Dixit took over as the NSA in the UPA government under Manmohan Singh. The report quoted an officer saying that Dixit, '... heard us out and gave instructions that there should be no discrimination on the basis of religion while recruiting competent officers. Days later he passed away and the instructions were not recorded on file and did not become official policy. So things continue to be the way they were.'

The Intelligence Bureau, the Central agency tasked with domestic intelligence, began accepting Muslims only during the P.V. Narasimha Rao government. The report said that the first handful of people who were hired as officers were assets in several anti-insurgency operations in Kashmir: 'They could identify with the sensibilities of the Kashmiris and were much more sensitive in their approach which paid off in 1994-95 when militancy was at its height. In fact, these officers helped us counter the Pakistani propaganda that was dominant in the Kashmir valley during that time,' the report said.

However, this policy was not pursued. I checked with sources in the government and in 2020, in the entire intelligence community of RAW, IB, National Technical Research Organisation and Military Intelligence, India only had a single Muslim officer. This had been the case for several years, I was told.

Elsewhere, in the security forces, the Sachar report secured data on 5 lakh of the 19 lakh people employed. Of the people employed in Border Security Force, Central Industrial Security Force, Sashastra Seema Bal and Central Reserve Police Force, the representation of Muslims was 3.6 per cent in the higher categories and 4.6 per cent in the lower. Almost all Muslims (96 per cent of the total) were in the lower levels, with only 2 per cent of them making it to Group A or Group B officer levels. The data from the military was not made available to the Sachar committee for whatever reason. However, in 1999, former defence minister Mulayam Singh Yadav said that of the over 1 million people in the Indian military, Muslims were only 1 per cent.

The observations made here are important because they could have led to action. Article 16(4) of the Constitution gives the State the authority to make 'any provision for the reservation of appointments or posts in favour of any backward class of citizens which, in the opinion of the State, is not adequately represented in the services under the State'.

The Venkatachaliah committee had said on this subject to the Vajpayee government: 'An effort needs to be made to carry out special recruitment of persons belonging to the under-represented minority communities in the police forces of states, paramilitary forces and armed forces.' Nothing was done on this by the Vajpayee government or the governments that have come since. Manmohan Singh, as noted, was attacked merely for saying he intended to fix the problem of State discrimination against Muslims.

The India Justice Report 2019 released by the Tata Trusts said that over fifteen years, from 1999–2013, Muslim representation in the Indian police has remained consistently low, at between 3 per cent and 4 per cent per cent outside Kashmir. The inclusion of Jammu and Kashmir pushes the national figure up to 8 per cent. Meaning there are more Muslim policemen among the little over 1 crore people of Jammu and Kashmir than there are in the rest of India's 130 crore population. A few states like Kerala, Tamil Nadu, Telangana and West Bengal include reservation for Muslims under the Other Backward Classes category. The report said that since 2013, the National Crimes Records Bureau annual report has ceased reporting the level of Muslim representation in the police.

The postal department had 2.7 lakh employees of whom 5 per cent were Muslim, most in Group D. In universities, Muslims were 3.7 per cent of the teaching faculty, half of the SC/ST number which was at 7.4 per cent.

Excluded and discriminated against by the State and facing discrimination from large parts of society, Muslims have the highest proportion of self-employed people in India (39.4 per cent), more than Hindus as a whole (29.6 per cent) and SCs/STs (22.9 per cent). Muslim women (29.1 per cent) were twice as likely to be self-employed in a household enterprise than Hindu women (14.9 per cent). Informal sector employment in Muslims in urban areas was 92.1 per cent compared to 76.9 per cent for Hindus. Muslim men who worked in no fixed place or from home were 45.3 per cent. For Hindus, the number was 38.1 per cent.

Patterns of exclusion and discrimination were found to exist by the Sachar committee also with respect to Muslim citizens benefiting from government schemes. In Kerala, Muslims were over 30 per cent of those identified as below the poverty line, but only between 5 per cent and 18 per cent of BPL scheme beneficiaries, except for three programmes on tuberculosis (where they were 28 per cent), cooperative credit (25 per cent) and blindness 21 per cent). In UP, Muslims were over 23 per cent of the poor but their share of schemes was between 3 per cent and 14 per cent for all schemes except two.

Even in states that were considered to be relatively better, the share of Muslim beneficiaries of government schemes was under their share of the population. They have the poorest access to healthcare according to the National Sample Survey data. They had the lowest access to urban public access to hospital deliveries and the second lowest (after SC/STs) in private hospitals. In rural India, Muslims have the highest number of births delivered by a non-trained assistant.

Integrated Child Development Schemes touched only 7.6 per cent Muslim children from the ages of 0-6 compared to 10.2 per cent among SC/STs and 12.5 per cent among OBCs.

The number of Muslim children who are covered by the mid-day meal programme nationally are 22.8 per cent, compared to 28.1 per cent for all Hindus and 34.7 per cent for SC/STs. Only the general category is lower at 19.1 per cent, presumably because it educated its children in schools where these meals were not served.

The Sachar report says, 'Muslims, especially women, have virtually no access to government development schemes. They experience discrimination in getting loans from the Jawahar Rozgar Yojana for below poverty line beneficiaries, in getting loans for housing, in procuring widow pensions.'

The report said also that while it was not easy to identify all the causes for the marginalisation of Muslims in these schemes, one was the 'lack of Muslim participation in the political process and governance, especially at the local level'. The enhancement of this in electoral politics by parties and policy making by government was important.

Despite being burdened by disadvantages, on many social issues, Muslims are ahead of Hindus. Their sex ratio of 986 is much higher than the national average (Gujarat's is only 890). Their infant and under-five mortality rates are better than the national average.

And yet Muslims are so casually stigmatised that the report concluded that 'Muslims live with an inferiority complex as every bearded man is considered an ISI agent.'

Though it is an outstanding and thorough document, the Congress party no longer even refers to the Sachar Committee report and usually avoids speaking of Muslims and their plight for fear that it will be seen as the party of Muslims and couched as being 'anti-Hindu'. The Modi government continues to report to Parliament on the implementation of the Sachar report's findings and what it has done to alleviate the disparity and the discriminations faced by Muslims in India. The last such status update was given on 31 March 2019. While the update conflates what the government has done under its various umbrella schemes (such as Swachch Bharat and Ujjwala), rather than targeted ones, it still flows from the idea and the acceptance that India's minorities are more deprived than the rest of us.

Before the 2014 elections, Narendra Modi said in an interview that when the Sachar Committee came to Gujarat to take inputs for the report, it asked him: 'What did you do for the Muslims?' To this, Modi replied that he did nothing for the Muslims of Gujarat. He will do nothing for the Muslims of Gujarat. He further said that he did not do anything for the Hindus either.

This was a clever answer, as is to be expected from Modi. But it avoided the question and evaded the facts as they stand. Given that the government accepted the findings of the Sachar

Committee report, it was bound to ensuring its recommendations be implemented and the discrimination and disparity in Indian society reduced.

Instead, Modi and his party continued with the demonstrable untruth, even after they had won two terms in power, that India's Muslims were being 'appeased'.

7

KEEP THE FAITH (OR ELSE)

The Constituent Assembly debate on religious freedom happened on 6 December 1948. It came after meetings of the Minorities Committee and the committee on Fundamental Rights, which discussed the issue in detail and produced a text which is today Article 25. It reads: 'Right to freedom of religion: Subject to public order, morality and health and to the other provisions of this Part, all persons are equally entitled to freedom of conscience and the right freely to profess, practise and propagate religion'.

The key word here is propagate, which the dictionary defines as to spread and promote, and to breed. The context in which the word was debated by India's Constituent Assembly was that of conversions, specifically by Christians.

Gujarat's K.M. Munshi, the Hindu conservative, was part of group that arrived at the text and he said of the word 'propagate' that: 'I know it was on this word that the Christian community laid the greatest emphasis, not because they wanted to convert people aggressively, but because the word "propagate" was a fundamental part of their tenet.' And 'so long as religion is religion, conversion by free exercise of conscience had to be recognised.' People must not fear the idea of a right to propagate, Munshi said, because 'whatever conversions take place ... are only the result of persuasion and not because of material advantages.'

In the Interim Report on Fundamental Rights dated 1 May 1947, Frank Anthony had spoken to the committee and said: My community (he was an Anglo-Indian) does not propagate. We do not convert, nor are we converted. But I do appreciate how deeply, how passionately millions of Christians feel on this right to propagate their religion.' Anthony, the founder of a school network around India, congratulated the majority for retaining 'in spite of its contentious character' the words 'to propagate', 'a right which is regarded as perhaps the most fundamental of Christian rights.'

In the Assembly debate, L. Krishnaswami Bharathi of Madras, said of the Minorities Committee group that 'they had come to the conclusion that this great Christian community ... should be allowed to propagate its religion along with other religious communities in India.'

Pandit Lakshmi Kant Maitra of West Bengal spoke of the 'additional right to propagate' (the word was added specifically into the draft text after deliberation on the issue of conversions) and that 'we must be very careful to see' that 'we do not deny anybody the right not only to profess and practice but also to propagate'.

The only opposition in the Constituent Assembly to what had become a consensus on the right to propagate religion came from a twenty-six-year old man from Odisha, who wanted the word propagate removed. This was Loknath Misra, brother of Ranganath Misra who would later become Chief Justice of the Supreme Court, and uncle of Dipak Misra, also to become Chief Justice. Loknath Misra opined that Hindus had already obliged Indian minorities by not declaring India a Hindu State. In his words, by choosing secularism, the 'maximum of generosity' that a 'Hindu-dominated territory' could give its minorities was given (he was reading out a manuscript—Nehru noticed and objected). This generosity was being abused by 'making propagation a

Fundamental Right', said Misra, asking that Hinduism 'be given a fair deal, if not restored to its legitimate place after a thousand years of suppression'.

His said his fear was that widespread conversions, especially to Christianity 'which had worked out the policy of peaceful penetration by the back-door on the outskirts of our social life' would affect Hindus. He didn't have a problem he said, with propagation. 'If people should propagate their religion, let them do so', but 'only I crave, let not the Constitution put it as a fundamental right and encourage it'. His opposition also came from an understanding of the right to propagate as meaning the right to convert.

Misra's bid to remove the word 'propagate' was rejected as were his views on the threat to Hinduism. T.T. Krishnamachari said that Dalits became Christian because of the status it gave them, that Hindu reform would deter such conversions, and that the right to propagate also applied to Hindus and Arya Samajists who were free under the wording of this law to carry out their conversion activities, which they called 'shuddhi'.

The point here is that the meaning of the word 'propagate' was understood by all as the right to, in Munshi's words, 'persuade people to join their faith'. That is, to convert.

The word 'freely' in the Fundamental Right was deliberate. The State would regulate only that activity which was not concerned with religion itself. The law's qualifying clause reads: 'Nothing in this article shall affect the operation of any existing law or prevent the State from making any law regulating or restricting any economic, financial, political or other secular activity which may be associated with religious practice.'

But what would happen instead in India as we will see is that the State would step in to not only remove the right to propagate but also the right of the individual to change her religion.

V.P. Bharatiya, writing in the *Journal of Indian Law Institute* ('Propagation of religion: Stanislaus Vs State of MP', Vol. 19,

No. 3, July-Sept 1977), says the specificity in the debates gave the impression that the inclusion of the word propagate 'is reserved for Christians only, that it is for conversions only, and that it creates a specific fundamental right to convert' and that 'the rejection of the amendment seeking to regulate aspects of conversion proper suggests that the intention of the framers was ... not to exclude conversion from the ambit of propagation.'

Ambedkar was present in the debate but did not speak. He said he had nothing to add to what the others had said in defence of the right to propagate. It should be noted that Ambedkar's original draft submitted to the Constituent Assembly's committees bore the words: 'right to profess, to preach and to convert, within limits compatible with public order and morality'. He was satisfied that propagate meant the same thing. He would himself leave Hinduism and convert to Buddhism together with more than 3 lakh other Dalits in Nagpur on 14 October 1956.

In the debates, Kasturiranga Santhanam of Tamil Nadu said he foresaw that the problem would not be the fundamental right itself but the words before it. He said: 'What is important are the governing words with which the article begins, viz. "Subject to public order, morality and health".'

Before Independence several princely states had laws regulating conversions. Kotah, Bikaner, Jodhpur and Udaipur in Rajasthan and Surguja and Kalahandi in Chhattisgarh and Odisha respectively, were among them. The Surguja State Hindu Apostasy Act of 1945 vested in the king the power to allow conversions. The Udaipur State Conversion Act of 1946 required all conversions of Hindus to other faiths to be registered officially. The fear was that the lower castes would leave Hinduism if conversion was easy for them. This was compounded by the reality that Hinduism itself could not convert because outsiders would come without caste, something unacceptable to the doctrine of orthodox Hinduism. This problem of a depleting Hindu population has remained on the mind of those who have worried about freedom of religion in India.

In 1954 and 1960, two private members' bills seeking to regulate conversions were introduced in Parliament.

They were the Indian Conversion (Regulation and Registration) Bill of 1954, which sought to license missionaries and have those converting register themselves with magistrates and in 1960 came the Backward Communities (Religious Protection) Bill aimed at preventing Dalits and Adivasis from converting. Neither passed. Both these bills sought to regulate conversions and neither touched the fundamental right to propagate religion.

In 1967, Odisha became the first state in independent India to pass a law against conversion, the Freedom of Religion Act. The law said no person shall convert or attempt to convert anyone by use of force, inducement or fraudulent means. Force included 'the threat of divine displeasure or social excommunication.' This meant that speaking of the promise of heaven and the fear of hell constituted actual force.

The State had plucked propagation out of the list of fundamental rights and dropped it into the Indian Penal Code. From here on, propagation, both in the sense that spreading of scripture and converting, was no longer a guaranteed right to be enjoyed freely by the citizen, but a crime to be punished by the State.

When challenged in the high court, Justice Ranganath Misra (brother of Loknath referred to above) hearing the matter observed: 'Threat of divine displeasure numbs the mental faculty; more so of an undeveloped mind' and therefore 'the actions of such person thereafter are not free and according to conscience'.

Rules for the Odisha law required the priest performing a conversion to inform the district magistrate of the place, date and time of the ceremony, and the names and addresses of those being converted.

This became the model for all future laws in other states. The following year came the Madhya Pradesh law which prohibits 'allurement' in propagation and punishes those violating this with a year in jail and, if the convert is a woman, Dalit or Adivasi, then two years like the Odisha law.

When it was challenged, the Madhya Pradesh High Court upheld the law saying it 'established the equality of religious freedom for all citizens by prohibiting conversion by objectionable activities such, as conversion by force, fraud and by allurement'. The Odisha law was struck down by its high court on the issue of jurisdiction, saying that the state government had no power over freedom of religion, a fundamental right which was in the domain of the Centre.

The Supreme Court then upheld both laws in 1977 (Stanislaus versus Madhya Pradesh), concluding that regardless of Article 25, there could be no such thing as a fundamental right to convert. Legislation regulating this was valid and that the word 'propagate' in the right did not mean convert but merely to communicate one's faith. The court undid at a stroke what the Constituent Assembly had deliberately pushed for.

The right to communicate one's faith was already available to Indians under freedom of speech, also a fundamental right. The history of the inclusion of the word propagation and the meaning read into it by the framers of the Constitution was disregarded by the court. The Supreme Court also demoted the right to freedom of religion and removed it from the exclusive province of the Centre. It said the State was entitled to regulate the 'law and order' aspect which qualified the fundamental right.

Faizan Mustafa and Jagteshwar Singh Sohi (*Freedom of Religion in India: Current Issues and Supreme Court Acting as Clergy*) write that 'the right to convert was actually included in Article 25, and, as such, the decision of the Supreme Court in Stanislaus not only was erroneous but also led to instability in society, as Indian Christians feel they have been cheated in this matter. The assurances given to them in the Constituent Assembly on the inclusion of the word propagate have not been fulfilled, and the government has done nothing to remedy the situation arising out of the highly restrictive interpretation of the term propagation by the Supreme Court.'

Pratap Bhanu Mehta ('Passion and Constraint', *Seminar 521*, 2003) wrote about the court's finding that the Odisha law did not violate the right to propagate made no sense: 'If a person spoke to transmit tenets, he may not be punished, but if he harboured hopes that the person being addressed would accept the truth of his religion and convert, he would not be protected.'

Mehta added that the court interpreted freedom of religion to purely mean the right not to be targeted, and that conversion was objectionable. And that mention of divine displeasure or rewards constituted an attempt to convert by fraud. 'The court seems to assume throughout that people are somehow not capable of managing "religious" ideas they receive, particularly if they are from lower castes,' he wrote.

The court's removal of the right to propagate immediately led to laws in other states. The following year (1978), came laws in Andhra Pradesh, Arunachal Pradesh and Tamil Nadu. In 2006, under the BJP, Chhattisgarh, which had inherited the Madhya Pradesh law,[9] removed regulation on conversions to Hinduism through an amendment saying that 'the return to ancestor's original religion or own original religion by any person shall not be construed as conversion'.

In 2003, under Narendra Modi, Gujarat passed a law that essentially removes all freedom of religion for Gujaratis. It

---

9. Chattisgarh was carved out of Madhya Pradesh in 2000 and hence had inherited its state-level laws.

requires individuals changing their faith to fill out a form telling the District Magistrate the reasons they were choosing to convert; their occupation and monthly income; how long they had been in the faith they were converting out of; to reveal whether they were Dalit or Adivasi; the date and time of their conversion; the names, addresses and ages of themselves and all in their family; the names and addresses of all guests attending the ceremony.

If they did not do so within ten days of their conversion, they faced one year in jail.

The person propagating has to fill out another form with all of the details referred to above and must submit, one month before the conversion, an application to the District Magistrate seeking permission. The bureaucrat has one month in which to approve or deny permission. This denial of propagation obviously also affects the right of the person who wants to change their faith. One had to remain in the faith they were born in unless the government approved.

The District Magistrate must also maintain a register that has the number of applications received, approved, denied or pending which he must report every quarter. The coercion can be imagined.

Gujarat's Assembly was told in January 2020 that in the previous five years a total of 1,895 'applications' for conversion had been filed in the state. Gujarat had denied permission to convert to 889 individuals.

The government 'gave permission' to 1,006 applicants, almost all of whom were Dalits in Surat converting to Buddhism. The number of Dalit applicants to convert to Buddhism had swelled because in 2014, they had been denied permission to convert in a mass ceremony. The Modi government attempted to modify the law to exclude conversions from Buddhism and Jainism to Hinduism and vice versa from the State's regulation. Meaning that Jains and Buddhists would be seen legally as Hindus and therefore would not really be 'converting'. But this was objected to by Gujarat's Jains who resisted being clubbed wth Hindus and the modification was withdrawn.

The Gujarat law increased punishment for propagation to three years (four years if the convert was a woman, Dalit or Adivasi). But how the District Magistrate's denial of permission would work at the level of faith was unclear. One priest the writer interviewed said: 'Suppose I stopped believing in Christ today. This would be a conversion from being a believer to a non-believer. I am supposed to take permission from the State for this change, but I have already stopped believing.'

He said about Article 25 that '... we see the right to propagate as the individual having the right to believe in the god she chooses to and the right of the church to spread the message of salvation'.

The regulations have made it so difficult for individuals to change their faith that the Catholic Church in Gujarat has stopped offering the baptism ceremony to individuals wishing to take it. The church only baptises the children of Christians. The state and Hindutva groups continue harassment and have demanded to see the baptism register of churches, though this is a clear violation of the right to privacy of individuals.

The Gujarat law was challenged by rights activists in the Gujarat High Court, saying it violated constitutional rights under freedom of expression and freedom of religion. The state government did not respond to the notice from the court and the matter has remained shelved. In protest against the court, the activists withdrew the challenge. Gujarat's government meanwhile has aggressively gone after individuals under this law.

On 24 January 2020, the *Times of India* in Ahmedabad reported ('Women booked for converting her minor son to Christianity') about a single woman who had had her infant baptised at a church in Anand eight years before (in 2012). She was booked under the Freedom of Religion Act. The inquiry against her had been kept pending all these years but it was concluded on 3 January by the district collector, who ordered an FIR to be filed against her. The complaint against the woman originally came from a Hindutva group running a campaign against conversions.

This group, led by an individual named Dharmendra Rathod, had earlier filed the first complaint under the Gujarat Freedom of Religion Act in 2012, alleging that thirty-two Dalit Christians had been 'converted' in Petlad. The church said this was untrue because the children were Christians at birth and from Christian families who had been baptised at a public ceremony.

Dalits and Adivasis who convert are vulnerable, because the State insists on registering them on certificates as 'Christian Adivasi' making it difficult for the individuals to then secure their rights as members of Scheduled Tribes. We have seen this issue mentioned by the Sachar Committee in the previous chapter. In Gujarat, some Dalit converts to Christianity officially retain their Hindu faith, and therefore their caste and status, a process the church condones under the tradition of occult compensation. This term refers to the action of an individual seeking to recover their losses through an extra-legal act. In this instance, the use of stealth by Dalits to claim their right from a state which is denying it to them unjustly.

The BJP government actively goes after Gujarat's Dalit and Adivasi Christians as a way of blocking their conversions. On 7 March 2011, Gujarat High Court rejected a Dalit's access to benefits he had earlier received after the government claimed he had converted.

The court said that the man, Nimesh Zaveri, and his families would cease to enjoy their rights as Dalits despite having a certificate issued by the government.

This came after a committee claimed that he and his family had converted based on an affidavit from 1990 that he had converted in 1987, declaring that he would no longer be identified by caste but as an Indian Christian. On his sons' marriage cards, they were said to have been described as Christian.

A priest said that one reason that the polity and the law prevented the granting of rights to converts was the fear that they would en masse leave Hinduism. [10] 'Once you grant Dalit and Adivasi Muslims and Christians their rights as SC and STs, the floodgates will open,' the individual said. Asked why, the reply was: 'Because they feel oppressed.'

Propagation and conversion of the Dalits and Adivasis has been one of the bugbears of the RSS, coupled with its often-expressed fear that large numbers of Hindus are being bribed, coerced or duped into changing their faith. This happens, or so Hindutva's theories go, because of the financial inducements by missionaries, Muslims luring Hindu women into marriage ('love jihad') and the naivety of Indians, especially the Dalit and the Adivasi and also the Indian woman.

In its vision and mission text on its website, the RSS speaks about 'incessant conversions from the Hindu fold through

10. The worry that Dalits and Adivasis would leave the Hindu fold was echoed also in Article 25, which gives the State the authority for 'providing for social welfare and reform or the throwing open of Hindu religious institutions of a public character to all classes and sections of Hindus'. This is seen as creeping communalism. Academic Pritam Singh in his paper 'Hindu Bias in India's 'Secular' Constitution: Probing flaws in the instruments of governance', (*Third World Quarterly* Vol. 26, No. 6) asked, 'Why should a secular state be concerned with social welfare and reform of only Hindu temples?' His response was that 'it seems that the overriding concern behind these social reform measures was to prevent the exodus of the Dalits from the Hindu fold.' (quoted in 'Is there a Hindu bias in India's secular Constitution?', *scroll.in*, 2 February 2020). On the other hand, Hindu convervatives chafe at Article 25 for another of its provisions giving the State the right to regulate 'economic, financial, political or other secular activity which may be associated with religious practice'. This is used to manage the large temple trusts such as Tirupathi, Siddhivinayak and Sabarimala. Some Hindus feel this is intrusion, though the BJP itself has not been concerned about this much. The issue has been mentioned in only one BJP manifesto, in 2009.

money-power' and that 'the poor, the illiterate and the weaker sections in the society become an easy prey for exploitation and conversion to other faiths'.

It adds that 'the systematic alienation of the tribals, inhabiting remote forest areas, but who form an inseparable part of the Hindu society through proselytisation was another grave challenge that demanded immediate corrective measures ... They had all along been a most exploited lot and an easy prey for unscrupulous conversion by Christian missionaries.'

The RSS says, 'A mechanism to reconvert all those who had been knowingly or unknowingly proselytised to alien faiths and are now desirous of coming back to the Hindu fold was needed. The VHP was founded in 1964 to fill this need.' The VHP's efforts have 'succeeded not only in putting a stop to conversions in all its areas of operation, but also in bringing the converts back to the Hindu fold'.

The anti-conversion focus of the RSS and the VHP excludes conversions to Hinduism. These are 'ghar wapsi' (homecoming) for them, and not conversions. What the VHP does in converting people to Hinduism is according to itself neither allurement nor force. And it does not need permission under any law to do ghar wapsi because it feels converting people to Hinduism is unexceptionable unlike converting them to other faiths. Like the Chhattisgarh law referred to above, the proposed anti-conversion law in Uttar Pradesh submitted in 2019 also says conversion to Hinduism is excluded. It is conversions to Christianity and Islam that are the focus of the RSS.

But why do people convert? The narrative from the RSS is that propagation happens because of conspiracies and those who change their faith do so because they are duped. The history of conversions in India and especially conversions that happen in communities tells a different story. We need to examine it.

On 19 February 1981, news came from Meenakshipuram in Tamil Nadu of the conversion of about 1000 Dalits to Islam.

Atal Bihari Vajpayee and L.K. Advani sped to the town offering incentives, including the building of homes for the Dalits, if they reconverted, a process the RSS calls 'shuddhi' or purification.

A report from the state government explained why the Dalits were converting: 'From the discussions with the converted Scheduled Castes it was obvious that a longstanding social discrimination based on untouchability and indifference of Hindu society at large towards them was the major cause for the conversion ... With regard to drinking water there are separate wells in the localities of Pallans, Arunathathiyars and Thevars. Pallans (Harijans) have their own barbers. Harijans cannot get water from the wells of Thevar locality. There are three tea-stalls at Panpoli run by a Moopanar, a Thevar and a Muslim. Harijans can get tea at a shop run by the Muslim but not from the other two stalls.'[11]

The VHP sent a team that visited Meenakshipuram ('Sudden spurt in conversions of Harijans to Islam forces govt to study the issue', *India Today*, 15 September 1981). It concluded that 'the temptation for financial gain and assurance of protection from police appear to be the main reasons for conversions in Tamil Nadu...'.

But why should legal protection against vigilante violence be offensive? And so far as the 'temptation for financial gain' goes, the VHP alleged that, 'On the day of conversion on 19 February 1981 a grand function and feast was arranged and a lot of money was reportedly spent including Rs 500 per convert distributed at the time of conversion.'

On 18 November 2002, *India Today* went back to Meenakshipuram to speak to those who had become Muslim.

---

11. I am aware that 'Harijan' as a word is no longer acceptable to the Dalit community and the term 'Dalit' is currently prevalent. However, in the instances where I am quoting old reports, studies and so on, I have thought it fit to retain the original usage and not alter it. I have myself used the word 'Dalit' in the relevant contexts when commenting on the matters discussed.

One of them was Sheikh Madar Sahib, who was forty when he had converted. Asked if his conversion was forced, he said: 'Yes, I was forced ... forced by the upper-caste Hindus to run away from a system that treated me like a street dog.'

On 17 April 2019, the *Times of India* published a report ('In Meenakshipuram, conversions continue in hope of social dignity'). It spoke to individuals like Umar Kaiyam, a Dalit who used to be a Mookhan. As a primary school teacher he could not get anyone to rent a room to him. When he converted he got one immediately. Another man, Saifullah, said he collected paddy for the local temple. They used to treat him shabbily, he said, 'Now they call me "bhai".' Such stories will help explain why even though the change in social status may be marginal given their occupation, individuals choose to convert for dignity, respect and access. However the State in India has continued to view the issue through suspicion and from the majoritarian perspective, which is against freedom of religion.

In 2002, the Jayalalitha government introduced the Tamil Nadu Prohibition of Forcible Conversion of Religion Act. It had the standard references to force, allurement and fraudulent means and that anyone who 'converts any person from one religion to another either by performing any ceremony by himself for such conversion as a religious priest or by taking part directly or indirectly in such ceremony' was required to send notice to the District Magistrate. Punishment was three years or, if the convert was a woman, Dalit or Adivasi, four years in jail.

The law drew protests from minorities' organisations, Dalit groups and political parties who demonstrated on 24 October. DMK leader M. Karunanidhi said conversions like in the case of Meenakshipuram happened because Dalits were still the victims of the 'two-tumbler system' (where Dalits are served tea in separate tumblers or in coconut shells).

Orthodox Hindu groups mobilised in support of the law on 31 October. Kanchi Shankaracharya Jayendra Saraswathi spoke against conversions at the rally. *India Today* interviewed him and reported: 'The Shankaracharya was, however, evasive on atrocities against Dalits saying, "Every section of Hindu is assigned a job according to their qualification." Asked who fixed the qualification, the reporter says the pontiff turned aggressive: "We fix it."'

In protest against the law, thousands of Dalits converted to Christianity and Buddhism without approval from the local magistrate on 6 December 2002 (6 December is Ambedkar's death anniversary). BBC reported ('Crackdown over India mass baptism', 6 December 2002) that ten people had been arrested for this. The law remained unpopular and was repealed on 21 May, 2004.

On 2 December 2019, a twenty-foot wall erected to segregate Dalits from upper castes in a Coimbatore village fell after rains, killing seventeen Dalits, including nine children. The Dalits had sent a letter on 13 October 2018 to the local administration asking to be kept safe from the wall but this got no response, the *Hindu* reported ('Wall of discrimination fell on houses, allege Dalit, Muslim bodies', 3 December 2019).

In February 2020, *India Today* reported that 430 of the Dalits in the community had legally converted to Islam. The magazine spoke to some of these individuals, including Mohammed Abubaker, originally known as Marx. Abubaker said: 'We converted to Islam because of injustice and untouchability. Dalits cannot enter the Mariamman temple. Tea shops have discrimination here. We can't sit with other people equally on the bus.'

A young man named Sarath Kumar who now went by the name Abdullah said no Hindu spoke for them: 'Only the Muslim brothers stood with us and protested for us. Where is Arjun Sampath (leader of the Hindu Makkal Katchi) who said that he would voice for the Hindus who are persecuted? Where is that leader? Our Muslim brothers invite us to their houses. Hindus never called us. Would you make me enter the common temple? We could enter any mosque though. I have visited four to five mosques after converting. I worship god there with all levels of people.'[12]

In other parts of India, and especially in the Hindi belt, this freedom is unavailable. On 5 September 2014 *Indian Express* reported that Dalits in Madhya Pradesh had been arrested for choosing to become Muslim fourteen months previously, and then forcibly tried to be again made Hindu through ghar wapasi. The report said that 'a day after they were arrested for converting to Islam, four Dalits were "re-converted" to Hinduism by VHP and Bajrang Dal activists in a ceremony at the Hanuman Temple here. Calling it ghar wapasi, the Hindu organisations also brought in over half-a-dozen other Dalits who had expressed their willingness to embrace Islam, and subjected them to a 'purification' ceremony amid chanting of mantras by the temple priest.'

Two young men from the same family who had converted refused to participate in the 're-conversion' ceremony, the report said.

---

12. The denial of entry to Dalits into temples occasionally breaks out in the national news. The *Times of India* ('At Puri, priests block President Ram Nath Kovind's way, shove First Lady', 27 June 2018) reported how even the president of India was made unwelcome. Golwalkar's solution of the Dalit hiding his identity to be able to secure entry would not apply in such an instance. *Hindustan Times* ('Temple entry ban angers Dalits in Orissa village', 2 November 2006) reported hundreds of Dalits in Kendrapara threatening to convert over the issue. *DNA* ('Dalit denied entry in temple: Orissa government steps in to resolve issue', 25 June 2011) reported Dalits facing a socio-economic boycott by the upper castes in Puri for wanting to enter a Kali temple. The chairman of the National Commission of Scheduled Castes, himself a Dalit and also a member of parliament, was himself denied entry when he went to investigate the matter. ('Dalit MP denied entry in temple'. *News18*, 25 June 2011). This happens regularly to Dalits but does not seem to produce the outrage that is should. The *New Indian Express* ('Two priests booked for denying temple entry to Dalit girl', 17 January 2018) reported about an engineering student who was kept out of a Shiva temple.

On 8 December the same year, 385 Muslims were converted to Hindus at an RSS ceremony. After the event, the Muslims alleged they were misled into the conversion on the pretext of being given government benefits. A case was registered but no sanction for prosecution came, according to an *Indian Express* report the following year ('Agra "ghar wapsi": A year later, main accused out on bail as cops await govt. prosecution sanction', 8 December 2015).

Numbers: How many choose to change their faith in India?

Conversions in India have happened through communities. It is difficult for an individual to change her faith in India because ties to community and family are strong. For this social reason as well as the restrictions placed on the freedom of religion, the numbers of conversions in India are quite low. In its issue of 15 September, 1981 *India Today* reported that 'figures painstakingly tabulated by the Home Ministry showed that in the past fourteen months the number of conversions recorded—mostly of Harijans to Islam—numbered no more than 5,000.'

It added that though some conversions had been reported from north India, they were happening primarily in Tamil Nadu where, including the 1100 in Meenakshipuram, around 2,000 people had switched religions during the last eight months against less than 1,500 between 1944 and 1980.

On 7 March 2017, *Malayalam Manorama* reported the research by a non-profit organisation (Media Development and Research Foundation, Kozhikode) which showed 60 per cent of those who had converted in Kerala between January 2011 and December 2017 chose to become Hindus. Gazette records of changed names showed that 8,334 people had converted in the seven-year period, of whom 4,968 chose to become Hindu, of which the vast majority, 4,756, were Christian and 212 Muslim. Of the total, the number of women was 2,244 and the men 2,724.

Of the 1,864 who became Muslim, 78 per cent were previously Hindu, again with men and women converts being roughly equal. And of the 1,496 who became Christian, 95 per cent were Hindu, with 720 women and 776 men. Six individuals chose to become Buddhist, of whom five were Hindu, one was Christian and there were a total of two women and four men.

There is no official data from the State on this. However, a report in the *Times of India* a couple of years before that ('Nearly 6,000 converted to Islam in Kerala in 5 years: Report', 15 July 2016) quoted an 'intelligence report' filed by the police showing that 5,793 people had converted between 2011 and 2015. Of these about half were men and half women. Hindus converting were 4,719 with 1,074 being Christians.

These numbers over the years, whether from Tamil Nadu, Gujarat or Kerala pale before the conversions done by the VHP. On 26 October 2019, PTI reported the VHP saying it had converted 25,000 Muslims and Christians, mostly Adivasis, to Hinduism in 2018.

On 8 January 2016, PTI reported VHP leader Pravin Togadia claiming at a rally that his organisation had converted more than five lakh Christians and 2.5 lakh Muslims to Hinduism in the last ten years.[13]

'In the last ten years, we did ghar wapsi of more than five lakh Christians and 2.5 lakh Muslims. Our rate of ghar wapsi used to be around 15,000 each year. But last year, we crossed the mark of 40,000, which is excluding the figures of RSS,' Togadia said, adding 'if Hindus need to be in majority in India and to save our religion, we have to engage in many more ghar wapsi drives to bring crores of others into our religion.'

To this end, he said the VHP 'wants a bill which will make it difficult to convert people to other religions'.

---

13. *DNA*, 8 January 2016, https://www.dnaindia.com/india/report-75-lakh-muslims-christians-re-converted-in-last-10-years-vhp-leader-pravin-togadia-2163725

On 13 December 2015, *rediff.com* interviewed the man who would go on to become chief minister of Uttar Pradesh ('Yogi Adityanath proposes anti-conversion law, without ban on "reconversion"). 'We have reconverted several lakh Muslims and Christians over the past ten years,' he claimed, speaking of the activities of his organisation, the Hindu Yuva Vahini, 'What I am doing is simply taking such people back to their old home from where they were weaned away through inducement or coercion.'

He explained why he wanted the exemption for his own conversions from the law: 'So what if someone's ancestors were converted to Islam or Christianity several hundred years ago? Time is of no consequence. Therefore all those Hindus who were compelled to switch over to Islam during Mughal emperor Aurangzeb's rule—when the maximum mass conversions took place—should get exemption under the new law that the BJP wants to legislate.'

The Hindutva movement against religious freedom has turned particularly nasty in another area that it refers to as 'love jihad', meaning the luring away of women by Muslim men with the express intention of converting them. This is a relatively recent allegation and, as we will see, an entirely false one.

Its history begins officially on 10 December 2009, when Kerala High Court announced it had found indications of 'forceful religious conversions under the garb of love' in the state, and asked the government to consider enacting a law to prohibit such 'deceptive' acts. 'Under the pretext of love, there cannot be any compulsive, deceptive conversion,' Justice K.T. Sankaran said.

He accepted he had no evidence to show that 'love jihad' existed, but spoke nonetheless of a 'plan to trap brilliant upper caste Hindu and Christian girls from well-to-do families'. Thus began a spate of news stories around the speculation that there was such a thing as 'love jihad'. And into this stepped the RSS to stir up trouble and spread conspiracy theories.

On 27 November 2017, at a VHP Dharma Sansad in Udupi, the organisation's regional convenor Gopal G said 'Muslims must stop love jihad, otherwise we will send our youths from the Bajrang Dal to attract Muslim girls.'

On 23 December 2017, Indo-Asian News Service, it was previously known as India Abroad News Service (IANS), reported that 'over 100 workers of the BJP and other Hindu outfits, including dozen-odd leaders, were booked in Ghaziabad on the charge of clashing with police and rioting over the marriage of a Hindu woman with a Muslim man'.

On 6 December 2017, a man in Rajasthan hacked a Muslim labourer to death and set his body on fire while being recorded by his nephew. He spoke about love jihad in the video. On 22 December 22, *IANS* reported RSS leader Indresh Kumar as saying, when asked about the incident, that 'those indulging in love jihad will meet the same fate'.

On 1 May 2018, Kerala police registered a case against the VHP's Sadhvi Saraswati for a speech in Kasaragod in which she said: 'Your sister ties the rakhi on your wrist. You, in return, gift her clothes, jewellry and sweets. But along with that, gift her a sword also, so that even when a love jihadi glances at her, she would be brave enough to behead him and offer it at the feet of Bharat Mata.'

On 4 September 2018, PTI reported the VHP saying it would launch a campaign in West Bengal's schools and colleges against the 'ills of love jihad'. On 29 July 2019, ANI reported a BJP leader from Barabanki telling a gathering that 'cows at the houses of Muslims should be taken back. When we consider girls from our homes going to their homes love jihad, shouldn't we consider "gau mata" going to their homes love jihad too? Cows should be taken back from them at any cost.'

On 24 September 2018, *The Statesman* reported that 'a Hindu woman and a Muslim man, both fourth-year medical students of LLRM Medical College, were badly beaten by VHP men on suspicion of love jihad when they were studying at the latter's house in Medical Thana area of Meerut.' ('Love Jihad | Two medical students thrashed by VHP activists in Meerut')

The two were later handed over to the police where the duo had to sit for several hours. The police later handed over the girl to her parents and the boy was also set free, the report said.

On 22 May 2018, a sub-inspector Gagandeep Singh, saved a twenty-three-year-old Muslim youth after a mob of Bajrang Dal and VHP members assaulted him for being with a woman in Uttarakhand's Ramnagar.

There has been no evidence or demonstration that the phenomenon of love jihad exists and this should be obvious. The assumption that young couples are mingling not because they always have but because of something else requires a closed mind. On 14 September 2020, the *Indian Express* reported ('A case just fell flat, but VHP push makes UP police probe love jihad)' that under pressure from the Sangh, the administration would approach eleven inter-faith couples and investigate their relationship.

On 4 October 2015, Cobrapost published an investigation called 'Operation Juliet: Busting the myth of love jihad'. The reporters on the story spoke to RSS, BJP and VHP leaders including Union minister Sanjeev Kumar Balyan, sitting BJP MLAs and MPs and various officers of the RSS and VHP.

The findings of the story were that they misused public support for mounting pressure on police and local administration to nullify interfaith marriages.

They filed fake rape and kidnapping cases against Muslim men who marry Hindu women. They used fake documents showing women as minors so as to implicate the Muslim men.

They also found that not a single woman they claimed to have rescued ever sought their help saying she was a victim of love jihad.

On 4 February 2020, the Modi government told Parliament that there was no such thing as love jihad, in response to a question about whether the government was aware of the observation of Kerala High Court on the issue.

'The term "love jihad" is not defined under the extant laws. No such case of love jihad has been reported by any of the central agencies,' junior home minister G. Kishan Reddy said.

Hindutva created the narrative in public, spread the theory, encouraged violence and then denied its existence in Parliament. Like other invented phrases like 'urban naxal' and 'tukde tukde gang', 'love jihad' is a concoction that has been used for Hindutva propaganda and violence against citizens and then disowned at the altar. However, the poison has spread, including into the judiciary.

Over the years, India's laws on religious freedom have become more regressive, particularly in BJP states. On 20 November 2017, Uttarakhand High Court 'suggested' that Madhya Pradesh's Freedom of Religion Act be adopted by the state legislature, in order to put an end to what it said were sham conversions for the purpose of marriage. The judges said, 'It needs to be mentioned that the Court has come across number of cases where the inter-religion marriages are being organised. However, in few instances, the conversion from one religion to another religion is a sham conversion only to facilitate the process of marriage. In order to curb this tendency, the state government is expected to legislate the Freedom of Religion Act on the analogy of Madhya Pradesh Freedom of Religion Act.' ('Curb tendency of religion conversion for marriage, formulate Act: Uttarakhand HC', *Times of India*, 20 November 2017).

The Court accepted that 'it is not the role of the Court to give suggestions to the state government to legislate', but justified the suggestions 'due to (the) fast-changing social milieu'. The observations were made while the court was hearing the case of a Muslim man who had converted to Hinduism. The court had earlier asked 'whether the respondent Atul Sharma has converted to Hinduism merely for the sake of marriage or he has converted for all other purposes, is a disputed question of fact which can only be determined by a competent court of law separately'.

It ordered his wife, an adult, to be sent to a girls' hostel, 'in order to 'allay the fear of parents' while acknowledging that she was a major.

Uttarakhand's Freedom of Religion Act was passed within a few months of this judgment. It legitimised ghar wapsi as not being conversion by saying that any person 'coming back to his ancestral religion' shall "not be deemed conversion under this Act'.

The law included a new prohibition related to the case mentioned above. It said would prohibit conversion that happened because of a marriage. Meaning a woman or man could not take up the faith their partner belong to. The law says such a marriage will be invalidated by the courts.

The only way that a couple of different faiths can get married and retain their faith in India currently is through the Special Marriage Act. Even here the state has put up obstacles. They must apply for permission and this application with their names is pasted on the magistrate's notice board for a month. This is monitored by Hindutva groups who harass the couple and their families. The *News Minute* ('Kerala interfaith couples harassed by right wing vigilantes using marriage notices') reported on 20 July 2020, that hundreds of couples were being bullied and harassed after their marriage notices were posted in public.[14] Their details were being passed around on WhatsApp groups

14. Five days later, the Kerala government said it was ending this practice because of the harassment couples faced. ('Inter-Religious Marriages: Following Complaints Of Misuse, Kerala Govt Stops Publication Of Notice Of Marriage In Website', *Live Law*, 25 July 2020)

with threats. The report said that the documents were posted on the website of the Kerala government's Registration Department, and anyone could download them.

The momentum against religious freedom and the acceptance of the Hindutva narrative is increasing. On 21 November 2019, the UP Law Commission under Justice Aditya Nath Mittal presented a draft bill to CM Adityanath against conversions that excludes conversions to Hinduism from attracting the law. It has this line—'provided that, if any person reconverts to his immediate previous religion, shall not be deemed to be a conversion under this Act'. Ghar wapsi and shuddhi would not be considered conversions.

The bill increased punishment to five years (seven in the case of women, Dalits and Adivasis). It reversed the burden of proof on the person proselytising, and they must prove their innocence once charged, rather than requiring the state to prove them guilty. It requires anyone wanting to change their faith to fill out a form one month in advance, to the district magistrate. It also requires the person changing their faith to send a declaration on a form after their conversion within a month of the conversion. It requires the district magistrate to 'exhibit a copy of the declaration on the notice board of the office' till he confirms their conversion.

Justice Mittal's draft bill is accompanied by a report which contained the observation: 'Some organisations are enticing Hindus, especially SC/STs, to convert for their own gains. In the process, these organisations are making people insult their religious traditions and rich culture.'

The cover page of Mittal's report has the visual of a man in begging posture. Four disembodied hands are offering him cash, medicines, a baton with the word 'job' on it and one holding out a Bible. Chapters in the report include 'Recent newspaper cuttings regarding forcible conversions', 'anti-conversion laws in neighbouring countries, 'pre-independence and post-independence anti-conversion laws in India', 'anti-conversion acts of various states of India along with comparative study' and 'proceedings of UP Legislative Assembly regarding anti-conversion'.

Mittal's draft recommends that there be total restriction on conversion by marriage in UP. It says, 'The majority of conversions are regarding the members of Scheduled Castes and Scheduled Tribes on the ground of allurement, better education, better lifestyle and other aspects.' The UP Bill, the eleventh such law in India, also introduced a specific section on women and love jihad.

As a result of these laws India has been falling in the index of nations that have religious freedom. In 2016, India scored 'high' on the Pew Research Center's Index of Government Restrictions on religious freedom. India rose from 4.8 in 2007 to 5.1 on the index, compared to 2.8 for the world.

Afghanistan, Bangladesh, Israel, Pakistan, Sudan and Ethiopia were among the other nations with restrictions as severe as India's. In 2019, India again scored 'high' while scoring 'very high' on the Social Hostilities Index.

In Conclusion

The freedom to propagate and the freedom to practice religion freely given to Indians by the Constitution and its authors have been taken away. The Hindu majoritarian thrust of the State and its actors against other faiths has eroded the freedom the minorities explicitly asked for and were given by the Constitution's framers.

A few strands become apparent as we examine the issue here.

Firstly, the nomenclature is deliberately deceitful. The laws are named to suggest they represent emancipation but they actually do the opposite. The Orissa Freedom of Religion Act takes away freedom to both convert and to proselytise. It does not grant it. Ditto the Madhya Pradesh Freedom of Religion Act, the Gujarat Freedom of Religion (Amendment) Act, the Arunachal Pradesh Freedom of Religion Act, and the acts of Chhattisgarh, Himachal Pradesh, Jharkhand, Uttarakhand and Rajasthan. The only honestly named law was the one that was repealed: The Tamil Nadu Prohibition of Forcible Conversion of Religion Act.

Secondly, none of the laws appear to show any understanding of the reality of caste and the reasons why many would want to consider converting out of their humiliation. There is a demand side to conversion based on discrimination and marginalisation and India's laws on freedom of religion fail to acknowledge it.

Thirdly, it appears that the intent of the state on this matter is to restrict religious freedom from a majoritarian perspective: the fundamental right of Muslims and Christians to propagate is sought to be blocked, as is the will of the individual seeking to change faith. And that this has been the case whatever party or formation has been in office. The introduction of registration and permission and investigation into an act of personal belief is to impede, if not to outright prevent, as can be seen in the Gujarat cases.

Fourthly, assumptions and accusations and urban myths are taken to be facts. The judiciary is complicit here as the beginning of the myth of love jihad in Kerala High Court shows. The Freedom of Religion Bill submitted by its law commission to the government of Uttar Pradesh uses the word freedom 306 times and the word conversion or convert 1,013 times, showing where the priority is. It uses 'liberty' thirteen times but 'allure' ninety-two times, 'induce' fifty-five times and 'force' 198 times. The word Hinduism features in eighteen places, but Islam in eighty-four and Christianity in 110. The bill is written with a set of assumptions, backed by little other than prejudice against minorities.

Fifthly, the legislatures have infantilised Dalits and Adivasis, by raising the quantum of punishment for converting them specifically. And in doing so they have made it more difficult for the most marginalised Indians to change their faith, even one whose chains they seek to break free of. In the Orissa High Court case this observation was made by the judges: 'Threat of divine displeasure numbs the mental faculty; more so of an undeveloped mind and the actions of such a person thereafter, are not free and according to conscience.'

These laws also manifestly violate the right to privacy. Why must individuals reveal their identity, background, income and the reasons they wish to convert to a district magistrate? It is a matter touching their most personal and private self. And why must they submit a list of the guests attending a private ceremony? The reason of course is that it gives the State leverage to harass and dissuade.

Sixthly, the judiciary has weighed in against individual liberties and against fundamental rights using specious arguments. The one sound judgment by the Orissa High Court against the first law was undone by the Supreme Court through a tenuous and unconsidered judgment. Its disregard of a basic constitutional violation, that of a state to overturn a fundamental right, cannot be seen in benign terms.

Seventhly, the judiciary has in similar fashion been patriarchal and patronising towards women. The Supreme Court and high courts have all indulged in the confinement of adult women who have committed no crime but have been suspected by the judges of some moral wrongdoing. In the Hadiya case in 2017, two male judges of Kerala High Court said of an adult woman married to a Muslim that 'her marriage being the most important decision in her life, can only be taken with the active involvement of her parents'. They gave 'custody' of her to her father though Hadiya, an adult, did not consent to parental custody. Instead of freeing her immediately, the Supreme Court ordered a National Intelligence Agency investigation into her marriage.[15]

Eighthly, the numbers of conversion cases are not significant as the data over half a decade, official data in the case of Gujarat, and Kerala show. Tamil Nadu's sensational cases appear to be triggered by immediate and localised factors rather than the success of proselytisation.

Identities are not easy to discard and to assume that people would do so lightly is to be unaware of fundamental human attributes. India is a nation of communities and separating oneself from one's clan through individual conversion is difficult.

On the other hand, if their own numbers are to be believed, the VHP is the largest and most successful proselytising body in India.

Ninthly, there is a hypocrisy under which these freedom of religion laws operate. Conversion into some faiths, Hinduism and Buddhism specifically, is not considered conversion and allowed to proceed unregulated, and the VHP actually does this. But conversion out of Hinduism to other faiths must be regulated so tightly as to make it impossible, as the BJP wants. In some states—Rajasthan, Arunachal Pradesh and Uttar Pradesh's draft bill—this discrimination is so naked as to be written into law.

Tenthly, the laws are accelerating further away from liberty with time. More states are adopting 'freedom of religion'. The punishments for exercising freedom are also getting more severe. The 1967 law in Odisha had maximum punishment of one and two years (the latter for offences against women, Dalits and Adivasis). Madhya Pradesh and Gujarat upped this to three years and four years respectively. UP has proposed five years and seven years and reversed the burden of proof, shifting it from

---

15. The allegation was that Hadiya, a 24-year-old homeopathic student, was deceived into marrying her husband Shafin Jahan and forcibly converted to Islam.

the State to the individual. Uttarakhand's 2018 law expands the law to include marriage and allowing annulment by the state of a purely personal and private act. The Centre is also invested in the issue, with home minister Amit Shah saying that a central anti-conversion law was coming under the Modi government.

On the ground as well, the ending of religious freedom in India is being noticed. And things are getting worse quite quickly on this front. For instance, a Law Library report for the US Congress accepted that 'despite criticism of India's anti-conversion laws, some human rights bodies, including the United States Commission on International Religious Freedom (USCIRF), have acknowledged that these laws have resulted in few arrests and no convictions'. The US State Department's International Religious Freedom reports published in 2010 and 2011 also noted few arrests and no convictions under various anti-conversion laws during the respective reporting periods.

After Narendra Modi took power this has begun to change. USCIRF highlighted arrests under the freedom of religion laws. The Law Library report refers to some:

In April 2017, three Christians were arrested in Khandwa and booked under the anti-conversion law. *Hindustan Times* reported on the incident, mentioning the arrests of Amar Singh, 35, of Burhanpur, Kishor Barela, 30, of Kalukhedi, and Prabhakar Barela, 39, of Jalgaon in Maharashtra. The paper also mentioned similar arrests in the previous two years: 28 December 2015: Three preachers arrested from Morani village, Barwani; 18 January 2016: Twelve arrested from Dhar district; 23 May 2016: Three arrested from Satna district; and 23 June 2016: Two arrested from Rewa district.

A Catholic nun and four tribal women were detained in June 2017 at Satna after a complaint by the Bajrang Dal. In July 2017, Christians protested in Ludhiana after Sultan Masih, pastor of the Temple of God Church, was murdered in public based on suspicions of his engaging in the conversion of others.

The US State Department also highlighted an incident in its 2017 report. Police arrested seven Christian pastors on 4 December while they were holding a meeting in a private home. The following day, a court sent them to fourteen days in judicial custody for carrying out a forcible conversion campaign.

In December 2017, police arrested seven Christian preachers in Mathura. The same month, police in Madhya Pradesh arrested a Christian priest and questioned members of a seminary after the Bajrang Dal 'accused them of trying to convert villagers to Christianity by distributing Bibles and singing carols'.

The USCIRF report of 2019 concluded that 'in 2018, religious freedom conditions in India continued a downward trend' and the report of 2020 said that 'in 2019, religious freedom conditions in India experienced a drastic turn downwards with religious minorities under increasing assault'.

In May 2018, four people were held and another eleven investigated in Simdega, Jharkhand over a Christian wedding ceremony. In June 2018, sixteen were arrested for conducting a group prayer in a home in Dumka, Jharkhand. In July 2019, UP police arrested four Christians for organising prayer meetings without permission. In September 2019, Jharkhand police arrested two Catholic priests accusing them of practicing forced conversions.

The 2019 report said that 'anti-conversion laws have gone into effect in seven states: Odisha, Madhya Pradesh, Chhattisgarh, Gujarat, Arunachal Pradesh, Himachal Pradesh, and Jharkhand'.

The 2020 USCIRF report said, 'Authorities predominantly arrest Muslims and Christians for conversion activities' but 'Hindutva groups pursue mass conversions through ceremonies known as ghar wapsi, without interference'.

It said of the anti-conversion laws that they 'create a hostile, and on occasion violent, environment for religious minority communities because they do not require any evidence to support accusations of wrongdoing'.

The First Amendment of the United States Constitution says, 'Congress shall make no law respecting an establishment of religion, or prohibiting the free exercise thereof; or abridging the freedom of speech, or of the press; or the right of the people peaceably to assemble, and to petition the Government for a redress of grievances.'

India has taken away the freedoms of its citizens by inverting their rights with the 'reasonable restrictions' qualifying them. The restrictions have overwhelmed and strangled the liberties.

The fundamental right—'freely to profess, practise and propagate religion'—does not exist. The right resides with the State which will decide whether or not you may change your faith and whether or not you may propagate it.

Against the express wishes of the Constituent Assembly, the fundamental right has been comprehensively taken away from India's minorities, and especially its Christians.

8

APARTHEID AHMEDABAD

Poor people forced to live clubbed together is what we know as a slum. An ethnic group forcibly relegated to certain neighbourhoods is a ghetto. The former have no means to go elsewhere. The latter have no choice even if they have the means. Apartheid means separateness and refers to the policy of South Africa of forcing the black Africans in ghettos. They could only live in fixed spaces by law.

When segregation in the United States was legally ended in the 1960s, the government passed laws that sought to integrate the races, like the Fair Housing Act. It prevented discrimination in the buying and selling of properties which was keeping the races separate.

All across Gujarat, in all major cities and in several towns, the government has done the opposite. Muslims are deliberately forced into ghettos through a law called the Gujarat Prohibition of Transfer of Immovable Property and Provision for Protection of Tenants from Eviction from Premises in Disturbed Areas Act.

The law requires citizens in particular parts of cities to seek permission from the government before selling their property or changing their tenant and filters them by religion. The application must list the name of the buyer and the seller and includes an affidavit that the sale has been without coercion and at market price.

The law was initially meant to be temporary and to protect during an episode of communal violence, those who would be vulnerable to forced eviction or could be coerced into eviction. But Gujarat under the BJP has used the law, renewing it and extending it across the state, to keep Muslims out of other neighbourhoods than those traditionally Muslim. And it criminalises attempts to integrate, permanently separating Muslims from Hindus.

The law says that if the state government feels that the intensity and duration of a riot is such that an area is 'disturbed', it isolates the area under the act for a specified period. When satisfied that the area has 'ceased to be disturbed', the government can rescind the notification and buying and selling properties can go back to being unregulated.

What has happened instead is that thirty-five years after the law was introduced and eighteen years after the 2002 riot, the law remains active even in cities when there is no violence. And it is being expanded through the addition of more geographical areas and placing more restrictions on Muslims and creating more hurdles to their leaving their ghettoes. Every three years, on 30 June, the law has been renewed for another three years.

In 2009, the Modi government amended the Act to give discretionary powers to the collector to hold an inquiry suo moto and to take possession of property under the Act. In July 2019, another change was introduced. Previously, property sellers had to apply for permission to transfer their property and register their consent on affidavit. Now, it would not matter even if the sale was with free consent, and the fair value was paid to the owner. The collector could stop a sale of property if he felt at his discretion that there was any 'disturbance in demographic equilibrium' or 'improper clustering of persons of a community' or 'likelihood of polarisation', if the transfer took place.

The collector could reject an application for the legal transfer of a property after making assessment on these grounds. Punishment for transferring property without clearance was raised to six years in jail (it was six months when the law was first introduced).

Modi's new law also allowed the state government to form a 'Monitoring and Advisory Committee' to keep a check on the demographic structure in neighbourhoods. This committee would advise the collectors on whether or not sales could be permitted.

Writing in *Counter Currents* ('Disturbed Areas Act: A tool to fuel the communal divide', 10 August 2019), Aman Mansuri explained that when the law was written in 1985, 'Land mafias used to take advantage of the insecurity of people during the time of riots and coerced them to sell their property at a cheaper rate. The Act was introduced to save people from such exploitation.' Mansuri reported that in Ahmedabad alone, there were 770 neighbourhoods, some 40 per cent of the city, which were notified as being disturbed.

A scholar I spoke to said that when the law had been originally framed, 'the intent was noble: to prevent ghettoisation. We know that the 1980s were a particularly violent phase in Gujarat's history with caste clashes, religious violence, the rise of BJP and VHP. Hence, there was a real fear about Muslims selling their properties at a cheap value to flee to safety and Hindus doing the same in Muslim-dominated areas. Hence, the law. Of course, its application changed over the years, particularly after the 1991 Act.'

By this time the state was using it not to protect vulnerable individuals, but to ghettoise Muslims.

In May 2018, two activists, Nishant Varma and Danish Qureshi, challenged the constitutional validity of the Act in Gujarat High Court. The petitioners cited Gujarat's reports to the National Crime Records Bureau which consistently showed that the state does not witness communal violence at a higher rate than other states. But the state government had still been increasing coverage of the law to cover more localities across the state. The activists asked why, if the NCRB reports were true and communal harmony prevails in Gujarat, there is a need for the Disturbed Areas Act.

I spoke to Qureshi who said permission was refused on the grounds that the area was communally sensitive to violence even though there were no FIRs filed to show that. He said the law had produced the strange reality that even foreigners could buy places in neighbourhoods that Gujarati Muslims could not.

When the BJP government legislated the 2019 change in the law, Congress MLA Imran Khedawala opposed it for its targeting of Muslims. He said it was ironic that the BJP was insisting that all Indians be allowed to buy property in Kashmir when Indians couldn't even buy it in their own state of Gujarat. Why this double standard and why was it that the BJP had claimed it had brought peace to the state when it was also continuing to officially say that its cities were disturbed? Why was this law still required thirty-five years after it was written, he asked, saying that the law violated the constitutional rights of Muslims.

The changes in the law have taken place amid the BJP vastly increasing the geographical areas where it is applicable. In 2017 and 2018, the BJP notified parts of Surat—where no large-scale violence took place even during the 2002 riots—and Bharuch as disturbed, because of a demand from BJP MLAs. As of August 2019, there were 770 parts of Ahmedabad alone that were declared disturbed.

On 25 February 2020, the Disturbed Areas Act was imposed in the town of Khambhat after violence against Muslims. *First Post* reported that the decision came after a mob of over 5,000 people gathered by the Hindu Jagran Manch was addressed by BJP leaders who raised communal slogans and called for all Muslim families to be ousted from Khambhat.

The *New Indian Express* reported Gujarat's minister of state for home Pradeepsinh Jadeja as saying that 'such clashes are happening because of demographic changes. As demanded by the people of Khambhat, the government has decided to start the process of imposing the Disturbed Areas Act in areas where such incidents are happening regularly ... We have taken this decision to stop further changes in the local demography.' ('Gujarat government to impose Disturbed Areas Act in parts of Khambhat after communal clashes', 25 February 2020)

On 7 December 2019, the town of Anand was declared disturbed and notified. A report in the *Times of India* said this was after a campaign since June that year, run by the Hindu Jagriti Manch and presided over by BJP councillor Himesh Mukhi, following a property deal between a Hindu and Muslim on one of the main roads. A rally was held against it on 19 June and twenty-nine BJP councillors sought implementation of the act.

The act is currently in force in large parts of the state's three largest cities, Ahmedabad, Vadodara and Surat, and also in Bharuch, Kapadvanj, Anand and Godhra. These are also the places Gujarat's Muslims are concentrated, effectively ghettoising them permanently.

On 13 March 2020, *Indian Express* reported that the Gujarat Assembly rejected Khedawala's bill to repeal the Disturbed Areas Act. The Bill was supported by Khedawala's fellow Muslim Congress MLA Gyasuddin Shaikh, but was voted down and even in the Congress there is no appetite to push for its repeal. Activist Qureshi, who challenged the law, said that in the three decades that the law had been periodically renewed, it had never previously been opposed in the legislature.

On 4 June 2020, Gujarat imposed the Disturbed Areas Act in more of Ahmedabad covering areas in the Vatva and Narol police station jurisdiction. Chief minister Vijay Rupani announced the decision, saying it was 'to provide safety and security to the people of Gujarat'. The decision came after Hindus opposed the redevelopment of some Muslim neighbourhoods.

PTI reported ('Disturbed Areas Act extended to more localities in Vadodara', 22 August 2020) the addition of three more neighbourhoods in Baroda after a demand by BJP MLA Manisha Vakil. None of the areas had seen communal violence in the eighteen years after the Godhra riots.

One scholar I spoke to explained how Muslims were being prevented in areas like Ahmedabad's Paldi from redeveloping old and dilapidated housing schemes. Redevelopment would mean the construction of high-rise buildings with more flats in them than in the original structures built in the 1950s or 60s. This would mean more Muslim families moving into the neighbourhood, something that the Jains of Paldi found offensive (Rupani is also Jain). They blocked this by declaring Paldi disturbed though it has not seen any violence let alone be vulnerable to distress sales.

The intent of the BJP is clear here and the bureaucracy follows their directions. On 18 March 2020, *Indian Express* reported that the Gujarat High Court had struck down the order of a Vadodara official rejecting the sale by brothers Dinesh and Deepak Modi of their shop to Onali Ezazuddin Dholkawala and Iqbal Hussain Asgar Ali Tinwala. A sale deed was executed and presented before the sub-registrar for registration.

The official conducted an inquiry through the police on whether the transfer was taking place of free consent and if the transfer was likely to 'affect the balance in the majority Hindu/minority Muslim strength' or 'affect the neighbourhood' or if there is 'a likelihood of a law and order problem in future'.

The official concluded that 'there could be a possible law and order situation, which was also reiterated by the deputy police commissioner, following which the deputy collector rejected the application for the transfer of property'.

The judge who reversed this noted that the police inquiry was 'completely out of context with the provisions of the Disturbed Areas Act'. The judgment observed, 'It is undisputed that the property in question was sold on a fair value and with free consent, as it is evident from the statement recorded by the seller and the purchaser. When the scope of inquiry is that of free consent and fair value, the role of neighbours in the context of such sale becomes irrelevant.' But of course, the neighbours are part of the problem.

On 22 September 2019, the *Indian Express* reported that the sale of a Rs 6 crore bungalow by a well-known businesswoman, Geeta Goradia, to another well-known businessman and educationist Faizal Fazlani was blocked after fifty residents challenged the sale ('Vadodara Collector orders probe into sale of property under Disturbed Areas Act').

Vadodara District Collector and Magistrate Shalini Agarwal stayed the sale. In December the Gujarat High Court again found her intrusion to be non-maintainable and let the sale go ahead. But such victories are rare against a nasty State and a polarised society. The officials often neither approve nor disapprove of a sale, keeping it pending long enough for the buyer and seller to lose interest. And since Gujaratis know of the law, they steer clear of properties in the Disturbed Areas. Often the neighbours apply so much pressure that the buyer and seller back off.

On 25 November 2019, *Indian Express* reported ('As Vadodara residents protest, owner cancels plan to sell property to Muslim') that the sale of a house was reversed because of the objection of neighbours.

Among other things, the Hindu residents said that if Muslims came into the neighbourhood, property prices would drop. The society had 170 houses of which two were owned by Muslims and a third was leased by a Muslim. The Disturbed Areas Act was not needed here because the neighbours successfully kept the Muslim out. During their protest against the lawful sale, the report said, 'Police were present in the area to ensure law and order.'

The *Times of India* reported ('Man booked for concealing religion to sell his property in Gujarat', 31 August 2020) that a Parsi man had been booked under the Disturbed Areas Act for selling his property to a Muslim after a neighbour objected. The complainant, Manish Malhotra, said that the man selling his property, Feroze Contractor, 'concealed his religion' while dealing with a Muslim family.

The Disturbed Areas Act is part of a concerted action by the VHP to keep Gujarat segregated. In April 2014, as the campaign for the Lok Sabha was on, a video of VHP leader Pravin Togadia was circulated in which he gave suggestions to Gujaratis in Bhavnagar on this matter. He said Muslims could be kept out of Hindu neighbourhoods in two ways.

'First, that the government applies the Disturbed Areas Act, which has been applied in Ahmedabad and elsewhere. If this Act is applied in Hindu-majority neighbourhoods, Muslims will be forbidden from buying property. Not even through a power of attorney. For this, put pressure on the government and get it done.'

Togadia said the second way was to 'consult a lawyer, forcibly occupy the building and put a Bajrang Dal board and then we fight it out in court. If a case is filed, we'll fight it out and if Rajiv Gandhi's killers were not hanged none of us is about to be hanged. When they come to take possession we'll sort them out.' He also said: 'I've done this before, and I've kept possession of a building for a long time through a Bajrang Dal board. The Muslim lost his money and the building both. The case kept being fought out in court.'

He asked the crowd to 'try to get the law changed by the government. For that, get together, put it in writing and hold a press conference, and make a demand of the government. That they apply the Act and ensure that in Hindu majority areas no Muslim be allowed to buy property.'

Where property had already been sold, Togadia said the Hindus should 'gherao him in his shop that is such an attempt to frighten him. We should not run away, his shop we should shut instead. This is an aggressive war strategy. You go for the gherao of his shop, and put a board of the Bajrang Dal or Vishwa Hindu Parishad.

'Announce at the press conference that if the building is not taken back in forty-eight hours then thousands of us will arrive for a gherao of his shop.

'And go with stones and rocks, and burn tyres. Create the atmosphere of a riot. Announce the programme to gherao the Bohra's shop.[16] Come there in full strength. Women should be in front. And sisters, listen: we do not run away. We chase them off. That is our way. Go to their shops and chase them from there. Organise programmes to spit on them when they come out. They have to come out, right? There's no punishment for spitting on people.'

Such is the nastiness that accompanies a prejudiced law in a highly communalised society. The forced ghettoisation of Muslims also helps the BJP direct development away from their areas. A newspaper report from 12 September 2020 spoke of how the Centre and the Gujarat government had kept Ahmedabad's largest Muslim area out of a scheme aimed specifically at developing minority areas.

The report ('Ahmedabad's largest Muslim ghetto excluded from minority-specific development plan', *Ahmedabad Mirror*) said twenty-four minority concentration areas (MCA) of

---

16. The Bohras are a Gujarati Muslim community, many of whom are businesspeople.

Gujarat had been identified for development work under the PM Jan Vikas Karyakram (PMJVK). Juhapura, the largest Muslim neighbourhood of Ahmedabad, had been left out of the Rs 200 crore programme though Jain and Buddhist neighbourhoods had been included for works like the building of hostels, skill development centres and education and social development facilities.

Writing in the *Indian Express* ('The segregated city', 26 May 2018) Christophe Jaffrelot and Sharik Laliwala said Ahmedabad had become the most segregated Indian city on Hindu-Muslim lines.

After the 2009 amendment which gave powers to the collector to hold a suo motu inquiry and even take possession of property, BJP revenue minister Anandiben Patel claimed the law was to help prevent ghettoisation. Instead, the writers said, 'The exact opposite has been achieved. Ghettoisation and spatial segregation in urban Gujarat is at its peak. Juhapura, an all-Muslim locality, often derided as the "Wagah of Ahmedabad" or "mini Pakistan", is the quintessential example of this phenomenon.'

Juhapura was a mixed neighbourhood established in 1973 as a colony for Sabarmati river flood victims. 'Riot after riot, Hindus left and more Muslims fled for safety to Juhapura and could not return to their original homes, a process fuelled by the Disturbed Areas Act. Currently, it is home to more than three lakh Muslims and Ahmedabad has more Muslims at its periphery than in the old city, their traditional home. Post-2002, elite Muslims—lawyers, professionals, doctors, people in business, judges, IAS-IPS officers—migrated to Juhapura as elite Muslim localities, including Paldi, were attacked for the first time. Juhapura has become a full-fledged ghetto with economic heterogeneity but ethnic homogeneity.'

The writers also remarked, 'Ghettoisation not only segregates people but also leads to neglect of basic public amenities. In

Juhapura, the State is almost absent in education and healthcare ... The impact of ghettoisation due to riots and the Disturbed Areas Act is manifest in Gujarati society. Since Hindus and Muslims no longer live next-door, their children cannot meet daily or play together, limiting social relations. They are strangers to each other, a phenomenon that perpetuates myths about each other's communities.'

Laliwala has written elsewhere ('Gujarat's enduring Muslim ghettoes', 15 July 2019, scroll.in) that although ghettoisation in urban Gujarat had found some media and scholarly attention in the last few years, the resultant deliberate erasure of Muslim representation in electoral politics had been neglected. 'Since the Muslim population has been restricted to ghettoes, their geographical spread remains limited—in turn, their political relevance as a major voting block does not acquire significance, allowing political parties to ignore their concerns, legitimate or otherwise.

'The effect of the spatial stagnancy of urban Muslims is clearly visible on the representative aspect of democracy. With the rise of Hindutva politics in Gujarat, more than five Muslim MLAs have never entered the Gujarat Vidhan Sabha from the 1990s. In fact, it is exactly the accommodation of Muslims by the Congress party in Gujarat during the 1980s that provoked a motley of upper-caste groups and Patels to organise in the form of the BJP on the plank of Hindu unity.'

The activist Qureshi said that in the constituencies of Jamalpur and Bapunagar, there were about 5,000 houses in each locality that Hindus could not sell because the government did not want to shift the balance of voters and make the constituencies competitive. The effectiveness of the combined efforts to marginalise Gujarati Muslims can be seen in the data. In the Gujarat Assembly, their numbers fell from eleven in 1980 to three in 2017. Less than 2 per cent representation for a community that has 10 per cent of the population.

They won't be able to have any weight in many constituencies except where they are densely populated—places like the old city, industrial areas, or Juhapura in the case of Ahmedabad. But, Laliwala says, they won't have much voice to shape electoral outcomes in rest of the city, let alone send one of their own to Parliament.

The last time that Gujarat sent a Muslim to the Lok Sabha was Ahmed Patel from Bharuch in 1985, the year when the Disturbed Areas Act was introduced.

9

SUPREME COMPLICITY

India's election law forbids appeals in the name of religion. Over the years, the Indian judiciary and especially, the Supreme Court have progressively worked their way around this to allow the functioning of majoritarian electoral politics, and relax, bend and break the rules for its spread. Along with jurisprudence, the Supreme Court judges have held forth on theology, and defined Hindutva not as the exclusionary ideology that Hindutva's inventors and adherents say it is, but as a benign 'way of life'.

This in turn has allowed appeals in the name of Hindutva to become acceptable as an election platform and as a basis for canvassing. Asking for a vote in the name of Hindutva is not a communal appeal, but an appeal to India's heritage. India arrived at this place, as we will see in this chapter, after a series of judgments and court observations which have over time endorsed Hindu majoritarianism and sanctified it, making appeals to voters on the basis of faith and communal division valid. This progression climaxed with a remarkable judgment from the Supreme Court which tells us that even promising a Hindu Rashtra to Hindu voters is not a communal appeal.

The election law referred to here is the Representation of the People Act of 1951, which has a clause saying that candidates cannot ask for votes on the basis of religion directly or indirectly.

The exact words are that an 'appeal by a candidate (or his agent or by any other person with the consent of a candidate or his election agent) to vote or refrain from voting for any person on the ground of his religion, race, caste, community or language or the use of, or appeal to religious symbols ... for the furtherance of the prospects of the election of that candidate or for prejudicially affecting the election of any candidate' is a corrupt practice. The law was written while the trauma of Partition was still being felt and its framers felt that India ought not to be put again through the divisiveness that sprang up when religion was mixed with politics. In essence, the election law bans the use of religion, including religious symbols.

In 1964, the Supreme Court heard the case of Jagdev Singh Sidhanti versus Pratap Singh Daulta. The court had to decide whether the symbol 'Om' could be regarded as a religious symbol. A candidate, Sidhanti, had used it in an election in Punjab before it was divided between Punjab and Haryana. His opponent Daulta said that Sidhanti as part of the Arya Samaj had organised the Hindi agitation of 1957, 'the real object of which was to promote feelings of enmity and hatred between the Sikh and the Hindu communities in the state of Punjab on the ground of religion and language' to promote their prospects in the general elections to be held in 1962.

To that end they held meetings in the Haryana region of undivided Punjab and appealed to the electorate to vote for Sidhanti 'on the ground of his religion and language', using a religious symbol—a flag called 'Om Dhwaj' (Om flag)—in all these meetings.

The losing candidate sought judicial intervention and the High Court held that Sidhanti had indeed violated the Representation of People Act. Sidhanti then appealed against the verdict. The Supreme Court said that if Daulta could establish that the 'Om' flag was a religious symbol, the question then would arise whether the use of or appeal to the 'Om' flag was made in the campaign with Sidhanti's consent.

On the matter of Om being a religious symbol, the court said: 'The expression "Om" is respected by the Hindus generally and has a special significance in the Hindu scriptures. It is recited at the commencement of the recitations of Hindu religious works.'

It quoted sources including some Western dictionaries to show that Om was the sacred syllable used in invocations, at the commencement of prayers, at the beginning and the end of Vedic recitations, and as a respectful salutation. And also that it was also subject of many mystical speculations.

Having looked at all this, however, the Supreme Court concluded, 'It is difficult to regard Om which is a preliminary to an incantation or to religious books as having religious significance.' What it meant is that though Om often occurs at the beginning of a religious text, it was not according to the court part of the text itself and therefore not a religious symbol. The court offered more wisdom on the issue, classifying Om not as a religious symbol but a 'spiritual' one (it offered no explanation of what this difference was or meant). Om had a 'high spiritual or mystical efficacy', the court said, but, 'the attribute of spiritual significance will not necessarily impart to its use on a flag the character of a religious symbol in the context in which the expression religious symbol occurs in the section with which we are concerned'.

In the court's opinion a symbol was only something that stood for or represented something else, whether material or abstract. In order for something to be called a religious symbol, it would therefore have to be a 'visible representation of a thing or concept which is religious.' This appeared to exclude Om and its use on a flag does not symbolise religion, or anything religious. In the court's words: 'It is not easy therefore to see how the Om flag which merely is a pennant on which is printed the word "Om" can be called a religious symbol.'

Having thus done away with the idea of Om being religious, the court said that even assuming it was religious, the case would rest on whether or not it could be established that it had been used by Sidhanti or his agents with his consent to further his candidacy. The burden of proof in such things lay on Daulta and the court determined that he was unable to prove it and so Sidhanti won the appeal. The observations the Supreme Court made regarding Om would remain on its record and be used in other judgments.

That same year, 1964, another case came up where one of the points raised was again on the use of religious symbols in an election (Ramanbhai Ashabhai Patel versus Dabhi Ajithkumar Fulsinji). This time the dispute was over the symbol of the Dhruva Star. Once again, the actual issue and decision were not ultimately as important as the court's observations.

In this instance, the Supreme Court concluded that it was 'impossible to say that any particular object, bird, or animal could be regarded as a symbol of the Hindu religion'. This was because 'the basic concept of Hindu religion is that the supreme being is in every "inanimate" object, plant, creature or person, i.e., in the entire creation and that the entire creation is within the Supreme Being.'

Given this, 'it would not be possible to say that any particular object is a symbol of the Hindu religion'. The court accepted that it was true that various deities in the Hindu pantheon were associated with specific objects, birds or animals. Shiva was associated with a trident and a coiled cobra round his neck; Vishnu with the cobra and the eagle; Lakshmi with the lotus. But this did not make that object religious in nature. 'Does it mean then that if a person uses a lotus or a cobra or a trident as his election symbol he will be appealing to the religious sentiments of the people?' the court asked, answering: 'The answer must be clearly in the negative.'

However this idea that religion could not be associated with any specific symbols was true, according to the Supreme Court, only for Hinduism. The court said its observation could not apply to other faiths: 'If they are told that they should cast their vote for a particular candidate whose election symbol is associated with a particular religion just as the cross is with Christianity, that will be using a religious symbol for obtaining votes.'

But, 'in the case of the Hindu religion, it is not possible to associate a particular symbol with religion, the use of a symbol even when it is associated with some deity, cannot, without something more, be regarded as a corrupt practice within the meaning of the Act'.

(L.K. Advani has described in his autobiography how the BJP landed the lotus as a symbol. He writes that after the Jana Sangh folded up and the party lost the use of the diya [oil lamp] symbol, he went to the Election Commission. He was told by Chief Election Commissioner S.L. Shadkar that it was too late for the BJP to register a symbol it wanted but instead of allotting one to it, Shadkar showed Advani a list of symbols available to independents. Advani picked the lotus and says, 'Shadkar, who knew that we had chosen the lotus to be in the BJP's flag' gave it to the BJP.)

In the Dhruva Star case, the court quoted the judgment in Sidhanti's case to observe that the use of pennants with 'Om' inscribed on them did not to fall within the prohibition' of the Act because 'Om does not symbolise religion or anything religious. Undoubtedly, it has great spiritual or mystical significance. For according to the Upanishads it is from the primordial sound Om that this phenomenal universe was projected and that this universe exists in and ultimately dissolves in Om. It is thus everything including God or Ishwara and the Supreme Brahman.' The court had accepted that 'Om is sacred to the Hindus', but felt still that 'the use of pennants on which

Om was inscribed did not amount to use of or appeal to a religious symbol'.

This idea that Hinduism's symbols were exempt from the rules that applied to other religions was taken further after the rise of the BJP and its aggressive communal appeals.

In 1995, Rajasthan High Court heard a case against BJP leader Bhairon Singh Shekhawat. During an Assembly election campaign, at a rally on 27 October 1993, Shekhawat made an appeal in the name of Lord Ram. He referred to the demolition of the Babri mosque and the construction of a temple.

Shekhawat began his speech with 'Jai Shri Ram', and said this was a slogan akin to Vande Mataram which Gandhi had used to drive the British out of India. Just as Vande Mataram was popular during the Independence movement, Jai Shri Ram was popular now and would see the departure of the Congress. He said the main question was whether a temple should be built at the site of the mosque.

The Congress was saying that the mosque would be reconstructed and the idols placed in it removed. Would the crowd accept this removal? If they wanted to see a temple constructed they would have to stand by Shekhawat. Lord Ram was for all and the proof was that when someone died, it was said that Ram had quit his body.

He ended by saying that the date of polling fell on Dhanteras and this would bring his own election expenses down.[17] People would buy portraits of Lakshmi seated on a lotus and it would be impossible to for people not to vote for the BJP after that.

The court found that 'no particular portion of the speech has been pointed out as offending' because the entire speech had

---

17. Dhanteras is the first day that marks the time of the festival of Diwali in India which is something of a three to four day affair (variations by region, of course, exist). The festival is celebrated as 'Lakshmi Puja'. Hence the reference in the following sentence.

been submitted as evidence rather than specific portions. 'Even the communities or classes between which hatred was intended to be or promoted were not specified. It was not specified as to whether hatred was promoted or attempted to be promoted. It was not alleged that reference to the demolition of the structure of Babri Masjid and construction of Ram Temple was for the promotion of hatred. Merely saying that it was in the context of promotion of hatred would not suffice,' the court said, striking the allegations out.

The court said that though the speech was attacked at the time when it had been given as being offensive, 'it would be clear that when he (Shekhawat) spoke in regard to building of the temple of Shri Ram at his birth place, he was not canvassing that the temple should be built at the place where the mosque stood'.

This was because, the court said, that Shekhawat had never accepted it as having been a mosque in the first place: 'If in a dispute as to whether a particular structure was a temple or a mosque, if a person contends that it was a temple and was never a mosque, his statement cannot be branded as communal or an appeal in the name of religion.'

The court reasoned that the Babri dispute and demolition was not in fact a communal issue because 'though normally a majority of Hindus are likely to have an opinion in favour of the structure being a temple and a majority of Muslims are likely to have an opinion that the structure was a mosque' there would still be 'some Hindus of the opinion that the structure was a mosque and, therefore, temple should not be built there and some Muslims of the opinion that the structure was originally a temple and, therefore, it should be handed over to Hindus for building a temple there. The division of opinion on such a property dispute may not always be on communal lines.'

An issue cannot be called communal, the court is saying here, unless the disagreement shows in 100 per cent of the population on every side of a divide.

The court also said that the Congress Party 'which is a national party, having unquestionably a Hindu majority in its membership and not a Muslim majority of members, was perceived to have an opinion that the structure was a mosque is enough proof' (of this fact that not every individual on either side agreed with their larger community and therefore this was not a communal issue at all).

The court added that it could not be reasonably said that every Muslim was a supporter of the mosque and every Hindu was an opponent of the mosque. The question was, therefore, not a communal one. 'It was at best a question of politico-historical opinion and everyone was free for (to) have his own view on the point and a right to express it freely irrespective of his religion.'

Shekhawat was blaming the Congress here and not Muslims, the court observed, and so there was no appeal to religion in the speech. So far as the references to Lord Ram and Goddess Lakshmi went, the court said that 'the gods and incarnations of Hindus cannot be contained within the limits of religion. They have with passage of time transcended all barriers and have entered the social psyche of the masses.'

It may have been relevant to speak about them as at 'a time when religious sects believing in different Gods were separated from each other and were at logger-heads. "Shaivas" (those who believed in God Shiv) and "Vaishnavas" (those who believed in God Vishnu) were distinctly recognised religious denominations. At that time it might have been relevant to invoke sympathies or garner support in the name of Lord Shiva or Lord Ram or Lord Krishna.'

However, in the court's opinion 'a synthesis was then arrived at and it came to be largely believed that all sects were only different paths to reach the same goal'. Because of this, 'Lord Ganesh and Goddess Sarasvati came to be regarded as symbols of learning quite apart-from their religious significance and Kuber and Laxmi became symbols of wealth apart from their place in the Hindu religion'.

This was why, 'normally social functions in India, though not even remotely connected with religion, begin with Ganesh Vandana or Saraswati Vandana. Even government functions have been known to begin with certain invocations and ceremonies which had their roots in the religious practices of Hindus.'

And so, the court said, 'It must be accepted that Ram, Krishna, Laxmi, Ganesh and several other Gods of the Hindus have religious as well as non-religious significance depending on the context ... In Indian society they are taken to be ideals to be emulated.' It then came up with some examples: 'If ideal relationship of brothers is to be described example of "Ram-Laxman" is given. Ideal couple is referred to as "Lakshmi Narayan" or "Sita-Ram". An ideal government is described as "Ram-Raj" and an ideal servant is described as "Hanuman". That has become a manner of speech. Thus, unless used in the religious context, these names of Gods have little religious significance. Reference to Ram, Krishna, Ganesh, Saraswati and Laxmi in a speech, therefore, cannot per se be taken as reference to or use of religious symbols or an appeal on the ground of religion. By themselves, these names have ceased to arouse religious feelings and to that extent can be said to have been secularised.'

Thus the court concluded that 'in the context in which the respondent is said to have referred to "Ram" and "Laxmi" in his speech, it cannot be said that he was appealing to vote for him on the ground of religion or was making any use of or making any appeal to religious symbols.'

With such philosophical flourishes and sophistry did India's judiciary made the cross unacceptable during an election campaign but allowed Om and all other Hindu symbols, for they were not religious figures at all but representative of some universal cosmic truth. Judges determined that even the primary deities of Hinduism were not actually religious figures and could be used and invoked in election rallies. And that communalism could exist only where every single individual on every side was divided on the issue, and for this reason Hindutva's divisive politics did not constitute communalism.

Dr Ramesh Yashwant Prabhoo versus Prabhakar Kashinath Kunte, 11 December 1995

The charge of violating the Representation of People Act here was based on three public speeches by Bal Thackeray in November and December 1987 in canvassing for a Shiv Sena candidate.

The High Court found Thackeray's speeches 'were all in very intemperate language and incendiary in nature which were appeals to the voters to vote for Dr Prabhoo because of his religion, i.e., he being a Hindu, and the speeches also promoted or tended to promote enmity and hatred between different classes of the citizens of India on the ground of religion.'

Thackeray's speech included the words: 'We are fighting this election for the protection of Hinduism. Therefore, we do not care for the votes of the Muslims. This country belongs to Hindus and will remain so.' In the *Urdu Times,* the report appeared with the headline *'Shiv Sena ko Musalmanon ke voton ki zarurat nahin hai'* (Shiv Sena did not need the votes of Muslims).

At the second rally, Thackeray said: 'Hinduism will triumph in this election and we must become recipients of this victory to ward off the danger on Hinduism, elect Ramesh Prabhoo to join with Chhagan Bhujbal who is already there. You will find Hindu temples underneath if all the mosques are dug out. Anybody who stands against the Hindus should be showed or worshipped with shoes. A candidate by name Prabhoo should be led to victory in the name of religion.'

At the third: 'We have come with the ideology of Hinduism. Shiv Sena will implement this ideology. Though this country belongs to Hindus, Ram and Krishna are insulted. (The opposition) valued the Muslim votes more than your votes; we do not want the Muslim votes. A snake like Shahabuddin is sitting in the Janata Party, a man like Nihal Ahmed is also in Janata Party. So the residents of Vile Parle should bury this party.'

The Supreme Court quoted other extracts from the first speech: 'All my Hindu brothers, sisters and mothers gathered here ... Today Dr. Prabhoo has been put up as candidate from your Parle ... But here one cannot do anything at anytime about the snake in the form of Khalistan and Muslims ... The entire country has been ruined and therefore we took the stand of Hindutva and by taking the said stand we will step in the legislative assembly ... Unless we step forward strongly it would be difficult for us to live because there would be a war of religion ... Muslims will come, what will you Hindus do? Are you going to throw "bhasma" (ashes) on them ... We won't mind if we do not get a vote from a single Muslim and we are not at all desirous to win an election with such votes ... There is a dire need of the voice of Hindutva and therefore please send Shiv Sena to the Legislative Assembly ... Who are these Muslims? Who are these "lande" (derogatory reference to circumcised men)? Once Vasant Dada had called me when he was chief minister. He told me that rest was fine, but asked me why I was calling them 'lande. But if it is correct that they call us "kafir" (i.e. non-believer) then we will certainly call them "lande"... They should bear in mind that this country is of Hindus, and shall remain of Hindus ... if Shiv Sena comes to power everybody will have to take "diksha" (i.e. initiation) of Hindu religion.'

Second speech: 'The victory will not be mine or of Dr. Prabhoo or of Shiv Sena but the victory will be that of Hinduism. You will be instrumental in victory and you should become instruments for the same. At last you have the right to get rid of the difficulties faced by your caste, creed, gods, deities and Hindu religion ... Therefore, I want to say that today we are standing for Hinduism ... Whatever mosques are there, if one starts digging under them, one will find Hindu temples ... If anybody stands against Hindustan you should show courage by performing pooja with shoes ... And a person named Prabhoo who is contesting the election in the name of religion must be elected. A soldier like Prabhoo should go to the assembly.'

Third speech: 'It will do if we do not get a vote from any Muslim. If anybody from them is present at this place he should think for himself. I am not in need of their votes. But I want your vote ... You must send only Dr Ramesh Prabhoo of Shiv Sena, otherwise Hindus will be finished. It will not take much take for Hindustan to become green.'

In Thackeray's defence, the famous advocate Ram Jethmalani said that what his client had said was protected by Article 19 which gave citizens the right to free speech. The right was conditional only on the maintenance of public order and unless this was prejudiced or compromised by the speech, it could not be restricted by the election laws.

Jethmalani's other argument was over the word 'his' in the line 'appeal by a candidate or his agent or by any other person with the consent of a candidates or his election agent to vote or refrain from voting for any person on the ground of his religion...'

Jethmalani argued that only a direct appeal for votes on the ground of 'his' religion and that too subject to its tendency to disturb public order was within the scope of the law. And secondly, he argued, what Thackeray was doing was not soliciting votes on behalf of Hinduism but on behalf of Hindutva, which was not a religion at all but Indian culture.

The court observed that both sides referred copiously to the meaning of the word 'Hindutva' and 'Hinduism'. Jethmalani had emphasised that Hindutva is related to Indian culture based on the geographical division known as Hindustan. The defence lawyer Ashok Desai had said that the word 'Hindutva' used in election speeches was an emphasis on Hindu religion and its communal aspects.

The court said Jethmalani's second point about 'his religion' was valid, however it needn't be a direct appeal (such as 'vote for A because he is Hindu' or 'do not vote for B because he is Muslim') to be found violating the Act.

Similarly, speeches with a secular stance alleging discrimination against a particular religion and promising removal of the imbalance could not be treated as an appeal on the ground of religion, as the thrust was on promoting secularism. 'In other words,' the court said, 'mention of religion is not forbidden so long as it does not amount to an appeal to vote for a candidate on the ground of his religion or to refrain from voting for any other candidate on the ground of his religion.'

The bench then went on to consider Jethmalani's other point, that Hindutva was not an appeal to religion. Here is where the court performed a magic trick. It first went on to try and show how Hinduism was a way of life and not a religion, and then, without citing any evidence, made Hindutva a synonym of Hinduism.

It said that considering Hindutva 'as depicting hostility, enmity or intolerance towards other religious faiths or professing communalism, proceeds from an improper appreciation and perception of the true meaning'. This true meaning had apparently emerged from earlier Supreme Court judgements.

The bench quoted Sastri Yagnapurushadji versus Muldas Brudardas Vaishya, a 1966 judgment in which the Supreme

Court had waxed philosophical: 'When we think of the Hindu religion, we find it difficult, if not impossible, to define Hindu religion or even adequately describe it. Unlike other religions in the world, the Hindu religion does not claim any one prophet; it does not worship any one God; it does not subscribe to any one dogma; it does not believe in any one philosophic concept; it does not follow any one set of religious rites or performances; in fact, it does not appear to satisfy the narrow traditional features of any religion or creed.'

The court added: 'It may broadly be described as a way of life and nothing more. Confronted by this difficulty, Dr. Radhakrishnan realised that "to many, Hinduism seems to be a name without any content. Is it a museum of beliefs, a medley of rites, or a mere map, a geographical expression?" Having posed these questions which disturbed foreigners when they think of Hinduism, Dr. Radhakrishnan has explained how Hinduism has steadily absorbed the customs and ideas of peoples with whom it has come into contact and has thus been able to maintain its supremacy and its youth. The term "Hindu", according to Dr. Radhakrishnan, had originally a territorial and not a creedal significance. It implied residence in a well-defined geographical area.' (The reference is to Dr. Sarvepalli Radhakrishnan, philosopher and the second president of India.)

That is how 'the several views set forth in India in regard to the vital philosophic concepts are considered to be the branches of the self-same tree. The short cuts and blind alleys are somehow reconciled with the main road of advance to the truth.'

But it also said that earlier judgments indicated that 'no precise meaning can be ascribed to the terms Hindu, Hindutva and Hinduism; and no meaning in the abstract can confine it to the narrow limits of religion alone, excluding the content of Indian culture and heritage'.

What the court was convinced of was that the term 'Hindutva' 'is related more to the way of life of the people in the subcontinent'. And so it was 'difficult to appreciate how in the face of these decisions the term Hindutva or Hinduism per se, in the abstract, can be assumed to mean and be equated with narrow fundamentalist Hindu religious bigotry, or be construed to fall within the prohibition of the Act'. It repeated that Hindutva was 'indicative more of a way of life of the Indian people and are not confined merely to describe persons practising the Hindu religion as a faith'.

The court quoted *Indian Muslims: The Need For A Positive Outlook* by Maulana Wahiduddin Khan, (1994) which said: 'The strategy worked out to solve the minorities problem was, although differently worded, that of Hindutva or Indianisation. This strategy, briefly stated, aims at developing a uniform culture by obliterating the differences between all of the cultures coexisting in the country. This was felt to be the way to communal harmony and national unity. It was thought that this would put an end once and for all to the minorities problem.'

This, the court said, 'indicates that the word "Hindutva" is used and understood as a synonym of Indianisation, i.e., development of uniform culture by obliterating the differences between all the cultures co-existing in the country.'

The court concluded that it was wrong to say that references to Hindutva were automatically negative against other faiths: 'It is, therefore, a fallacy and an error of law to proceed on the assumption that any reference to Hindutva or Hinduism in a speech makes it automatically a speech based on the Hindu religion as opposed to the other religions or that the use of words Hindutva or Hinduism per se depict an attitude hostile to all persons practising any religion other than the Hindu religion.'

It added: 'The fallacy is in the assumption that a speech in which reference is made to Hindutva or Hinduism must be a speech on the ground of Hindu religion so that if the candidate for whom the speech is made happens to be a Hindu, it must necessarily amount to a corrupt practice.'

The misuse of the expression 'Hindutva' to promote communalism could not alter the true meaning of the word and would have to be checked, the court said. 'It is indeed very unfortunate, if in spite of the liberal and tolerant features of Hinduism recognised in judicial decisions, these terms are misused by anyone during the elections to gain any unfair political advantage. Fundamentalism of any colour or kind must be curbed with a heavy hand to preserve and promote the secular creed of the nation. Any misuse of these terms must, therefore, be dealt with strictly,' it said.

Whether or not a speech made in the name of Hindutva fell under the prohibition of the Act would, the court said, have to be determined by the facts in each case.

The court found Thackeray's speeches violative not of secularism but the morality and decency qualifications of free speech. The bench said: 'We cannot help recording our distress at this kind of speeches given by a top leader of a political party. The lack of restraint in the language used and the derogatory terms used therein to refer to a group of people in an election speech in indeed in to be condemned ... the offending speeches in the present case discarded the cherished values of our rich cultural heritage and tended to erode the secular polity. We say this, with the fervent hope that our observation has some chastening effect in the future election campaigns.' The judges were J.S. Verma, N.P. Singh and K. Venkataswami, with Verma writing the judgment.

It may be noticed that in all judgments we have seen, the observations by the judiciary on Hindutva were given as obiter dicta, statements made in passing. They were not essential to the judgment itself. The lengthy exposition on Hindutva in the case against Prabhoo was not material in the finding against him. Similarly, the matter of Om not being a religious symbol was discussed in depth but set aside because it could not be proven that the symbol was actually used. And Shekhawat's references to building a temple on the Babri mosque demolition site and the rest of his speech were found to be acceptable because the Babri issue was not a communal one, and Hinduism was inseparable from Indian culture.

This separation of the court's commentary and observations on Hindutva from the judgment would not be so for another case the Prabhoo case bench (Verma, Singh, Venkataswami) heard on the same day, concerning the man who was then chief minister of Maharashtra, the Shiv Sena's Manohar Joshi.

Manohar Joshi versus Nitin Bhaurao Patil & Another on 11 December 1995

Joshi's 1990 election to Dadar Assembly constituency was overturned by the Bombay High Court in 1993. His opponent successfully convinced the court that the facts showed that the BJP and Shiv Sena had systematically exploited disputes to seek votes in the name of Hindutva, a communal offence attracting disqualification.

The petition listed the things that were seen as offensive in the Hindutva platform, and especially, Bal Thackeray's speeches. These included propagating:

a) Hindus and the Hindu religion are in danger;

b) That only the BJP and Shiv Sena could protect Hindus and the Hindu religion;

c) That the Congress and Janata Dal had failed to protect, and would not protect Hindus and the Hindu religion and for this reason their candidates were unfit to be elected;

d) That Hindus suffered and would continue to suffer indignity, discrimination and unequal treatment;

e) That the problem in states like Kashmir, Punjab and Assam had arisen because of the pampering of minorities;

f) That Hindus must unite and fight the attack on them and their religion and say with pride that they were Hindus;

g) That Hindus owed a duty to their religion and if necessary must give their life for it;

h) That minorities, and particularly the Muslims, were treated more favourably for their votes than Hindus.

Some of the specific things that were said at the rallies were:

1) To handle the Congress hoodlums the Shiv Sainiks could take law in their hands and use firearms if necessary (Thackeray).

2) To save Hindutva, people had to vote for the BJP-Sena candidates (Pramod Mahajan).

3) Rajiv Gandhi did not know what his own religion was, and had no right to speak on Hinduism (Mahajan).

4) The result of these elections would not only depend on everyday issues like food and clothing, but also whether the flame of Hindutva would burn brighter or be extinguished. If it died, the anti-national Muslims would transform India to Pakistan. If the flame grew, the Muslims would be turned to ash (Mahajan).

5) Rajiv Gandhi speaking on Hindutva was like a prostitute lecturing on fidelity. The country was again headed for partition. It was necessary in these circumstances that the BJP-Shiv Sena combine be elected (Mahajan).

6) (Referring to Rajiv Gandhi): Wife Christian, mother Hindu, father Parsee and therefore, himself without any (Hindu) culture/teaching ('vevarsi') (Mahajan).

The speeches at these meetings had been tape-recorded, widely reported on and were also taken down in shorthand by police personnel present there. Manohar Joshi himself had said at a meeting in Shivaji Park on 24 February 1990 that 'the first Hindu State will be established in Maharashtra'. Other speakers said that on Joshi being elected, and the BJP-Sena alliance establishing a Hindu Government, jobs would be given to all Hindus. The tapes showed that other faiths had been referred to as traitors and betrayers of India.

The petition said that 'under the guise of protecting Hindu religion/Hindutva the said cassettes attack other religions and whip up lowered instincts and animosities. The concept of secular democracy is totally eliminated. It generates powerful emotions by appealing to the Hindu voters to vote for the candidates of the alliance on a false impression given to voters that only the alliance and its candidates can protect Hindu religion.'

The Supreme Court judged that many of the things spoken could not be considered because the petition had technical deficiencies (such as the fact that the petition said it was based on the Hindutva plank and not the individual acts of Joshi and his agents). On the broad facts the court said that it had settled the issue of Hindutva in the Prabhoo judgment delivered earlier in the day.

'We have already indicated in the connected matters that the word "Hindutva" by itself does not invariably mean Hindu religion and it is the context and the manner of its use which is material for deciding the meaning of the word Hindutva in a particular text,' the court said. 'It cannot be held that in the abstract the mere word "Hindutva" by itself invariably must mean Hindu religion.'

On the issue of the establishment of Hindu Rashtra, the court said: 'In our opinion, a mere statement that the first Hindu State will be established in Maharashtra is by itself not an appeal for votes on the ground of his religion but the expression, at best, of such a hope. However despicable be such a statement, it cannot be said to amount to an appeal for votes on the ground of his religion.'

The judgment, written again by Justice Verma, added, 'We cannot hold that it constitutes a corrupt practice, even though we would express our disdain at the entertaining of such a thought or such a stance in a political leader of any shade in the country. The question is whether the corrupt practice as defined in the

Act to permit negation of the electoral verdict has been made out. To this our answer is clearly in the negative.'

All the quotations the Supreme Court produced were regarding Hinduism, not Hindutva. It is Chief Justice Verma who makes the conflation. What the Supreme Court endorsed in these judgments was Savarkar's view that Hindutva was abstract Indian culture in general.

The court does not touch upon what Savarkar and the RSS then go on to say—that non-Hindu Indians are excluded from this identity. The court also does not consider that only the RSS and its affiliated groups use the word 'Hindutva'. It is not a synonym for Hinduism. It is not a phrase of use in any religious text and a word of modern coinage specifically introduced to cast non-Hindus as some sort of civilisational enemy.

The court said it was wrong to assume that references to Hindutva were automatically hostile to non-Hindu faiths. But that is the very definition of Hindutva according to Savarkar. The Supreme Court has no problem and little qualm in effortlessly blending the observations by Radhakrishnan on the philosophy of Hinduism with the politics of Hindutva, a twentieth-century term coined to exclude Muslims and Christians. Had Verma quoted Savarkar's two-nation theory of Hindutva, would the speeches still have been exonerated? The section disallowing appeals to religion was specifically written into the law by the Constituent Assembly to avoid the sort of campaigning that accompanied Partition.

In the S.R. Bommai case, only a year before the Hindutva judgments, the Supreme Court had observed that it was clear that if any party sought to fight the elections 'on the basis of a plank which has the proximate effect of eroding the secular philosophy of the Constitution it would certainly be guilty of following an unconstitutional course of action'. But this was ignored and actually overturned by Verma in the Manohar Joshi case.

The RSS journal, *Organiser*, said in an editorial on 24 December 1995: 'The Supreme Court has put its seal of judicial imprimatur on the Sangh ideology of Hindutva by stating that it is a way of life or state of mind and that it is not to be equated with religious fundamentalism.'

On its website, the Vishwa Hindu Parishad says under the heading 'Definition of Hindutva':

'The meaning of the term "Hindutva" is often misconstrued by politicians. It is a way of life and is synonymous with Bharatiyata (Indianness) and the concept encompasses all sections of the Indian society. The Supreme Court of India, in its judgement dated 11 December 1995, defined Hindutva as follows:

'The development of Hindu religion and philosophy shows that from time to time saints and religious reformers attempted to remove from the Hindu thought and practices element of corruption and superstition and that led to the formation of different sects. Buddha started Buddhism; Mahavir founded Jainism; Basava became the founder of Lingayat religion; Dhyaneshwar and Tukaram initiated the Varkari cult; Guru Nanak inspired Sikhism; Dayananda founded Arya Samaj, and Chaitanya began the Bhakti cult; and as a result of the teachings of Ramakrishna and Vivekananda, Hindu religion flowered into its most attractive, progressive and dynamic form. If we study the teachings of these saints and religious reformers, we would notice an amount of divergence, there is a kind of subtle indescribable unity which keeps them within the sweep of the broad and progressive Hindu religion.'

On the court's dismissal of the idea of Hindu Rashtra being an appeal to religion, lawyer A.G. Noorani wrote in *Constitutional Questions and Citizens' Rights* (Oxford University Press, 2005): 'In one fell blow, the wall of separation which the founding fathers built so laboriously to keep religion and politics apart is destroyed. Elections can be fought to make India a theocratic state.' And Justice Verma's 'profuse expressions of disapproval are neither relevant nor effective. It is his ruling on the law and his construction of the facts which matter. Both are manifestly, demonstrably wrong.'

'Election candidates do not waste time expressing hopes in order to titillate the electorate. They know that its vote will be given against promises and pledges. "(The first Hindu State) will be established" is not an expression of hope but a pledge by a Shiv Sena leader at a meeting in a predominantly Hindu locality. If this is not the seeking of votes "on the ground of his religion", what is?'

The Supreme Court picked quotations out of context. The one attributed to Maulana Wahiduddin Khan saying Hindutva aimed at developing a uniform culture by obliterating the differences between all of the cultures of India as a solution to the minorities' problem was quoted approvingly.

Noorani writes that 'far from supporting the learned judge's contention, the quote refutes it thoroughly. It was not in praise of Hindutva or its euphemism "Indianisation" but in their censure. The paragraph preceding it lamented that Hindus did not treat the partition as "just an incident in past history". The subsequent strategy "to solve the minorities problem" through Hindutva or Indianisation, sought to impose a uniform culture by obliterating the differences between all of the cultures coexisting in the country.

'Unlike Justice Verma who quotes this to imply approval of this process, the Maulana disapproved of it. He is for the coexistence "of all the cultures in our diverse land".'

To the Supreme Court, Hinduism is a way of life (as it says in Sastri Yagnapurushadji versus Muldas Brudardas Vaishya) and Hindutva is also a way of life (Dr Ramesh Yashwant Prabhoo vs Prabhakar Kashinath Kunte).

The quotation in the Prabhoo case where the judges go weak at the knee 'when we think of the Hindu religion, we find it difficult, if not impossible, to define Hindu religion or even adequately describe it' is taken from the Sastri Yagnapurushadji case.

The judges go on to say that unlike other faiths, Hinduism has no prophet, no one god, no one dogma, no one philosophy and no one set of rites. They conclude that 'in fact, it does not appear to satisfy the narrow traditional features of any religion or creed'.

The case they were quoting was about a sect of Gujaratis called Swaminarayan who were insisting that they were not Hindus and for this reason did not have to follow the Harijan Temple Entry Act. Essentially, they were claiming to be non-Hindus to keep Dalits out. Even if the reasons were abhorrent, surely freedom of religion entitled them to claim the founding of a new faith. The judges, after having delivered their homily on how Hinduism did not satisfy the features of any one religion, went on to insist that the Swaminarayan sect was, in fact, Hindu.

Hindutva is a way of life but Lingayats in Karnataka, a community which wants to be classified as separate from Hinduism, are to this day, resisted by Hindutva. *India Today* reported ('Centre rejects minority religious tag to Lingayat and Veerashaiva communities: Who are they?', 12 December 2018) that the Modi government had rejected the recommendation of the Karnataka government to grant religious minority status to communities asking for it. 'Lingayats and Veerashaivas are demanding status of a separate religion for a long time,' the report said, 'The Karnataka State Minorities Commission constituted a seven-member panel to look into the demand for minority status and the committee recommended in favour of the demand.' The Modi government refused to let this happen.

This is insistence on uniform culture and comes from a fear of meaningful diversity. The Ramakrishna Mission (Bramchari

Sidheshwar Shai versus State of West Bengal) similarly has been blocked by courts from exiting Hinduism as it sought to do legally and the law appears to make it impossible for a sect the courts consider to be 'Hindu' from leaving.[18]

The opinion of the court as to what constitutes Hinduism or Hindutva is often at odds with reality. The court says Om doesn't have religious significance. However, Om is in fact a religious symbol, and its use can offend those believing in the Hindu faith. The *Daily Telegraph* reported such an incident ('Brewery apologises after use of Hindu symbol on beer bottle sparks protest') on 28 December 2018. A group called the Universal Society of Hinduism forced a company to remove the Om symbol from its bottles and asked its executives to go for sensitivity training.

On 30 March 2020, it was reported from Nevada that the pizza chain Papa John's was forced to remove the Om symbol from its advertising after Hindus protested.

The judiciary's understanding of the Babri issue is that it can only be considered communal if 100 per cent of the Hindus stand opposed to 100 per cent of the Muslims (as it did in Shekhawat's case). On the basis of this logic, no issue can ever be termed 'communal'. It is the division and hatred and violence

---

18. Groups like the Ramakrishna Mission and Jains have sought to be classified as minorities for different reasons. The Constitution gives India's linguistic and religious minorities the right to operate freely their own educational institutions. This comes from the Constituent Assembly's sentiment that all Indians have access to their mother tongue as the medium of instruction. This was needed given the large numbers of non-native language speakers and migrants all across India's states. The right (Article 30: 'All minorities, whether based on religion or language, shall have the right to establish and administer educational institutions of their choice') gives religious and linguistic minorities independence in their institutions from the State on such things as setting a fee structure and exempts them from following reservations for recruiting teaching and non-teaching staff and for admitting students. The Jains wanted minority status to evict tenants from their temples properties in urban spaces ('What minority status will mean for Jains', *Business Standard*, 22 January 2014) as well as reservation for Jain students in Jain-run institutions.

produced that makes something communal, not the size of the consensus behind it.

A challenge to the Prabhoo and Joshi judgments was made in 2016. The petitioners said that the Hindutva 'way of life' had led to demands of homogenisation and assimilation of minorities and Dalits and Adivasis in the Hindutva way of life.

It said, 'Hindutva has become a mark of nationalism and citizenship. The interpretation has curtailed faith in secularism, which is the basic feature of the Constitution.' The challenge was unsuccessful, with the Supreme Court refusing to hear it citing a procedural technicality, and the Hindutva judgments continue to give the RSS and the BJP the validity with which to further their agenda.

At a campaign rally during the Gujarat Assembly elections in December 2007, Narendra Modi raised the issue of a Muslim man, Sohrabuddin Sheikh, and his wife whom Gujarat police had murdered. What should have been done with the man? The crowd responded: 'Kill him!' Complaints to the election commission drew the response from the EC that 'it could only rebuke, not punish'.

In March 2009, during the general elections, BJP candidate Varun Gandhi at an election rally in UP said: *'Yeh panjaa nahin hai, yeh kamal ka haath hai. Yeh katwon ke gale ko kaat dega chunav ke baad. Jai Shri Ram! Ramji ki jai! Varun Gandhi kaat daalega!'* (This is not the [Congress symbol] 'hand', this is the hand of the 'lotus' [BJP's symbol]. It will cut the throats of the [derogatory expletive referring to circumcised Muslims] after the elections. Jai Shri Ram.')

Gandhi was arrested for the speech and the EC 'requested' the BJP to drop him as a candidate, which the BJP refused to do. What would have happened if the candidate had been a Muslim speaking in this language against Hindus can only be imagined.

10

THAT MOSQUE IN AWADH,
AND OTHERS IN GUJARAT

The Supreme Court's endorsement of Hindutva shines through in what is likely its most appalling decision, on Ayodhya in 2019. The court's judges demonstrated sleight of hand by saying the demolition of the Babri Masjid was illegal, but at the same time handed over the property to those who had destroyed it. The court made much of being led by reason and secular principles in arriving at its wisdom. It also had to go through contortions when denying Muslims justice on damage to religious properties in another, less well-known matter as we will see here. But first we return to the place whose modern history begins the same time as the Jana Sangh, where the seed of the BJP's rise was planted and whose legacy lives with us and will remain with us for a long time: an elegant, three-domed structure that now exists only in memory and in photographs.

A mosque built in Ayodhya in 1528 first became the site of a dispute in 1856 when violence between Hindus and Muslims broke out in the vicinity of the structure. The British built a separation, a railing, six feet or so in height which would allow the Muslims to pray in their mosque while giving access to Hindus to the courtyard outside. In 1885, a man claiming to be the mahant of Ram Janmasthan filed a suit demanding that permission be granted to build a temple in the courtyard of the mosque. This suit was dismissed and an appeal the next year was also dismissed following a visit by the district judge. A second appeal also failed. Each time, the British courts ordered a status quo, meaning that the Muslims would continue to pray inside the mosque while the Hindus had limited rights to pray in the courtyard.

In 1934, Hindus damaged a part of the mosque structure, which was repaired by the British. After this event only Friday prayers were offered. The last such prayer was on 16 December 1949. On Thursday, 22 December 1949, idols were smuggled into the mosque and installed under the central dome. The administration knew the desecration was being planned and about to happen, but allowed it. (A seven-part series in *The Quint* ['Ayodhya Part 1: Ram Lalla and a contrived miracle', 11 November 2017] found that 'the city's four top administrators were adamant on executing the plan to place Ram's idol inside the Babri (masjid)'. They included District Magistrate K.K. Nayar, Superintendent of Police Kripal Singh and Judge Thakur Bir Singh. The work *Ayodhya: The Dark Night—The Secret History of Rama's Apperance in Babri Masjid* by Krishna Jha and Dhirendra K. Jha has discussed the episode in great detail. Nayar would become a Jana Sangh Lok Sabha MP in 1967, having planted the seed inside the mosque which would sprout in time and give Hindutva control of the Indian State.)

An FIR was filed against the trespass, but the idols were allowed to remain. Muslims were not allowed to pray any longer, and the mosque was locked up the same day. The property was then attached by the government and handed over to a receiver.

The next month, on 16 January 1950, the Hindu Mahasabha filed a suit demanding to be allowed to conduct pooja. The same day a judge passed an order allowing daily pooja. A series of suits then followed seeking to take over the property from the receiver.

In 1961, the Sunni Waqf Board filed a suit seeking removal of the idols and possession of their mosque.

In 1986, a suit was filed seeking the unlocking of the mosque's gates so that Hindu devotees, who had to be outside the gates, could have darshan of the idols that had been smuggled in. The court ordered the opening of the mosque to Hindu worshippers with the acquiescence of Rajiv Gandhi's government.

That year, the Vishwa Hindu Parishad's campaign asking that the mosque be removed and a temple built in its place gathered momentum and entered the realm of popular politics. The new president of the BJP, L.K. Advani, saw the opportunity to mobilise against Muslims and threw himself and his party behind the demand.

In 1989, Rajiv Gandhi, who was then prime minister, allowed the VHP to lay the foundation stone of a future Ram temple on the assurance that the mosque would remain intact. The same year a suit was filed on behalf of Ram asking that the property be handed over to 'him'. In 1991, the BJP state government of UP acquired the area, saying it would be developed for tourism. The high court allowed this. A challenge by Muslim groups to this acquisition was dismissed.

The BJP and RSS groups then began threatening other mosques, including in Kashi and Mathura. In July 1991, the Union government enacted a law which barred the conversion of places of worship from one religion to another and that the 'religious character of a place of worship existing on the 15th day of August, 1947 shall continue to be the same as it existed on that day'.

The law however added that 'nothing contained in this Act shall apply to the place or place of worship commonly known as Ram Janmabhoomi-Babri Masjid situated in Ayodhya in the state of Uttar Pradesh and to any suit, appeal or other proceeding relating to the said place or place of worship.'

The BJP was accused of leading a mob to the site on 6 December 1992, and of demolishing the mosque. Riots followed in which over 2,000 Indians were killed. Within a few hours, a makeshift temple came up where the mosque had stood.

On 21 December a petition was filed in the Allahabad High Court by a man saying it was his fundamental right to worship Ram in that temple. The court agreed and said every Hindu had the right to worship at his birthplace.

A worried Union government under P.V. Narasimha Rao promulgated an ordinance a few days later, acquiring the land and sending a reference to the Supreme Court for it to determine if there had been a temple under the mosque's debris.

The Muslim groups again challenged this acquisition of their property and again lost. The Supreme Court told them that a mosque was not essential to the practice of Islam and their prayer could be offered anywhere. It allowed the makeshift temple to stay and allowed pooja to continue.

In 2003, excavation was ordered at the site and the Archaeological Survey of India found that there had been a structure or several structures under the debris dating back to the twelfth century. There was nothing to show what had happened in the 400 years between then and the construction of the mosque, the report said, though it is clear in history that Awadh was in continual possession of Muslims from the Delhi Sultanate to the Mughals during this period. The report did not show that the remains of this previous structure had been used in making the mosque.

There was in fact no sign of a temple, later reports would show. The survey also found human remains but this was not included in their report.

After this was submitted, the Allahabad High Court ordered the property split into three with a third each being given to the Muslims, one agitating Hindu party and to Ram himself. All three parties appealed to the Supreme Court which stayed the order and asked for mediation between the parties, which failed.

On 9 November 2019, the Supreme Court handed over the entire site to Ram, the last entrant to the dispute, and ordered the formation of a trust and the building of a temple. The reason given was a lack of proof from the Muslims showing that they possessed the property continually. The revenue records, grant papers and the British gazetteers were rejected as insufficient. The court also found that there was no evidence of a temple under the mosque.

It said that the idols had been illegally smuggled into the mosque and it found that the demolition of mosque was illegal.

It noted that 'the damage to the mosque in 1934, its desecration in 1949 leading to the ouster of the Muslims and the eventual destruction on 6 December 1992 constituted a serious violation of the rule of law'.

However, it chose not to give justice to the Muslims on the dispossession of their land and the demolition of their mosque, asking them to accept land somewhere else that the government would allot it. This was not part of the Muslims' plea and in fact they had consistently rejected the VHP's demand for the same thing: that they surrender the Babri Masjid and take land elsewhere.

Since the court called the demolition of the mosque illegal, the question asked immediately was: how would it have adjudicated on the dispute had the demolition not occurred? Would the Supreme Court have ordered the mosque to be demolished and handed over the land to Ram? Of course, it would not have. This question shows how flawed in logic and justice the judgment was. What the court did was condone the demolition after making noises about criticising it.

The Supreme Court judgment was consistent with the behaviour of the Indian judiciary and administration. The status quo which the British courts had kept intact was changed every time under the Indian judiciary with verdicts against the Muslims and they continually denied Muslims their access and their rights and ultimately, their property.

Each time, militant Hindu groups aggressively changed the situation on the ground, whether it was the courtyard, the smuggling in of the idols, the allowing of pooja, the opening of the gates to Hindus, the allowing of shilanyas, the demolition, the construction of the makeshift temple, the acquisition of property by the State, the casual dismissal of the Muslim right to pray while allowing Hindu prayer at the site, the ordering of an archaeological survey into what was essentially a land-grab, the subsequent disregard of the survey's findings, the ordering of mediation through a Hindu figure (Sri Sri Ravi Shankar) who made comments asking Muslims to surrender their claim, the lack of action against those who demolished the mosque, and finally, the handing over of the mosque property to those who had demolished it. The record is long and shameful.

The court pretended to have arrived at its conclusions not on the basis of faith, but law. It said: 'A finding of title cannot be based in law on the archaeological findings which have been arrived at by ASI. Between the twelfth century to which the underlying structure is dated and the construction of the mosque in the sixteenth century, there is an intervening period of four centuries. No evidence has been placed on the record in relation to the course of human history between the twelfth and sixteen centuries. No evidence is available in a case of this antiquity on (i) the cause of destruction of the underlying structure; and (ii) whether the pre-existing structure was demolished for the construction of the mosque. Title to the land must be decided on settled legal principles and applying evidentiary standards which govern a civil trial.'

The court said, echoing a previous judgment by Allahabad High Court, that it had no evidence that prayer was offered at the mosque from the time that it was constructed in 1528 to 1857 though it refers to the Babri Masjid as a four-century-old mosque. It does not itself offer any evidence of disuse and is careful not to call the mosque defunct. On the other hand it did not ask the Hindu groups to prove that they had possession of the mosque property prior to 1856 before handing it over to them: their devotion was sufficient. The court ignored the dividing barrier put up by the British and treated the property as a whole and handed over the entire property to the Hindus.

The court ignored or did not accept documentary evidence that included continual maintenance being sent to the mosque as a waqf property from before the time of the Nawabs of Awadh right down to the British period.

While holding that 'the Muslims have been wrongly deprived of a mosque which had been constructed well over 450 years ago' the court felt that splitting the property up three ways as recommended by the high court was legally unsustainable. The disputed sited measured only 1500 square yards and therefore, the court said, 'Dividing the land will not subserve the interest of either of the parties or secure a lasting sense of peace and tranquillity.' And therefore it, concluded, it should be given in entirety to Ram Lalla, the juristic entity who the court itself said illegally entered the mosque in 1949. And this juristic entity of Ram Lalla was given the property through the trusteeship of those same parties who participated in the demolishing of the mosque.

Journalist K. Venkataraman, writing in *The Hindu* on 9 November 2019, said that the tolerance of Awadh's Muslims to Hindu encroachment into the mosque and its courtyard cost them against aggressive Hindu tactics.

He wrote: 'In the ultimate analysis, the non-interference by Muslims in Hindu patterns of worship in Hindu shrines such as the Ramchabutra and Sita Rasoi worked against their cause, with the Supreme Court now holding that it proved that the Muslim claim was non-exclusionary.' This punished the tolerant.

On the other hand, he added, 'By repeatedly challenging the Muslim mode of worship, Hindus managed to come across as those with unimpeded possession in the outer courtyard, and with a partial stake in the inner courtyard too.'

He said a close reading of the judgment showed that the entire property had not in fact been declared in favour of the Hindus though they were ultimately given total possession.

The Supreme Court's decision to instruct the government to set up a trust and start building a temple is a breach of the secular character of the State. A nine judge bench in the S.R. Bommai case had observed that the 'State is neither pro-particular religion nor anti-particular religion. It stands aloof, in other words maintains neutrality in matters of religion and provides equal protection to all religions.'

C. Rammanohar Reddy, writing in *The Hindu* on 12 November, said: 'You do not have to be a legal person to be embarrassed on reading such a ruling. The essence of the 1,045-page judgement was that the Hindus had complete right to worship in the outer courtyard of the Babri Masjid since 1858, while the Muslims' right to pray in the inner courtyard was contested. Therefore, possession of the entire disputed plot goes to the Hindus, for a temple to be built by a trust constituted by the government, no less.'

NALSAR University of Law vice-chancellor Faizan Mustafa, writing with Aymen Mohammed in the *Indian Express* ('Ayodhya judgment is a setback to evidence law', 10 November 2019) observed: 'The judgment will be remembered for the victory of faith over the rule of law as the Supreme Court considered religious beliefs even in deciding a property dispute, and despite conceding that faith cannot confer title, it still went ahead to give property to worshippers on the basis of faith. The court should not have any say in matters of freedom of religion, but deciding title suit on the basis of faith is a thorny proposition. In brief, it is the red letter day for the constitutional right to religion but a setback to property law and a setback to evidence law with differential burden of proof being demanded from different parties.'

In an interview to *Business Standard*, Mustafa said, 'Faith cannot be above the Constitution. The Constitution itself recognises freedom of religion subject to public order, health, morality and other fundamental rights. Thus freedom of religion is confined to what is an "essential or core beliefs" of a religion. Here court did not seek any proof of birth of Lord Ram at the disputed site as an integral part of Hindu religion. The mere assertion of belief was considered sufficient. By not undertaking essentiality test that court has been following in the freedom of religion cases, the court went against its own judgments and favoured one particular party's faith-based argument. Moreover considering faith as part of one's religious beliefs for Article 25 is one thing but taking it into account in a property dispute is an entirely different proposition.'

Mustafa was asked if there had been an injustice to the Muslims. He replied: 'Yes, they were wronged and that's why restitution has been provided in the form of five-acre land. But then, restitution means restoring parties to the original position. Ideally, the court should have accepted their right to possession and then said that since structure is not there anymore, we are handing it to Hindu parties invoking powers under Article 142. Construction of the mosque within the disputed site as ordered by the High Court would have enhanced our reputation in the world as a secular country that believes in pluralism. We lost this opportunity. Even if the land had been given to Muslims, civil society and Muslim intellectuals would have persuaded the Sunni Waqf Board to give up this land for the construction of a grand Ram temple.'

The court did not doubt the Hindu claim that Ram's birthplace was underneath the mosque's central dome. It was not required to be an essential practice, as was the argument when namaz was refused at the site. At that time the Supreme Court found that a mosque was not an essential part of Islam. The Supreme Court's position on this has remained inconsistent and appears to be aimed at easing the path of Hindutva. On the other hand, where minority rights have been asserted and claims for justice have been raised against Hindutva's violence, the Supreme Court has chosen not to curb majoritarianism.

On 30 September 2020, a CBI court acquitted Advani and others in the BJP, absolving them in the demolition of the mosque. They were found not guilty of charges including incitement to violence, conspiracy and unlawful assembly. The last named charge was demonstrably true: they were indeed present and in unlawful assembly. The court disregarded a meeting recorded by the police which said it had taken place the day before the demolition at BJP leader Vinay Katiyar's house where Advani had been present. At that meeting, the BJP's Kalyan Singh, then the chief minister of Uttar Pradesh, was reported to have said that there was a stay on construction of the temple, not on the demolition of the mosque ('Acquittals in Babri demolition case are a blot on CBI, it must be liberated from political influence', *Indian Express,* 1 October 2020). But the court determined that the demolition was spontaneous. Thus ended the decades-long saga of that mosque in Awadh. It was not the only place where the judiciary found against the rights of India's minorities when it came to the damaging and destruction of their religious sites by majoritarian mobs.

In 2017, the Supreme Court heard the appeal of Gujarat's government against its high court's order that it repair minority religious places damaged during the 2002 riots.

In 2012, the Gujarat High Court had asked the Modi government to make a survey of those mosques, dargahs, graveyards, khankahs and other religious places and institutions desecrated, damaged or destroyed by Hindu mobs. Under the court's supervision and guidance the government would have to repair and restore these properties and also compensate the trusts and institutions owning them.

The Gujarat High Court based its judgment on a Supreme Court judgment in 2008 concerning churches damaged in Odisha after a riot against Christians. The government had not given compensation on the grounds that there was some dispute concerning the land the churches were standing on. The court said that the government 'may formulate a scheme regarding these religious places and take appropriate decision'.

The Modi government framed a policy to hand over Rs 50,000 each to places of worship destroyed except to those in the middle of the road (usually old Muslim shrines built before the modern city came up) or those that were illegal. It would not pay for repairing or rebuilding, arguing that the state fund which was raised through taxes could not be spent on restoration or construction of religious places. It went against the freedom of citizens' religion that their money was being spent by the government on building religious places. It quoted Article 27 of the Constitution: 'No person shall be compelled to pay any taxes, the proceeds of which are specifically appropriated in payment of expenses for the promotion or maintenance of any particular religion or religions denomination.'

The Modi government argued further that the deletion of the right to property from the fundamental rights (under Article 19[1][f]) meant that these damaged religious places need not be restored or repaired. The courts had never ordered compensation for the breach of any right other than Article 21 (protection of life and liberty) and the Modi government argued that the right to freedom of religion was not protected under Article 21. It also said that it did not know how to ask its officers to assess the damage and even if they were able to do so how it would be distributed among the various title holders of the properties.

The lawyers representing the demolished and damaged places seeking compensation said mob attacks on religious places of worship were an attack on the religious symbolism of people who held them sacred. The destruction of these places belonging to the weaker sections of the society by a dominant group was to inflict humiliation on them and thereby violates Article 21 of the Constitution, the protection of life and liberty in addition to a violation of their freedom of religion. Fundamental rights could not be compartmentalised as the Modi government was claiming, they argued.

If the State failed to protect large scale destruction of places of worship belonging to the weaker or less dominant section of the people it resulted in breach of Article 21 and the State was obliged to give equal protection of law to all. This was one of the facets of secularism, especially when the State had failed in its obligation to maintain law and order.

The Supreme Court said that it would not use the word 'victim' in this case because it did not refer to individuals. It said it would also disregard the opinion of international jurists and courts as irrelevant. The court accepted that the 'protection of property and places of worship is an essential part of secularism'. However it sided with the Modi government and overturned the Gujarat High Court order.

The court agreed with the Modi government that Article 27 would be violated if the State offered taxpayer money for religious purposes. However, as Faizan Mustafa has pointed out, Kerala annually gives Rs 46 lakh to Travancore Dewasom Board and Tamil Nadu annually gives Rs 13.6 lakh for the maintenance of Hindu temples. The Supreme Court's argument that taxpayer money couldn't be used to rebuild Gujarat's demolished and damaged monuments is flawed.

I have a personal story that connects with the vandalism in this instance in Gujarat. Wali Muhammad Wali, who died in 1707, was the first poet of Urdu, acknowledged as being so in a couplet by Mir Taqi Mir. Wali is called Wali Daccani because he was born in Aurangabad, but also Wali Gujarati because that is where he lived and was buried.

Wali's elegant grave had stood outside the gate of the police commissioner's office and was a shrine worshipped as the 'Cheeni pir ka mazar' (the saint of the tomb made of China).

On 28 February 2002, during the Godhra riots, a mob tore down Wali's little tomb in Ahmedabad and dug up his grave. An idol of 'Hulladio Hanuman' (riotous Hanuman) was placed over the rubble. Overnight, the road was tarred and now no sign remains of the tomb. It was one of the first violent acts against Muslims in that long and barbarous pogrom.

I looked at Wali's works and discovered poetry that connected him with the people who had vandalised his grave.

One was a masnavi, *Taarif-e-Shehr Surat* (In Praise of Surat City), the other, excerpted below, was a ghazal, *Dar Firaaq-e-Gujarat* (On Separation from Gujarat):

Parting from Gujarat leaves thorns in my chest
My heart—on fire!—pounds impatiently in my breast
What cure can heal the wound of living apart?
The scimitar of exile has cut deep into my heart
My feet were bound, and in sorrow I did tire
My heart singed rapidly, like a hair over fire
Gaze into my heart and see the garden of the lover
Where the flowers of winter riot in my blood's colour
It is with regret that in the end I see my friends depart
So rise from the empty tavern and steady yourself, my heart
And thank God's mercy, O Wali!
He let that passion remain

The heart's still anxious to catch a glimpse of my Gujarat again

(Translation mine)

I read out *Dar Firaaq-e-Gujarat* to Modi in his office in Gandhinagar in 2003 and asked him to guess who the poet was. He could not say. When I told him it was Wali, and the government should do him justice, Modi's response at first was that something was already being done about it, but by the end of the conversation he added that the evidence that the demolished grave was Wali's wasn't clinching enough for him and he would have to think about it. Nothing was ultimately done.

11

PUNISHING CRIMES THAT DIDN'T HAPPEN

In 2019, India passed a law that makes Muslim men criminally liable for a private wrong. This was done through criminalising an utterance of divorce. It refers to Muslim men instantly divorcing their wives by saying the word 'talaq' (meaning repudiation) three times in succession in one sitting, hence the phrase 'triple talaq'.

The act was referred to in Islam as 'talaq biddat', meaning an innovation or a heresy. It was disapproved and even sinful as a form of divorce, though, if delivered, it was seen as valid by many jurists in the dominant Sunni school of jurisprudence (triple talaq is invalid for Shias). Data appears to show that some 200 divorces in this manner occur annually in India. A report ('Around 248 cases of triple talaq in India, says Ravi Shankar Prasad', *The New Indian Express*, 12 December 2018) said that between January 2017 and December 2018, the Centre had information on 248 cases, adding that in the same period of two years, media reports had spoken of 477 cases.

The approved manner of separation, called 'talaq sunnat', by a Muslim man is the utterance of talaq on three separate occasions over three months (menstrual cycles) and with the proviso that no intercourse between the couple takes place. During this period, the pronouncement of divorce is revocable.

The three months are a sort of cooling-off or reconciliation period and meant to ensure that divorce does not happen in haste or anger, which is why it is the 'approved' form and instant divorce is seen as an innovation or heresy.

Muslim women have a different process for initiating divorce, called 'khula', requiring them to obtain a decree on one of several specified grounds. A third category of Muslim divorce is one by mutual consent. Muslim marriage is not a sacrament but a contract. Divorce had to be introduced into Hindu law through legislation, but has always existed in Islamic law.

The law criminalising triple talaq was passed by Parliament following a Supreme Court judgment in August 2017 declaring triple talaq to be invalid through a split 3:2 judgment. The court did not declare the practice to be unconstitutional, as it was claimed by some press reports and by the BJP; merely void. It is important also to understand court did not strike down Muslim personal law and so the other forms of talaq remain legal.

The government's response was to quickly pass an ordinance and then later a bill which became the Muslim Women (Protection of Rights on Marriage) Act. It made Muslim men the only part of India's population to face jail for divorce. The law defines talaq here to mean triple or instantaneous talaq and reads:

'3. Any pronouncement of talaq by a Muslim husband upon his wife, by words, either spoken or written or in electronic form or in any other manner whatsoever, shall be void and illegal.

4. Punishment for pronouncing talaq. Any Muslim husband who pronounces talaq referred to in Section 3 upon his wife shall be punished with imprisonment for a term which may extend to three years, and shall also be liable to fine.'

Section 3 merely repeats what the court had already adjudicated: that a declaration of triple talaq was void. If an Indian man were to say it to his wife today, his action would not result in divorce and the marriage would remain intact per law. What was then the need to introduce punishment? The stated intention in invalidating triple talaq was to protect the woman. That was already achieved by the Supreme Court's judgment. The law punishes an act that hasn't happened.

No purpose appears to be served by criminalising the action. It keeps the marriage intact but jails the husband.

The law says it is triggered when a married Muslim woman or her relative by blood or marriage file a complaint against the man. This condition was altered from an earlier one which allowed anyone to file a complaint against a Muslim man alleging that he had uttered the three words. The mischief that could be caused had this been retained can only be imagined. The potential for this still remains, and relatives against a marriage or having a grouse against the husband have been given the space by the law to stir up trouble.

The law says that the man arrested cannot be released on bail until the magistrate 'after hearing the married Muslim woman upon whom talaq is pronounced' is satisfied there are reasonable grounds for bail.

This condition has introduced an additional category of bail in the law. India has bailable and non-bailable offences. In the former, bail is an automatic right. In the latter, bail is applied for and the magistrate determines whether it is to be given. By asking the magistrate to first listen to the woman, it takes away from his discretion. A lawyer I spoke to said the bail condition in this case was unusual: 'Bail is the rule, jail is the exception. Bail is granted for a variety of reasons—besides the primary fact that liberty is right unless there is a strong reasons to deny liberty,' the lawyer said, 'reasons for giving bail are things like deaths in the family or a ceremony and such things. Requiring the wife's consent imposes extraordinary judicial function on the wife and all aside affects the rights as an individual free citizen. The wife does not have to consent to bail even if I have stabbed the wife. Bail is an individual's right to liberty.' Here bail has been made conditional in a way it hasn't for any other offence.

What the court could have done was to declare a triple talaq delivered in one sitting as the valid delivery of only one utterance, leaving it for the man to still deliver the other two talaq utterances as prescribed over the following months. In fact, the Supreme Court quoted a previous judgment by Delhi High Court that actually did exactly this. Adopting it would have aligned triple talaq to talaq sunnat and resolved the issue but the court did not do this. It merely declared triple talaq to be invalid.

This was a problem essentially of the Hanafi sect of Sunnis. But the solution that has been sent by the Supreme Court and now by law covers all Muslim sects. This is in violation of Article 26, which gives freedom to manage their religious affairs to 'every religious denomination or any section thereof' to 'manage its own affairs in matters of religion'.

The law sends the man to jail and keeps the marriage intact. What is the position of the woman who, believing in the validity of triple talaq, receives it from her husband? The law forces her to remain in a marriage which she now considers illicit. It does not increase the woman's options. The law restricts them and it restricts her autonomy. The law says that the woman 'upon whom talaq is pronounced shall be entitled to receive from her husband such amount of subsistence allowance, for her and dependent children, as may be determined by the Magistrate.' But how is the husband to provide an allowance if he is in jail?

The vice-chancellor of NALSAR University of Law Faizan Mustafa wrote about the issue: 'From another angle, too, triple divorce is a unique case where the law is dictating to the orthodox Hanafi Muslim woman to continue in a relationship she considers sinful. If she thinks that as per her sect, her marriage has come to an end, forcing the continuance of sexual relations is nothing but tyranny unleashed by the law, which seriously undermines individual choice and autonomy.' ('Power, not justice', *Indian Express* 1 August 2019).

There was also a contradiction in the narrative that India was facing, Mustafa wrote: 'On the one hand, we have the bogey of so-called "love jihad" deployed to curtail the freedom to marry a person of one's choice and on the other hand, Muslim women are forced to continue with the same abusive husband who has given them instant triple divorce. We cannot say that the issue of women's entry into the Sabarimala temple is a question of faith and triple divorce is an issue of gender justice. This is hypocrisy of the highest order. Moreover, instant triple divorce should not be a crime when it is pronounced at the request of the wife. We should not curtail this right of Muslim women.'

He observed that Muslim marriage, unlike Hindu marriage, is a contract and not a sacrament. Hindu marriage vows promise continuation even on 'rebirth'. Muslim nikahnamas are contracts with specific deliverables and specific clauses which can trigger divorce (such as having a separate house, not being violent, not using triple talaq and so on). Such contracts were so common in the Mughal period that the conditions were referred to as the 'usual' ones in the marriage contract or nikahnama. It would have been appropriate to have approached the problem and its solution through the contractual route and insisting that all nikahnamas specify that triple talaq would not be used. Instead, the law promulgated by the BJP government has made the utterance a crime.

In September 2018, the ordinance (as it was still at the time) was challenged by Samastha Kerala Jamiyyathul Ulama, a religious organisation of Sunni Muslim scholars and clerics in Kerala, who moved the Supreme Court asking for the law to be declared unconstitutional, saying its only objective is 'to punish Muslim husbands'.

'If the motive was to protect a Muslim wife in an unhappy marriage, no reasonable person can believe that the means to ensure it is by putting an errant husband in jail for three years. Further, the offence is confined only to Muslim husbands,' their petition said.

'It is absurd that for an utterance which has no legal effect, whether spoken by Muslim, Hindu or Christian, it is only the Muslim husband who is penalised with a three-year sentence. Protection of wives cannot be achieved by incarceration of husbands,' the organisation said.

The court had already declared the utterance of triple talaq void and the marriage continues despite the utterance of triple talaq. If triple talaq has thus no legal effect, why should the government go ahead and make it an offence now, it asked.

On 25 March 2019, a bench comprising Chief Justice Ranjan Gogoi and Justice Deepak Gupta dismissed the plea saying that since it was an ordinance the court would not like to get into it. After the Act was passed on 31 July 2019, a Kerala woman moved court again. Noorbeena Rasheed's petition also said: 'The protection of women cannot be achieved by incarceration of husbands.' She questioned the provision allowing unaffected parties—relatives of the woman—the right to file complaints. The petition, one of many clubbed together against the Act, said that this provision could potentially destroy marital relationships in cases of false complaint.

The petitions said the punishment prescribed in the Act was graver than for offences like rioting and bribery under the Indian Penal Code for which there is a lesser punishment than instant divorce.

This is true. The three-year sentence for saying the word talaq three times is the same as IPC Section 148—rioting with a deadly weapon. Rioting is punishable by jail for up to two years, bribery by one year and adulterating food and drink by six months. Destroying a place of worship attracts a jail term of two years.

Proving this 'crime' is also going to be problematic. Given the burden of proof the criminal justice system requires for such harsh punishment as a three-year jail sentence, how is it to be proved beyond reasonable doubt that the man accused uttered words said in the presence of only the complainant, his wife? A conviction under this would lead to permanent damage. The inability to get a passport or get into government service are two outcomes. A conviction resulting in a fine, even a minor one, would keep the criminal conviction permanently on the husband's record. A civil fine, even of crores of rupees, incurred by an errant corporate executive would be less damaging than a thousand rupee fine for the 'crime' here.

Triple talaq is an instance of a private wrong, which should ordinarily attract civil law, not criminal. There is no danger to the State or society here for it to have been criminalised. It violates the principle of criminal law being used as a last resort (ultima ratio). It also violates Montesquieu's principle of punishment: 'Every punishment that does not arise from absolute necessity is tyranny.' There was no necessity here.

Triple talaq's criminalisation also goes against the recent trend of decriminalising offences related to morality. A year after the triple talaq judgment, on 6 September 2018, the Supreme Court decriminalised homosexuality, striking down the penal code's Section 377 which punished same sex relations with a ten-year sentence.

A few days later, on 27 September 2018, the Supreme Court held that adultery was not a crime. It struck down the penal code's section 497 which punished adulterers with a five-year sentence.

Elsewhere, the Indian State has failed to criminalise marital rape, though there has been a campaign against it. The rush by the Modi government to criminalise triple talaq must be seen in this light and compared to recent developments and advances in our laws. India continues to have a law criminalising bigamy. However, as Mustafa has pointed out, punishment for bigamy is punishing an actual act, that of a second marriage.

Triple talaq is invalid by law. Uttering it doesn't in fact end the marriage. It's strange to punish someone for a divorce that according to the State itself hasn't actually happened.

Writing in *The Tribune* ('The endgame of Triple Talaq', 21 September 2018), women's rights activist and lawyer Flavia Agnes asked what the law would give Muslim women: 'Will it save Muslim marriages, protect the Muslim woman's economic rights or ensure that she has a roof over her head, beyond what is stipulated under other existing statutes? Is this a magic wand that will save Muslim women from destitution stemming from triple talaq?'

No, she wrote. 'It will increase destitution among Muslim women. Because when a husband is jailed for pronouncing triple talaq, he will not be able to provide maintenance to his wife and children. Worse, it will not save her marriage. Is the end goal for a Muslim wife in a conflict marriage incarcerating her husband or securing her economic rights? I think the government has got its equations wrong.'

'How will a poor illiterate woman, who has been deprived of her shelter and sustenance, be able to follow up a rigorous and daunting criminal prosecution against her husband and secure a conviction? More importantly, what will the conviction give the aggrieved woman? Convicting the husband for three, seven or even ten years cannot ensure that she has food on the table to feed her children, money to clothe them and educate them, which are the primary concerns of any woman.'

If the ultimate desire of a Muslim woman is to save her marriage rather than break it, and ensure that her civil rights such as shelter and maintenance are protected, criminalising triple talaq is not the answer. Using the provisions of the Domestic Violence Act and challenging the talaq using the Supreme Court judgment would better ensure that the woman isn't deprived of her shelter and sustenance.

She pointed out that lakhs of women of faith (the traditional and conservative burqa-clad Muslim woman) had come out in large numbers in every city in protest against criminalising triple talaq.

Agnes added: 'If a large segment among campaigners against triple talaq does not support the move to criminalise triple talaq, then what is the justification for bringing out this Ordinance in great haste?'

The haste was of course political and ideological. The BJP was using the law as a stick to assault its primary enemy, the Muslims. The Supreme Court has said that seditious words and so called anti-national speech are not a crime in India. But saying this one word three times now means jail for Muslim men.

12

KASHMIR: OTHERWISE OCCUPIED

Jammu and Kashmir was India's only Muslim majority state. Sixty-seven per cent of the undivided state and 97 per cent of what is now the Kashmir part of the union territory (which comprises of Jammu and Kashmir, but excludes Ladakh) is Muslim. The state conditionally acceded to India in October 1947, being among the last princely states to come into the Indian Union. The 2011 census says the Kashmir region had 62 lakh Muslims and that about 1.6 lakh Kashmiri Pandits had left the Valley, many of them forced out, in 1990, after the Kashmiri movement for independence became militant.The Jammu region has about 50 lakh people of whom 65 per cent are Hindu and the Ladakh region around 3 lakh of whom around half are Muslim (who are culturally different from the Kashmiri Muslims, being of mixed extraction—see 'History of Muslims in Central Ladakh', *Tibet Journal*, Vol. 20, No. 3) and half Buddhist.

Kashmir's accession in 1947 was preceded by a Pakistani attack on it, during which a substantial part of the state was taken by the Pakistani raiders before the Indian army was deployed following the accession.

This part became known as Azad Kashmir in Pakistan and Pakistan Occupied Kashmir (PoK) in India. Jammu and Kashmir was known in Pakistan as Indian Occupied Kashmir while the world usually uses Indian administered Kashmir and Pakistan administered Kashmir, signalling the lack of legitimacy it sees in the occupation of the territories.

After the skirmish, India went to the United Nations to claim PoK. This came in a period when the Second World War had ended and the text of the Atlantic Charter was still fresh.[19] This was an agreement between the United States under Franklin Roosevelt and Britain under Winston Churchill that saw a post-war world where all people would have the right to self-determination.

The Indian foreign ministry website quotes a book (*The Kashmir Story*, B.L. Sharma, 1967) explaining what happened after the Kashmir dispute went to the UN Security Council:

'India was the first to suggest plebiscite as a peaceful method for resolving the Junagadh dispute with Pakistan. India made a similar offer for settling the Kashmir situation in 1947. The offer was reaffirmed in 1948 and when the UN Commission suggested plebiscite, India accepted the proposal. When the UN Commission (under Frank Graham) went to the subcontinent in 1951, it was India which not only wanted a plebiscite but wanted it as quickly as possible. In 1953, India reaffirmed its adherence to plebiscite as the best way of resolving the Kashmir problem in a joint communique issued by the Prime Ministers of India and Pakistan in New Delhi on 20 August. And yet a plebiscite could not be held.'

---

19. The Atlantic Charter was a statement issued on 14 August 1941 that set out American and British goals for the world after the end of the Second World War. The joint statement, later dubbed the Atlantic Charter, outlined the aims of United States and the United Kingdom for the post-war world as follows: no territorial aggrandisement, no territorial changes made against the wishes of the people (self-determination), restoration of self-government to those deprived of it, abandonment of the use of force, and disarmament of aggressor nations and provisions related to trade and other matters. The adherents to the Atlantic Charter signed the Declaration by United Nations on 1 January 1942, which was the basis for the modern United Nations.

The reason was sequencing. Pakistan was to withdraw its forces from the parts it was occupying first, per the UN Security Council Resolution Number 47 of 1948, but it chose not to do so without conditions. The work quoted by India's foreign ministry website says, 'The fact of the matter is that Pakistan never wanted a plebiscite. In spite of a plethora of statements of its leaders to the contrary, acceptance of plebiscite by its government was insincere. All available evidence goes to show that it did everything in its power to prevent a plebiscite from being held.'

Following this India also stepped back from its promise of plebiscite. The UN and its role became irrelevant over time from here on and in time the UN resolutions became a dead letter.

In 1949, India's Constitution added Article 370, as a temporary provision subject to the fulfilling of the plebiscite. Since the plebiscite never happened, the status of the Article became permanent.

Article 370 said that the power of India's Parliament to make laws for Jammu and Kashmir would be limited. This condition sprang from the Instrument of Accession signed by Kashmir's ruler Maharaja Hari Singh. His family, Dogra Rajputs from Jammu, who served the Lahore court, had after the death of Maharaja Ranjit Singh been given the Kashmir valley by the British in 1846, thus unifying for the first time Jammu with Kashmir and Ladakh.

Clause 3 of the document Hari Singh signed said, 'I accept the matters specified in the schedules hereto as the matters with respect to which the Dominion Legislature (meaning India's Assembly) may make laws for this state.'

The schedule attached listed four subjects for which India's Parliament could make laws for Kashmir: defence, including the navy and air force and cantonment areas; second, external affairs including treaties with other nations and emigration; third, communications including post and telephone and railways; and fourth, ancillary, specified here as elections to Parliament and limiting jurisdiction by courts except on those subjects to which the ruler agreed.

Did India ever intend to honour this agreement and did it ever do so?

Article 370 is the proviso which caused great offence to the RSS and the BJP but it is probably because they may not have known how empty it was. The agreement and its limitation on the intrusion of India into the autonomy of Kashmir was never taken seriously even by the Congress.

India progressively eroded these conditions over the years as it tried to forcibly integrate Kashmir. Initially, the state had a system of administration different from those of other Indian states. It had, from 1952 to 1965, a head of State known as the 'Sadr-e-Riyasat' and a prime minister, who was the head of the government. Later, this system was abolished[20] and the title of prime minister taken away as the official designation of the head of Kashmir's executive. The Kashmir legislature became a handmaiden of Nehru and later, of other Indian prime ministers, thus hollowing out the meaning of Article 370 over time. Pakistan tried to meddle directly through the sending of soldiers in 1965 who tried unsuccessfully to catalyse an insurrection. That war ended in a stalemate and the original borders after the 1947 skirmish, called the Line of Control, remained after a second war in 1971 because of which Bangladesh was formed.

The state spent a long period under president's rule, its biggest leader Sheikh Abdullah was jailed for a long spell, it had its chief ministers and its legislatures arbitrarily dismissed, and later went through sham elections with almost no turnout from a sullen population. The last vestiges of its autonomy, like its

20. The Sadr-e-Riyasat from 1952 to 1965 was Karan Singh, the son of the last Maharaja of Kashmir, Hari Singh.

Ranbir Penal Code, which was used instead of the Indian Penal Code, were stripped away in 2019 when the BJP revoked the special status under Article 370.

After 1990, Kashmir was being ruled more or less directly by Delhi and a large part of State power from then on was in military hands. The background to this was the winding down of the jihad in Afghanistan by the mujahideen groups armed and trained by America and Pakistan against the Soviets. And the eruption of an independence movement in Kashmir which swiftly took to militancy and was assisted by Pakistan which used its force of jihadi fighters to fuel violent insurrection.

The chief ministers had a limited say in what they could do. The army around the state and the paramilitaries on the streets of Srinagar were under the control of Delhi.

The violation of human rights in Kashmir began at this stage in full measure. In time, Kashmir's elections were largely believed to be rigged and a reluctant population and sullen people forced to vote to show the State was legitimate and the transfer of power from Kashmiris to bureaucrats and soldiers sent by Delhi complete.

In January 1990, Kashmir went under Governor's rule. In these circumstances through the Governor's Act No. 12 of 1990, Armed Forces Special Powers Act (AFSPA) came to Kashmir, never to leave.

The State's note in 1992 justifying the continuation of the area being declared 'disturbed' (and hence liable to be governed under the AFSPA) said that, 'at that time the militants/terrorists had posed a great challenge to the State administration' and that 'because of continued abetment and support from across the border to the militants it was felt that additional measures be taken to curb the militancy effectively and in a shortest possible time'.

By now, even the pretence of Kashmir's special status had been shed. While extending AFSPA in Kashmir, the government noted that 'in view of the urgency of the matter, it is not practicable to consult the Consultative Committee of Parliament on Jammu and Kashmir Legislation. This measure is accordingly being enacted without reference to the Consultative Committee.' In 2015, it was pointed out that the Disturbed Areas Act had lapsed in Kashmir in 1998 but ASPFA was still in force, apparently without sanction, but this was overlooked.

The key provision of AFSPA was the sweeping empowerment of individuals from the police and the military and the paramilitary to open fire 'if he is of opinion that it is necessary so to do for the maintenance of public order'. The forces could use force 'even to the causing of death' and would be immune from prosecution for their actions except with the sanction of the Centre.

They could destroy anything they thought was a hideout, a fortified position or shelter from which an attack could be made. And they could arrest and detain without a warrant anyone they wanted and could use force in effecting the arrest. What happens when you give armed men such freedom in a place that has been declared hostile by the State is not difficult to imagine.

On 23 February 1991, soldiers of 4 Rajputana Rifles came into the villages of Kunan and Poshpora in the remote northern district of Kupwara. The army asked the men to assemble outside and then entered their homes.

They remained there the entire night and allegedly raped the women of the village, from a fourteen-year old disabled girl to a seventy-year old grandmother ('Konan Poshpora mass rape: The silence of a night', *Indian Express*, 21 July 2013). The FIR mentions twenty-three rapes though the number was higher because many women chose not to disclose what they had gone through. Many of the survivors were teenagers not yet married. Forty women went to the Jammu and Kashmir State Human Rights Commission later saying they had been raped at

Kunan and Poshpora. Many of them had to be operated on after multiple rapes.

The first official to arrive was the deputy commissioner of Kupwara S.M. Yasin, who wrote that he felt 'ashamed to put in black and white the kind of atrocities and their magnitude'.

India dismissed the incident. Asia Watch, a part of Human Rights Watch, reported that: 'The alacrity with which Indian military and government authorities in Kashmir discredited the allegations of rape and their failure to follow through with procedures that would provide critical evidence for any prosecution—in particular prompt independent medical examinations of the alleged rape victims—undermined the integrity of the investigation and indicates that the Indian authorities have been far more interested in shielding government forces from charges of abuse.'

In October 2011, the State Human Rights Commission gave directions for reopening the case after hearing pleas from the victims from the village. It recommended the formation of a special investigation team, monetary compensation of Rs 2 lakh each to victims and prosecution of the head prosecutor who had ordered the case closed. Based on this, in 2014, the Jammu and Kashmir High Court ordered the government to pay the women. Nothing came of this because the state government, in which the BJP was now an alliance partner, opposed the compensation and appealed.

In February 2018, the Support Group for Justice for Kunan Poshpora Survivors filed another petition before the SHRC asking for an investigation. It provided the Commission with documentation of 143 cases of sexual assault between 1989 and 2017. In a 2019 report, the United Nations High Commissioner for Human Rights said this of the Kunan Poshpora survivors' attempts to get justice: 'Authorities continue to thwart attempts'. It noted that the state government petitioned the Supreme Court against the High Court's 2014 order that directed the state government to pay compensation to the victims within three months and reopen and reinvestigate the case and to prosecute a senior official, whom it accused of deliberately obstructing the investigation. The case remained stalled in the Supreme Court throughout 2018. In February 2020, the survivors told reporters they had given up and would not push for justice any longer ('Won't plead for justice anymore: Kashmir's "Mass Rape" survivors on 29th anniversary', *twocircles.net*, 25 February, 2020).

Those who have attempted to document incidents of rape have been abused by India's security forces. Human Rights Watch ('Rape in Kashmir: A crime of war', Vol. 5, Issue 9) reported that in November 1990, a surgeon at the Anantnag District Hospital was arrested after he had made arrangements for a gynecologist to examine seven women who had alleged that they had been raped by security forces. The women said security forces had broken up a wedding and raped all of them, including the bride.

Even when investigations are ordered, they did not result in prosecutions. A magisterial inquiry was ordered in the case of five women reportedly raped near Anantnag on 5 December 1991, but the magistrate's report was not submitted. According to the *Kashmir Times* of 14 January 1993, the state government had ordered inquiries into eighty-seven incidents of killings, rape and arson by the police. None of these cases resulted in criminal prosecutions, Human Rights Watch reported. Human rights organisations have consistently called for the Indian State to remove AFSPA but the Indian State has not responded or engaged with them.

The 1992 note regarding the continuation of AFSPA in Kashmir said that it was of 'temporary nature' and that 'actions taken under the Act have shown considerable improvement but the circumstances and the conditions due to which the law was enacted continue to be the same'. But it has continued all these years, shielding the men of the military, paramilitary and police from prosecution.

On 1 January 2018, the Rajya Sabha was informed by the government that the Defence Ministry had got fifty requests in twenty-six years from the Jammu and Kashmir government for permission to prosecute soldiers under AFSPA. It granted permission in zero cases. These include cases of soldiers accused of unlawful killings, torture and rape between 2001 and 2016.

An Amnesty India report published in 2015 looked at over a hundred cases and met with fifty-eight families and found that since 1990, no sanction had ever been given to prosecute those accused by the Kashmir government of crimes. A chargesheet is the document filed after an FIR is registered and on the basis of investigation, meaning the police had found evidence of a crime. However the Centre has approved none of the state's requests for justice.

The army says it conducts its own justice system, the court martial. These are opaque processes where the survivor or victim does not have access and shouldn't be used for crime unrelated to military discipline. However, this parallel court system has been allowed to soldiers trying fellow soldiers of crimes against civilians. On its website, the Indian army says it has investigated 1,026 allegations against its troops in Kashmir. Of these, it has dismissed 995 as being 'false/baseless'.[21] The numbers have not been updated on the website since December 2011.

An editorial in the *Economic Times* ('Pathribal fake encounter case: India's army's acquittal of accused soldiers a blot on democracy', 27 January 2014) describes what happens in these

---

21. 'Human Right Cell and Handling of Human Rights Violation Cases in the Army', https://indianarmy.nic.in/Site/FormTemplete/frmTempSimple.aspx?MnId=2ASv6/r4rRfw9BNyemcmhA==&ParentID=9Tinp5JWN1mKWXbay/DpnQ==

courts martial. The case discussed related to an attack in March 2000 during the then president Bill Clinton's visit to India. The army claimed it had attacked a hut which contained Lashkar-e-Taiba militants who had participated in a massacre of Sikhs in the village of Chattisingpora just before the Clinton visit.[22]

On 11 May 2006, after investigating the case the CBI filed murder charges against five serving army personnel from the 7 Rashtriya Rifles unit in the court of the Chief Judicial Magistrate of Srinagar. The CBI argued this was a case of 'cold blooded murder' and were not actions taken in the course of performing official duties, and so the perpetrators could not be protected. The Indian Army blocked the prosecution of five army personnel under Section 7 of the AFSPA. The Supreme Court of India upheld the army's action and asked it to decide whether it wanted to court martial them instead.

In September 2012, over twelve years after the murder of the five civilians in Pathribal, the Indian Army chose to bring the case before the military justice system and began proceedings in a general court-martial. On 24 January 2014 the Indian Army said it was dismissing all charges against five of its personnel due to a lack of evidence. According to the closure report filed in the Srinagar Chief Magistrate's Court, the Indian Army did not conduct a trial but instead dismissed the charges through a pre-trial procedure known as summary of evidence under Rule 24 of the Army Rules 1954.

The *Economic Times* editorial said that 'the army's self-acquittal of the Pathribal accused is a continuation of the cover ups of human rights violations in J&K and India's Northeast, where the military has a free hand in dealing out "justice" as it deems fit. This is a blot on our democracy.'

---

22. The Chattisinghpora, Pathribal, and Barakpora massacres refer to a series of three closely related incidents that took place in the Anantnag district of Jammu and Kashmir between 20 March 2000 and 3 April 2000 that left up to 49 Kashmiri civilians dead.

In another case, the paper reported on 11 July 2018 ('Machhil encounter: Life sentence of 5 army men suspended') soldiers were convicted of murdering three civilians but freed nonetheless by an army tribunal without explanation.

A report on the Amnesty research ('25 years of AFSPA in J&K demonstrates a failure of accountability, claims Amnesty', *www.scroll.in*, 1 July 2015) said that 'the sanction process is reportedly as opaque as the military courts. The reports state that victims' families were rarely informed of sanction decisions and so were unable to challenge them.'

Kashmiri victims' relatives have also found the military unwilling to part with information on inquiries into crimes or the conduct of court-martials. Neither did the military provide evidence for branding complaints 'false'.

Amnesty India's former law and policy director Shailesh Rai has pointed out ('India's court-martial system fails on all counts: competence, independence, impartiality', *www.scroll.in*, 1 July 2015) that for a court to be able to hold a fair trial, it must have at least three attributes—competence: judges must possess appropriate legal training and qualifications; independence: judges' appointments, promotions and security of tenure should not be open to the executive's influence; impartiality: judges should be and appear to be free of personal and institutional bias.

On all these counts, the Indian military justice system is deficient. It discounts legal training and qualifications, lacks independence from the military chain of command, and ignores conflicts of interest.

The flaw in processes is manifest. A court-martial is a temporary body assembled by a 'convening authority'—a senior military officer—after looking into the charges against an accused soldier. The convening officer also appoints the prosecutor and the defence counsel, who are all officers drawn from the military.

Members of a court-martial typically don't have any legal training or qualifications. U.C. Jha, a former Wing Commander in the Indian Air Force has written that the convening authority 'is not a lawyer and generally has no formal legal training' (*The Military Justice System in India: An Analysis,* Lexis Nexis, 2009).

Human Rights Watch reported that in seven courts-martial held between April 1990 and July 1991 involving incidents of rape, deaths in custody, illegal detention and indiscriminate firing on civilians by army soldiers, only one officer had been dismissed. The most severe punishment for the remaining officers was either a suspended promotion, or remarks of 'severe displeasure' in their files.

On 26 July 2020, the *Economic Times* published a report ('There are no set procedures or norms to sanction AFSPA cases: Defence ministry') of an application under the Right to Information Act by activist Venkatesh Nayak. It reported the defence ministry saying on affidavit that 'there are no official records containing details of procedure or the norms, criteria and standard that is required to be followed by the ministry while deciding the evidence submitted by the J&K government in prosecution sanction cases'.

In 2017, the Supreme Court ordered the CBI to investigate AFSPA violations in Manipur after a group of retired judges found that all six sample cases they examined were staged encounters. The accused were murderers whose prosecution was being denied by AFSPA. The judges, led by Justice Santosh Hegde observed, 'Normally, the greater the power, the greater the restraint and stricter the mechanism to prevent its misuse or abuse. But in the case of AFSPA in Manipur this principle appears to have been reversed.' Deaths in Manipur declined after this report to almost nil. Though the numbers are multiple times bigger in Kashmir and the accusations graver, India's Supreme Court has not shown similar interest in examining the cases of abuse by the army against Kashmir's Muslims.

Administrative detention, also called preventive detention, was the sum and substance of the Rowlatt Act that Gandhi opposed because of which the protestors had gathered at Jallianwala Bagh in 1919. It refers to the power of the government to arrest someone without having committed a crime. This is widely and liberally used in Kashmir through the Public Safety Act. It was introduced in 1978 to primarily deal with timber smugglers. It gives the State power to jail anyone without charge or trial for two years. The arrests and detentions of Kashmir's political leadership after the gutting of Article 370 in 2019 was under this law.

The Public Safety Act has been used to target journalists, human rights defenders, opposition parties and protestors. It has frequently been used illegally to jail even children. The law does not provide for judicial review and is abused by the government. Amnesty International reported that the State countered orders from the Jammu and Kashmir High Court by issuing another detention order, keeping people in jail without charge or trial for years ('Tyranny of a lawless law: Detention without charge or trial under the J&K Public Safety Act', Amnesty International India, 2019).[23]

The Supreme Court of India described this form of detention as a 'lawless law' but has allowed the State to use it and done nothing to remove it. The law violates India's commitment that it made when it signed the International Covenant on Civil and Political Rights in 1979, especially with regard to the right to liberty and the right to a free and fair trial.

The paramilitary in Kashmir uses a weapon for crowd control used nowhere else in India or the world. The pump action 12-gauge shotgun loaded with birdshot is fired into crowds regularly to disperse them. This is the same weapon that can be

---

23. Can be accessed at: https://amnesty.org.in/wp-content/uploads/2019/06/Tyranny-of-A-Lawless-Law.pdf

seen in movie scenes showing clay pigeon shooting. It fires the shot, meaning hundreds of ball bearing-like spheres, out of an unrifled barrel. The shot disperses widely with distance and one round can affect several people.

There have been hundreds of cases of Kashmiris being blinded by this weapon. Often people who haven't even been part of a protest but were inside their homes have been affected. A Right to Information request filed by rights groups has shown that even the armed forces are wounded by this weapon whose damage cannot be controlled. Between July 2016 and August 2017, at least seventeen people had been killed by the weapon, India's Parliament was told, and Kashmir's State Human Rights Commission documented 1,726 pellet gun injuries in 2016 alone. Kashmir's assembly was told by its then chief minister in January 2018 that 6,221 people in all had been hit, of whom 728 had eye injuries.

Despite the scale of the damage, only one inquiry into the use of the weapon in one death has been initiated. Twenty-one-year-old Riyaz Ahmad Shah was killed in August 2016, when a shotgun was fired into him at close quarters with the shell exploding in his abdomen leaving 300 pellets inside him. An FIR was filed for his death naming 'security forces'.

The effect of this weapon will be felt in Kashmir for a long time. Many people live with the dozens of metal pieces of shot inside their bodies and often, their face. Many, including children and infants, have been blinded and have had their lives damaged permanently. When challenged in court, the Indian government said it would replace the weapon but has not done so. The laxity and lack of interest by the Indian justice system in what has been going on in Kashmir can be seen by the fact that it thinks the weapon shouldn't be used but hasn't done much to stop it. On 14 December 2016 the Supreme Court told the government not to use pellet guns 'indiscriminately' and only after 'proper

application of mind'. Five months later it asked the government
to 'consider effective means other than the use of pellet guns'
('Supreme Court asks Centre to consider alternatives to pellet
guns in Kashmir', *Hindustan Times*, 5 May 2017). Nothing was
done and they continue to be used.

In August 2020, security forces opened fire on a religious
processon of Shias, blinding and wounding forty individuals
including boys ('Pellet Guns Fired On Srinagar Muharram
Procession, Leading To Blindings', *thewire.in*, 30 August 2020).
In September of 2020, the UN High Commissioner for Human
Rights Michelle Bachelet said at the UN Human Rights Council
that 'in the last one year in Jammu and Kashmir, incidents of
military and police violence against civilians continue, including
use of pellet guns, ('UN Human Rights Chief Raises Kashmir
at Start of HRC Session', *www.thewire.in*, 15 September 2020).
There is almost no resistance from India's political parties to the
use of the weapon and this has helped the State get away on this
and other issues where Kashmiri rights have been deliberately
trampled.

Owing to the prevalent state of affairs in Kashmir, its
economy has been forced to develop differently from other
states. Srinagar doesn't have access to the new economy with its
apps for online stores like Amazon or Flipkart, transport services
like Uber and Ola, and food and delivery services like Swiggy and
Zomato. Even messaging apps are frequently useless and social
media often doesn't work.

That's because the internet is often cut off in Kashmir and
high speed access on mobile almost never available. A United
Nations report in 2019 said, 'Kashmir continues to face frequent
barriers to internet access as the authorities continue to suspend
arbitrarily internet services. According to the United Nations
Educational, Scientific and Cultural Organisation (UNESCO),
South Asia reported the highest number of shutdowns in the

world between April 2017 and May 2018 with India accounting for the highest level of shutdowns in the world. Half of all internet shutdowns in India were reported from the Kashmir Valley.'[24]

A day before the Modi government gutted Article 370 and made Jammu and Kashmir a Union territory, the internet was cut off and remained cut off till the following year. The communications blockade continued for 213 days from 4 August 2019 to 4 March 2020. More than eleven months later, on 26 July 2020, the Kashmir administration told Delhi it 'had no objection to the restoration of 4G connectivity', according to a report in the *Indian Express* on that day.

The internet blockade is commonly used by India as a means of collective punishment. In the first four months of 2019, Kashmir had twenty-five instances of internet shutdown. In 2016, the blockade was 133 days long, from July to November. Even when the blockade is lifted, often only so-called 2G services are allowed. The government has 'whitelisted' websites which can be accessed while everything else including social media is banned. In 2018, it was reported that Twitter and Facebook had taken actions against a number of accounts for various pieces of Kashmir-related content because of removal demands from the Indian government.

The UNESCO report referred to above said that internet shutdowns 'pose a threat to human rights and block the public's right to know; and have emerged a significant tool of censorship by governments which are increasingly utilising shutdowns under the guise of security'.

India has for long run a parallel system of government akin to China's 'one country two systems' policy under which it governs Hong Kong differently from the mainland. In Kashmir there

24. Can be accessed at: https://www.ohchr.org/Documents/Countries/IN/KashmirUpdateReport_8July2019.pdf

operates a state that is tyrannical and where the citizen has no recourse to justice or rule of law or to democracy. The Supreme Court has said access to internet was a fundamental right but the government can ignore Supreme Court orders in Kashmir.

The ruler in Delhi can on a whim terminate elected governments, beginning with Sheikh Abdullah's in 1953 till the last one of Mehbooba Mufti in 2019. Today, Kashmir is a Union territory with no legislature, no elected representation and ruled by an envoy, Manoj Sinha (designated as Lieutenant Governor) sent by Delhi along with advisors. A pith helmet is all that is missing.

When the BJP took away Kashmir's statehood it kept hundreds of people belonging to various political parties in jail till these individuals signed a bond. This bond stated that they could not comment on Article 370 for a year. The document, reported by *India Today* on 21 October 2019 ('Freedom, conditions apply: Detained J&K leaders can't comment or hold rallies on Art 370 for a year, says bond') read: 'I undertake that in case of release from detention, I will not make any comments or issue statements or make public speeches or participate in public assemblies related to the recent events in the State of Jammu and Kashmir... for a period of one year.'

It also required a deposit of Rs 10,000 and the production of sureties who would lose Rs 50,000 if the individual did not keep to the terms signed on to.

An Amnesty India report ('Kashmir situation analysis and update') researched in September and October 2019, said that the state had admitted holding 144 children in jail, some as young as nine. The organisation said it could not speak to local representatives because they were either in jail or were afraid they would be sent back if they violated the bond.

After the Kashmir assembly was dissolved, its Lieutenant Governor passed an order that took away Kashmiri media's freedom ('J&K press demands roll back of new media policy', *The Hindu*, 6 July 2020). It gave the administration sweeping authority to control the content of the media, who would report, and most importantly, who would get money.

Called Media Policy 2020, this fifty-page document was 'in supersession of all previous orders'. The policy said it would 'focus on creating a sustained narrative on the functioning of the government in the media' so as to 'foster a genuinely positive image of the government'.[25]

This was required because 'the media has tended to focus on the security aspects'. The administration would 'thwart the efforts of anti-social and anti-national elements' and to that end would ensure that the 'antecedents of the paper/news portal as well as that of its publishers/editors/key personnel are duly gone into'. Newspapers and magazine and other journals already have to register before publishing so this was an additional process of getting a publication empanelled.

Before accrediting journalists, 'a robust background check including verification of antecedents of each journalist would be earned (sic) out with the assistance of the relevant authorities.'

The administration would 'examine the content of print, electronics and other forms of media for fake news, plagiarism and unethical or anti-national activities'. It would de-empanel those papers and journals found to have such content. Most importantly, 'there shall be no release of advertisements to any media' which questioned the 'sovereignty and integrity of India' or 'violate accepted norms' of 'behaviour'. Similarly, 'fake news or news with anti-social, communal or anti-national content' would be acted against.

The advertising lever is important because with no modern economy advertising telecom, apps or such things, the reliance of

25. Can be accessed at: https://kashmirlife.net/jammu-and-kashmir-media-policy-2020-236330/

Kashmiri media on advertising from the state is almost absolute. References to advertising occur in the Media Policy 2020 a total of eighty-nine times, making it clear to Kashmiri media that they had to behave or pay the price immediately. Even empanelled newspapers would have to toe the line. The policy says that 'empanelment of a newspaper, publication or journal would not per se guarantee placement of any advertisement or message from the government'.

The administration would also have a 'full-fledged social media cell in its repertoire for dissemination of information and monitoring of misinformation'. The rules under which information is gathered and disseminated and published in Kashmir is different than it is for the rest of India. The government, without defining what anti-national, anti-social or fake news was, would retain the authority to act when it found instances of these. The policy did not create any controversy in India. Kashmiri journalists protested on 6 July 2020, but this was not covered in mainstream Indian media.

Anuradha Bhasin, executive editor of *Kashmir Times*, said ('Jammu: New media policy wants journalists to "sing praises of the ruler"', *www.newsclick.in*, 9 July 2020) that the policy 'is going to completely silence, black out and even kill journalism. First, completely choke the finances of the organisation that is refusing to toe the line. Second, for individual journalists who are not toeing the line, the whole argument of fake news and being anti-national can be used against them.'

Reporters Sans Frontiers called the Media Policy 2020 'Orwellian' and 'Kafkaesque' saying that the administration had 'infinite space for interpretation, and will basically decide what is truth or false'. This is 'what usually happens in autocratic regimes, and it speaks volumes about the state of democracy in J&K'. ('New J&K Media Policy 2020 is 'Orwellian' and 'Kafkaesque', *www.twocircles.net*, 14 July 2020)

The interest of the world has changed with time about what is going on in Kashmir. During the decades of the Cold War from the 1950s to 1990, interest slowly waned as it became clear that the plebiscite would not happen. After 1990 for a few years when Kashmiris demanded independence and India responded with harsh military action, there was interest in the issue from human rights groups abroad and the media, which regularly reported what was going on.

The period after 9/11 and the 'war against terror' gave India the chance to apply pressure on Pakistan to end its support to armed groups. On 13 December 2001, there was a terrorist attack on the Indian Parliament in which fourteen people died. India blamed the Lashkar-e-Taiba and the Jaish-e-Muhammad and Atal Bihari Vajpayee mobilised the army for war. In response to pressure from India and US president George H.W. Bush, Pakistan's military leader Gen. Pervez Musharraf banned both these groups.

Following this, the levels of violence in Kashmir collapsed. Fatalities as recorded by the South Asian Terrorism Portal show that militancy began in full fashion in 1990, at the end of the Afghan war. In that year there were 1,107 deaths in Kashmir, including 862 civilians. The next year the number rose to 1393 with 614 'terrorists' killed. In 1993, the total was 1909 and the following year it was 2,567. The violence continued to rise, with total fatalities touching 3,288 in the year 2000, with 1808 'terrorists' being killed by India.

Violence peaked in 2001. That year 4,011 people died. It was the year of the 9/11 attacks and the global consensus was against such violence and the Parliament attack. After this, violence began to decline dramatically in Kashmir. In 2002, the toll was 3,098, in 2003 it was 2,507 and in 2004 it was 1,788. Fatalities kept falling every year for the decade of the Manmohan Singh government which took office in 2004, going under 1,000 in 2007, under 500 in 2009, and under 200 in 2011.

India blames Pakistan for militancy in Kashmir but doesn't credit it for the decline, which has come after Pakistan cracked down on the jihadi groups on its soil. There were 295 deaths from militancy in Pakistan in 2001. After Musharraf banned the militant outfits and began a crackdown, they fought back violently. Fatalities rose to over 1,000 in 2006 and over 3,000 the next year (when militants also made an attempt to assassinate Musharraf), over 6,000 in 2007 (the year Benazir Bhutto was killed by militants and another attempt was made on Musharraf) and peaked at 11,317 in 2009. After this, violence declined and in 2019, total fatalities were under 400.

In the last three full years of the UPA's rule—2011, 2012 and 2013—the fatalities remained under 200 (181, 121 and 172 respectively). In 2014 they were 189 and in 2015 they were 175. After this, India's long-term trend in decline in violence began to be reversed. Fatalities again crossed 200 in 2016, crossed 300 in 2017 and crossed 400 in 2018. Already by the end of October 2020, the number of those killed had crossed the fatalities of the entire previous year (283). Violence has again become an everyday phenomenon. It should be noted here that fatalities in Kashmir were twenty times higher in a period when there were no mobile phones and no internet. The denial of internet and mobile phone telephony to Kashmiris today is not for security and safety, but a collective punishment inflicted on the entire population.

Kashmir has paid an enormous price in blood over the last thirty years. Of a civilian population of less than a crore today, over 21,000 civilians have been killed, according to government data. Another 10,000 are missing. These are people believed to have been picked up by security forces, killed and their bodies disposed of without the family knowing. Another 25,000 have been killed and classified as militants, most of them Kashmiris. The security forces themselves have lost 7,000 men in Kashmir to the militancy. It is the absence of interest in the rest of India, the historical ability of the Indian Army to absorb great cost without seeking accountability from the political side of government, and the looking away by the rest of the world that has made this great slaughter possible.

A conversation that I had with a senior police officer in 2018 revealed that India had successfully mined and fenced almost the entire Line of Control, making it difficult for exfiltration and infiltration. Those wanting to be trained as militants could no longer go across to Pakistan and nor could those wanting to enter Kashmir, come in easily. It was no longer the foreigners who were the fighting the army and security forces in Kashmir, it was Kashmiris for the most part, if not entirely. This shows in recent reports, including the lionisation by locals of twenty-one-year old militant Burhan Wani, who was killed in 2016. It is not easy to stop this violence or to blame it on Pakistan. The world has begun to notice again and this time it is more intrusive than it has been in the past.

In June 2018, alarmed by what was happening in Kashmir under the Modi government, the Office of the United Nations High Commissioner for Human Rights (OHCHR) published its first-ever report on Kashmir, calling for an 'international inquiry into multiple violations' of the human rights of Kashmiris.

Titled 'Report on the Situation of Human Rights in Kashmir: Developments in the Indian State of Jammu and Kashmir from June 2016 to April 2018, and General Human Rights Concerns in Azad Jammu and Kashmir and Gilgit-Baltistan', it detailed abuses in both parts of Kashmir. Pakistan was urged to stop misusing its anti-terror law to persecute political activity and dissent, to remove the laws criminalising Ahmadis from the constitutions of Pakistan-administered Kashmir and Baltistan, and also to amend laws that limited freedom of expression and freedom of assembly.

India was urged to urgently repeal AFSPA, establish independent, impartial and credible investigations to probe all civilian killings since July 2016 and all abuses committed by armed groups; to provide reparations and rehabilitation to all injured individuals and to the families of those killed in security operations. It was also asked to amend the Public Safety Act to ensure its compliance with international human rights law, and demanded that all those held under administrative detention either be charged or immediately released.

India's response to the report did not address any of the issues factually. Instead, it accused the Office of the United Nations High Commissioner on Human Rights of 'personal prejudices'. This was Zeid Raad Al Hussein, a former Jordanian diplomat who is currently a human rights law professor at the University of Pennsylvania.

In 2019, the OHCHR released a follow-up report on Kashmir, under its new high commissioner, Michelle Bachelet, the former president of Chile. This time India called her report 'false and motivated'. Again, India chose not to address the facts. It will become more difficult for India to keep doing what it has been doing in Kashmir.

Part of the problem has been the aggravation by the Modi government of what was already a difficult situation. The gutting of Article 370 was accompanied by bombast from home minister Amit Shah who promised he would take back Aksai Chin, that part of Ladakh which had been lost to China after the 1962 war.

The move on Article 370 activated China, which launched aggressive actions on the Indian side of the Line of Actual Control in Ladakh, killing twenty Indian soldiers in savage hand-to-hand combat with primitive weapons in June 2020.

The Chinese action was not anticipated by the Modi government which appeared not to have thought through the strategic implications of what it was doing in Kashmir for its domestic Hindu constituency.

The question to ask is what has hollowing out and finally killing Article 370 achieved for India over all these years? There is no plan for the return of Kashmir Pandits as there has not been for thirty years. They are a mostly educated, urban and middle-class community that has dispersed and settled themselves in cities elsewhere. What does the prospect of a return to the Kashmir towns they left, till today lacking even the most basic connectivity of the rest of India, offer them? What opportunities do they have on return? Such things haven't been discussed or considered and it is one reason why despite often angrily raising their flight of three decades ago, the BJP has done nothing to act on it.

The stated reasons for the Article 370 action are untrue. This provision was not the cause of separatism, as Modi claimed when announcing the measure. It was not the cause of militancy either as he also claimed. Taking it away has not changed either of those things as events and the data show.

Is Kashmir any closer to India or any more firmly a part of India than it was six decades ago? The answer is that it is not. Its history since 1990 is one of progressive decline in the relations the state has had with the rest of India. Taking away its statehood, removing its elected leadership and jailing it, and governing it through non-Kashmiris are not acts of good faith, and nor are they seen as such by Kashmiris. How true is it today to say that Kashmir is not under occupation?

It seems clear that Kashmir's best period with India was the initial one when the terms of accession were most followed. As the agreement was hollowed out, the Kashmiris became more restive. Today, India is holding on to the state through force alone. Even the fig leaf of an elected assembly has been discarded.

A Kashmir that acceded to India under limited conditions and with autonomy was always seen for some reason as unacceptable right to India from the start. In the beginning because of the

Congress anxiety over Partition and its continuation of Muslim separatism and later, because of the BJP's Hindu nationalism.

It is now clear that the Indian inability and refusal to honour the instrument of accession made things progressively worse. In Kashmir, India started with a solution and ended up creating a problem.

13

ARTIFICE FOR THE HOLY COW

The Hindu values of prohibition and cow protection were smuggled into the Indian Constitution as secular principles. Hindus strongly wanted the ban on cow slaughter for religious reasons but at the same time didn't want to appear to violate the principle of secularism. They found a way to resolve this problem in the Constitution and then the Indian Supreme Court over time added its sophistry to the specious position.

The sociologist M.N. Srinivas says prohibition is a Sanskritic act, something that makes society more Brahminical. He defines a process called 'sanskritisation' as the giving up of alcohol and meat by lower castes, and the adoption of Sanskritic ritual, to raise themselves in the caste system. 'A lower caste was, in a generation or two, to rise to a higher position in the hierarchy by adopting vegetarianism and teetotalism, and by Sanskritising its ritual and pantheon,' he wrote. It was able to do this by separating its jati, or sub-caste, from those of similar stature, and taking on the manner of the jati above it.

All Brahmins except the Saraswats, Kashmiri Brahmins and Bengali Brahmins were vegetarian, Srinivas writes. This put pressure on the ones immediately below them in the caste hierarchy to give up meat if they wanted to be seen as equal. Similarly, eating beef and pork was more degrading than eating fish. Tapping and handling toddy, leather and butchery put a caste in a lower position. The use of alcohol and intoxicants in Hindu religious ritual is part of the practices of popular and indigenous cultures. Formal religious rites involve no alcohol and like beef, the idea of consuming the 'som' intoxicant in a ritual was given up long ago and made taboo.

In the Constituent Assembly, the claim was made (by Congressman B.G. Kher) that 'the drinking of liquor is one of the five deadly sins which the Smritis have laid down' and that not only Hindus and Muslims but even Christians viewed it as a sin.

When the point was made by members that alcohol was a part of Adivasi culture and ritual, Congressman V.I. Muniswami Pillai claimed that 'there is no such thing as require liquor, toddy, brandy or any such thing, at the time of the ceremonies of the aborigines'. He said that alcohol came to the indigenous people with the British and had left with them.

A spirited response to the Hindu conservatives came from B.H. Khardekar, an independent who represented Kolhapur. He said that the arguments being put forward in favour of prohibition did not hold. The first, that the Americans had adopted it, was flawed because the Americans had let it go. The second, that the Congress Party had pledged itself to it, did not matter because the Congress was only one political party after independence and did not represent the nation. The third, that the claim that Parsis and Christians were also in favour of prohibition, was bogus. And last, that Gandhi was in favour of it, did not hold because Gandhi was also against compulsion.

Khardekar also spoke of lost excise revenues which could be put to use to build the state and also quoted Harold Laski's *Liberty in the Modern State* in which he says prohibition infringes on personal liberty.

His is the most structured and factual intervention in the debate. But his primary arguments were dismissed by the others as being either of no consequence or resoluble. In absence of any pushback other than from Khardekar and a clear Congress desire to push this through on moral grounds, the amendment was accepted. Article 47 reads: 'The State shall regard the raising of the level of nutrition and the standard of living of its people and the improvement of public health as among its primary duties and, in particular, the State shall endeavour to bring about prohibition of the consumption except for medicinal purposes of intoxicating drinks and of drugs which are injurious to health.'

The provision was smuggled in under the cloak of health and well-being. But as the decades have shown, the obligation of the State in the first part, of raising the levels of nutrition and standard of living and improvement of health, and indeed these being its primary duties, has been followed in the breach. India stood 129th out of 189 nations in the 2019 United Nations Development Programme human development index which measures life expectancy, education and per capita income. Since independence, Gujarat has always been under prohibition but had an HDI rank of 14 among 25 Indian states in 2017 ('Human Development Index across Indian states', *State Bank of India*, Issue 94, FY 2019). Bihar, which is currently under prohibition ranked 25, the very last among all states surveyed. Prohibition in India is pushed always from the moral point, that of women's well-being and societal well-being. The point made by Srinivas, that it represented a Sanskritic act that was linked to caste, is never raised in Indian debates and the disapproval of drink is almost universal.

The article protecting cows was just as easy for the Congress to push through because of a Hindu consensus in favour of it. Ambedkar has written about his theory of caste Hinduism's beef taboo in his 1948 work, *The Untouchables: Who were they and why did they become Untouchables?* He says that beef-eating Hindus adopted a ban to separate themselves from Buddhists, who continued to eat beef (as they continue to do so today), and that this vegetarianism brought them and especially the Brahmins, a ritual purity.

'The 1910 Census Returns show that the meat of the dead cow forms the chief item of food consumed by communities which are generally classified as untouchable communities. No Hindu community, however low, will touch cow's flesh. On the other hand, there is no community which is really an untouchable community which has not something to do with the dead cow. Some eat her flesh, some remove the skin, some manufacture articles out of her skin and bones.

From the survey of the Census Commissioner, it is well established that untouchables eat beef. The question however is: Has beef-eating any relation to the origin of untouchability? Or is it merely an incident in the economic life of the untouchables?

'Can we say that the Broken Men began to be treated as Untouchables because they ate beef? There need be no hesitation in returning an affirmative answer to this question. No other answer is consistent with facts as we know them. In the second place if there is anything that separates the untouchables from the Hindus, it is beef-eating. Even a superficial view of the food taboos of the Hindus will show that there are two taboos regarding food which serve as dividing lines.

'There is one taboo against meat-eating. It divides Hindus into vegetarians and flesh eaters. There is another taboo which is against beef-eating. It divides Hindus into those who eat cow's flesh and those who do not. From the point of view of untouchability the first dividing line is of no importance. But the second is. For it completely marks off the touchables from the untouchables.

'The touchables whether they are vegetarians or flesh-eaters are united in their objection to eat cow's flesh. As against them stand the untouchables who eat cow's flesh without compunction and as a matter of course and habit.'

(Ambedkar in *The Untouchables* explores why, if Hindus once ate beef as the scriptures suggest, they developed a nausea against it. He theorises that the untouchables are those from Buddhist tribes who were defeated by the Hindus and chose not to come into Brahminism's fold after their defeat. They were a floating population of 'Broken Men' who were reviled then and continued to be, and marked by their consumption of beef, which the Brahminical Hindus had given up. 'The reason why Broken Men only became Untouchables was because in addition to being Buddhists they retained their habit of beef-eating which gave additional ground for offence to the Brahmins to carry their new-found love and reverence to the cow to its logical conclusion,' Ambedkar writes.)

By the time the Constituent Assembly discussed it, the issue had already had a divisive history of more than half a century. The first 'Gaurakshini Sabha', meaning cow protection group, was formed in Punjab in 1882 by Dayanand Saraswati of the Arya Samaj. It gave middle class Hindus a chance to defend the practices of their faith, usually under the hammer from reason, by pointing out to the cow's position in the rural economy and the use of manure as fertiliser and the utility of the bullock as a draught animal.

A popular movement in UP in the late nineteenth century likened cow slaughter to matricide and pressured Muslims to stop the Id sacrifice and prevented Dalits working with hide from doing their work. Kangaroo courts fined Hindus who sold their cows and bullocks to butchers ('Sacred Symbol as Mobilizing Ideology: The North Indian Search for a "Hindu" community' by Sandria B. Freitag).[26] Parallelly, Hindus had also been legally active on this issue, trying to insert cow protection into the blasphemy law. In 1888, the high court in the North West Frontier Province ruled that a cow was not a sacred object

---

26. Can be accessed at: https://www.jstor.org/stable/178470

under Section 295 of the IPC, the blasphemy law common
to India and Pakistan, which punishes anyone who 'destroys,
damages or defiles any place of worship, or any object held sacred
by a class of persons, with the intention of thereby insulting the
religion of any class of persons...'

In 1893, many cases were filed against Hindus in Azamgarh
for attempting to prevent Id sacrifices. Rioting broke out across
the country, killing dozens. This continued in the years leading
up to Partition, and cow protection was one of the primary
reasons for communal violence in north India.

This was the background to the Constituent Assembly
debating the issue of cow protection. Coming within months
of Partition, and with the Muslims at the receiving end of
accusations of treachery and breaking up Bharat Mata, they
could hardly put up a strong fight on an emotive issue such as
this. They went along with it on an assurance that was fraudulent
and which proved in time to harm Muslims and their interests.
This, of course, was always the point of the ban.

Article 48 of India's Constitution reads: 'The State shall
endeavour to organise agriculture and animal husbandry on
modern and scientific lines and shall, in particular, take steps
for preserving and improving the breeds, and prohibiting the
slaughter, of cows and calves and other milch and draught cattle.'

India's draft constitution did not refer to this prohibition
on cow slaughter. It was introduced into the Directive Principles
by the Hindu conservatives through subterfuge: as an economic
argument. But at the same time, those pressing for a ban kept
bringing up religious sentiment and also said, hypocritically, that
they did not want to impose a cow slaughter ban on unwilling
minorities.[27]

Two members, Seth Govind Das and Pandit Thakur Das
Bhargava, both of the Congress, even wanted to introduce a

---

27. Directive Principles are not enforceable by a court, but the principles are required
to be applied in making laws to establish a just society in the country.

ban of cow slaughter as a fundamental right (giving the cow enforceable and justiciable rights) instead of merely as a Directive Principle. Even a limited ban was unsatisfactory to many in the Congress. Ram Sahai of Indore wanted total prohibition and not a conditional one. Others wanted buffaloes, bulls and other cattle of all ages to be included in the ban.

In the end, Bhargava said the cow protectionists were agreeable to dropping their demand on the ban being a fundamental right. He said, 'I do not want that due to its inclusion in the fundamental rights, non-Hindus should complain that they have been forced to accept a certain thing against their will.' He assured the minorities that 'this problem should be solved in such a manner that the objective is gained without any sort of coercion'.

Granville Austin, the historian of India's Constitution, remarked on these proceedings: 'In the days of the British Raj, many Hindu revivalists had promised themselves that with Independence cow killing would stop. Those of this persuasion in the assembly believed that the time for action was ripe and, as a result of agreement in the Congress assembly party meeting, the measure passed without opposition. No one would have quarelled with the need to modernise agriculture, but many may have found the reference to cow-killing distasteful. There is good evidence that Nehru did. Generally speaking, however, Hindu feeling ran high on the subject, and one may surmise that those who opposed the anti-cow-killing cause bent with the wind, believing the issue not sufficiently important to warrant a firm stand against it. As various provisions of the Irish Constitution show that Ireland is a Roman Catholic nation, so Article 48 shows that Hindu sentiment predominated in the Constituent Assembly'

Writing in *Frontline* ('The ban on cow slaughter', 24 June 2016) A.G. Noorani said the cow slaughter bills were a 'monumental fraud' by the champions of the bill. He referred to a letter written on 7 August 1947, just a week before Independence, the soon-to-be president Rajendra Prasad wrote a letter to Nehru. It read: 'There are two points which I had for consideration at our meeting yesterday. I mentioned the agitation which is spreading with tremendous speed about the stopping of cow slaughter, but as everybody was in a hurry to go, the matter was not considered. I have been flooded with postcards, letters, packets and telegrams making a demand that cow slaughter should be stopped by legislation ... The Hindu sentiment in favour of cow protection is old, widespread and deep-seated and it has taken no time to rouse at this moment to a pitch when it is difficult, if not impossible, to ignore it. I think that the matter does require consideration and we must take a decision whatever it is after due consideration. The Hindu feeling on account of recent happenings is very much agitated and this movement, like the movement in favour of Hindi, is bound to gain strength more rapidly than we can imagine.'

Noorani asks us to note that Prasad 'made no pretences about the "economic factor"'. It was religion alone that moved him. The sophistry was left to Thakurdas Bhargava.

When the Constituent Assembly debated the issue on 24 November 1948, Bhargava of Haryana and Govind Das from Madhya Pradesh quoted figures showing a decline in India's bovine population as a reason for the ban. They also made the claim that there was no such thing as unproductive cattle (because a cow and a bullock were a 'moving manure factory'). But why would the population decline if keeping and feeding unproductive cows and bullocks was profitable? This they did not explain and the economic argument was secondary to the religious one. In his work, Austin had observed that 'Hindus slaughtered cattle too, of course, and in vastly greater numbers than did Muslims—a fact acknowledged by Bhargava'.

Their religious arguments were clearer and more direct. Seth Govind Das said cow protection was part of Indian culture, and culture was eternal and could not be imposed on an ancient nation such as India. Meaning that cow protection was and would remain an eternal law in India. Another Congressman, Prof. Shibban Lal Saksena from Uttar Pradesh felt that something having wide cultural adoption (as a revulsion to cow slaughter did) could only have come from science and that Hinduism was mostly based on such useful principles, which aligned economics with religion. He added that banning cow slaughter was important because vegetable oil (vanaspati) used as a substitute for cow ghee was unhealthy and in fact, dangerous (suggesting that it was absence of cow ghee that had led to consumption of vegetable oil).

Dr Raghu Vira of Punjab felt that constitutional freedom of expression meant that the nation would express itself collectively and civilisationally and forbid the killing of even a single cow. He said killing a cow was as horrible as killing a Brahmin. R.V. Dhulekar of UP said a cow had a higher status than one's mother, and those who would not turn to violence at the killing of their mother would take to arms over the killing of a cow. He added that India had a civilising mission which was a Hindu mission and to propagate this globally, a ban on cow slaughter was fundamental.

Given this conflation of religion and economics by the Congress in pushing for the ban, it was incumbent that there be clarity on why cows were being protected through the Constitution. This was left to the Muslim members to bring up.

Syed Muhammad Saadaulla, former Premier of Assam and member of the Drafting Committee, said: 'Those who put it on the economic front do create a suspicion in the minds of many that the ingrained Hindu feeling against cow slaughter is being satisfied by the back door. If you put it on the economic front,

292 OUR HINDU RASHTRA

I will place before you certain facts and figures which will show that the slaughter of cows is not as bad as it is sought to be made out from the economic point of view.'

Zahir-ul-Hasan Lari from UP said the majority was free to ban cow slaughter whether for religious or economic reasons. However, India should know that Muslims sacrificed cows at Eid and even in the absence of a ban Muslims were harassed, molested and jailed for cow and bullock slaughter. 'Therefore, if the House is of the opinion that slaughter of cows should be prohibited, let it be prohibited in clear, definite and unambiguous words,' he said. It was in the interest of goodwill and cordial relations between Hindus and Muslims that if Hindus wanted a ban on cow slaughter for religious reasons, 'this is the proper occasion when the majority should express itself clearly and definitely'.

He said Muslims were aware that their faith did not necessarily require them to sacrifice the cow; it permitted it. The question was whether, given the strong religious sentiments expressed by members of the Assembly, they would continue to extend to the Muslims the permission and privilege they had at the present. It was not so much interference with religion, he said, so much as with liberty. He asked the Hindu leadership to 'here and now make it clear and not leave it to the back-benchers to come forward and deliver sermons one way or the other'.

He said he did not want to get in the way of the Hindus protecting the cow but the economic argument was weak. Modern and scientific development of agriculture necessarily meant mechanisation and not the continued use of draught animals. His plea was not heard and the amendment was adopted.

Noorani wrote that 'the amendment had plain sailing, but only after (Bhargava's) vital assurance: "without using any sort of coercion". It was on the faith of this explicit assurance that the Constituent Assembly adopted the double-faced provision.'

Within months, states began legislating laws that made cow slaughter a crime. This was the coercion Noorani is referring to.*

West Bengal's Animal Slaughter Control Act of 1950 forbids the slaughter of cows under fourteen years of age. Exemption allowing slaughter of younger animals is made for religious, medicinal or research reasons. Punishment for violations is imprisonment up to six months and a fine of up to Rs 1,000.

The Assam Cattle Preservation Act of 1951 forbids the slaughter of cows unless they are fourteen years or older and judged by a bureaucrat to be unfit for work or breeding. It also allows slaughter of any cattle during the Id-ul-Zuha festival on 'such conditions as the state government may specify regarding privacy'. The State may allow slaughter for religious or ceremonial reasons. Punishment for violation is imprisonment for up to six months.

The Bihar Preservation and Improvement of Animals Act of 1955 forbids cow slaughter but allows the slaughter of bull and bullocks over twenty-five years of age. Female buffaloes which are both over twenty-five as well as incapable of giving milk or breeding also qualify. The law specifically allows the slaughter of bulls over three years of age 'dedicated in good faith to a religious purpose in accordance with any religious usage or custom'. The law bans the transport out of Bihar of cattle for any reason. It protects animals other than bovine, including horses, elephants and dogs. Punishment is imprisonment up to six months and a fine of up to Rs 1,000.

Punjab's Prohibition of Cow Slaughter Act of 1955 forbids the slaughter of all cow progeny and also bans the sale of beef. There is no reference to buffaloes in the law. Punishment for violations is jail up to two years and a fine of up to Rs 1,000.

---

*What follows over the next six pages is the sequence and progression of how Indian states began criminalising cow slaughter. Readers uninterested in the details can skip to page 299.

Tamil Nadu's Animal Preservation Act of 1958 bans the slaughter of cows and buffaloes under ten years of age, and if they are unfit for breeding or injured, diseased or deformed. Imprisonment is also up to six months for violation, like the Andhra and Karnataka acts.

The Orissa Prevention of Cow Slaughter Act of 1960 bans cow slaughter but allows slaughter of bulls and bullocks over fourteen years of age. Punishment for violations is imprisonment up to two years and a fine of Rs 1000.

Karnataka's Prevention of Cow Slaughter and Cattle Preservation Act of 1964 forbids cow slaughter but allows slaughter of bulls and buffaloes over twelve years of age or if they have become permanently deformed. Punishment for violations is up to six months in jail. Two attempts were made under BJP governments in 2010 and 2012 to introduce a harsher law more aligned to those in other BJP states in the north and seeking a total ban on slaughter but these were withdrawn in 2013. In 2020, a third attempt was made to bring about a change in law (*Frontline*, 'Farmers and Dalit organisations oppose Karnataka government's plan to bring Bill banning cow slaughter', 25 September 2020). The bill includes a ban on consumption of beef and increases the punishment to seven years.

Pondicherry's Prevention of Cow Slaughter Act of 1968 forbids cow slaughter but allows the slaughter of bulls over fifteen years of age or younger ones that have become unfit for breeding or draught. It also prohibits the sale of beef. The punishment is imprisonment up to two years. There is no reference to buffaloes.

The Andhra Pradesh Prohibition of Cow Slaughter and Animal Preservation Act 1977 allows the slaughter of male and adult female buffaloes and older bulls. It prohibits the slaughter of all cows and calves whether male or female and she buffalo calves.

The law forbids farmers from giving their animals for slaughter. Those buffaloes and older bulls which do qualify, would need a 'fit for slaughter certificate'. In case it is felt by the bureaucrat that the the animal was 'likely to become economical' by way of breeding, then the certificate would not be given. The law gives the government the power to enter and inspect any premises where an offence is suspected to have been committed. The penalty was six months in jail and a fine. A separate law dating to 1950 prohibits the sacrifice of animals and birds.

The Goa, Daman and Diu Prevention of Cow Slaughter Act 1978 bans cow slaughter totally without exceptions. However, the Goa Animal Preservation Act of 1995 allows the slaughter of bullocks and buffaloes certified as being uneconomical (no age is mentioned of the animal in the law) after the state set up a single abattoir. Punishment is up to two years in jail in the 1978 law and three years in the 1995 law. The Goa Animal Preservation Act of 2010 also forbids the sale of beef except when it is from another state and has been inspected and certified.

The Himachal Pradesh Prohibition of Cow Slaughter Act of 1979 was enacted under the Jana Sangh/Janata Party coalition government and bans all slaughter of any cow, whether young or old, just as the other states in the north and forbids the sale of beef. Punishment is imprisonment for up to five years. In 2010, the law was amended to ban the transport of cows outside the state. The law makes no reference to buffaloes.

The Delhi Agricultural Cattle Preservation Act of 1994 has an absolute ban on slaughter of cows of all ages, even if old. Its schedule of 'agricultural cattle' lists cows and calves of all ages, bulls and bullocks, but excludes bullocks. Passed by the BJP, the law reverses burden of proof and says, 'The burden of proving that the slaughter, transport, export, sale, purchase or possession of flesh ... shall be on the accused.' The law bans the possession of beef, including of animals slaughtered outside Delhi, with a punishment of one year in jail. There is no reference to buffaloes and they are allowed to be slaughtered.

Rajasthan's 'Govanshiya Pashu Vadh Ka Pratished Aur Asthayee Pravrajan Ya Niryat Ka Viniyaman Adhiniyam' or the Rajasthan Bovine Animal (Prohibition of slaughter and regulation of temporary migration or export) Act 1995 was passed under the BJP. It bans all slaughter absolutely notwithstanding custom and prohibits the possession and sale of beef. Transporters are liable as abettors and the burden of proof is on the accused. Punishment is imprisonment for up to ten years, and seven years if an animal is injured. The law makes no reference to buffaloes.

Maharashtra's Animal Preservation Act of 1954 (for Bombay State) originally allowed slaughter of all bulls and bullocks over fifteen years of age, and all bulls and bullocks of any age for religious reasons. It also allowed slaughter of those animals which were certified as not being useful for breeding, production of milk or draught. Imprisonment for violations was up to six months.

The law was amended in 1995 under the BJP-Shiv Sena government to include bulls and bullocks in a total ban. The law was only given approval by President Pranab Mukherjee under the BJP government in 2015. Punishment was imprisonment up to five years and possession of beef, including that from outside Maharashtra, was also criminalised. Burden of proof was on the accused. In 2017, Bombay High Court held the criminalisation of possession and reversal of burden of proof in the law to be unconstitutional.

The Uttar Pradesh Prevention of Cow Slaughter Act of 1955 was amended in 1979 and 2002. It prohibits all cow slaughter and also the sale and transfer of beef. In June 2020, the BJP government passed an ordinance increasing imprisonment up to ten years and a fine of Rs 5 lakh. The driver, operator and owner of the vehicle carrying animals suspected of being taken for slaughter would be charged unless they could prove their innocence. Expenditure incurred on maintaining seized cows would be taken from the vehicle owner. The Cabinet note approving the law said it 'will help it realise the dream of white revolution and promote agriculture in the cities and rural areas'. The law makes no reference to buffaloes.

Chhattisgarh's Agricultural Cattle Preservation Act of 2004 enforces a total ban on slaughter of all cattle whether young or old, whether cow or buffalo. It says the vehicle in which cattle is transported 'shall be seized and not released at least six months from the date of seizure or till the final judgment of the court (whichever is earlier)' if the State suspects the cattle are being taken for slaughter. The cattle will also be confiscated.

Like in Delhi, this law says that the burden of proof was on the accused, who would have to prove to the State's satisfaction that transport, slaughter or sale was not in contravention of the law. The law also penalises the possession of beef. It requires cattle traders to register themselves. The form for permission to transport cattle requires individuals to reveal their father's name and their caste. The law was amended in 2011, increasing punishment to seven years in jail, up from three years in 2004 and increasing the fine five times to Rs 50,000.

Jharkhand's Bovine Animal Prohibition of Slaughter Act was legislated by the BJP in 2005. It has an absolute ban on the slaughter of cows with punishment of jail upto ten years. The sale and possession of beef is also a crime with a minimum of one year in jail and a maximum of ten years. There is no reference to buffaloes in the Act.

Uttarakhand's Protection of Cow Progeny Act of 2007 was passed by the BJP within weeks of taking power that year. It has an absolute ban on cow slaughter. Possession of beef is also criminalised. The law requires all cows to be registered with the government. Punishment is up to ten years in jail. There is no reference to buffaloes.

The Madhya Pradesh Govansh Vadh Pratishedh (Sanshodhan) Adhiniyam 2010 has a total ban on cow slaughter. The law says it is an act 'to maintain communal harmony and peace' as well as 'for preservation and conservation of cow progeny'. Jail for possession and transport of cattle is up to three years and for slaughter is up to seven years. The 2010 law amended a 2004 law, raising punishment for slaughter up from three years. Again, it reverses the burden of proof and it is up to the accused to prove himself innocent. The law makes no reference to buffaloes.

Gujarat's Animal Preservation Act has been amended several times to ban cow slaughter absolutely without exception. In 2011, the Modi government changed the law to forbid the sale, display, transport, storing and purchase of beef or beef products. Buying beef is a criminal offence attracting three years in jail. Possession and storage of beef gets up to ten years in jail with a minimum of seven years.

In 2017 the law was amended again, increasing the penalty for cow slaughter to life imprisonment. Transportation of cows is allowed only between 7 a.m. and 5 p.m. Illegal transportation attracts up to seven years in jail. Vehicles found in violation and seized would remain permanently confiscated. There is no reference to buffaloes in the law, and they are allowed to be slaughtered.

Haryana's Gauvansh Sanrakshan and Gausamvardhan Act of 2015 has a total ban on all slaughter of cows including those that are 'disabled, diseased or barren'. It says even 'the removal of skin and hide from dead cows other than slaughtered cows by authorised person is not cow slaughter' only if 'authorisation from competent authority has been taken'. Punishment is jail up to ten years. The law makes no reference to buffaloes.

Sikkim's Prevention of Cow Slaughter Act was passed in 2017 by the BJP led North East Democratic Alliance. It allows the slaughter of all bulls and bullocks and protects only cows and their female progeny. Punishment for violation is jail up to five years.

The chronology of the various pieces of state legislation shows that cow protection laws have become harsher in India over time. And the meaning of the laws have taken them farther and farther away from the reason cited in Article 48.

The southern states (excepting Pondicherry) all have laws that allow slaughter of animals. Overall the southern states can be identified as being the ones that allow slaughter, allow transport of cows and bullocks, inflict less punishment for illegal slaughter, do not have prohibition (Pondicherry is the exception) on the sale of beef, do not reverse burden of proof from the state to the accused, and include buffaloes in their laws. They also do not have traditional and quasi religious names for their laws as do some of the states in the north, like Madhya Pradesh and Rajasthan.

Kerala has no ban on slaughter, along with Arunachal Pradesh, Manipur, Meghalaya, Nagaland and Mizoram.

It is the northern states, as the names of those individuals who participated in the Constituent Assembly debate on this issue also show, that are particularly agitated over the issue.

It will be noticed that Madhya Pradesh, Chhattisgarh, Gujarat, Himachal Pradesh, Jharkhand, Uttarakhand, Odisha, Rajasthan, Uttar Pradesh and Haryana are also on the list of those who have or are about to pass anti-conversion laws.

It is no exaggeration to say that today nobody fully understands India's cow slaughter laws. There is confusion arising from a full ban in some states to no ban in some and partial bans in others. There are bans on beef eating in some states, but not in other states. There are bans on the slaughter of some species of bovine but not others, on some cattle of a particular age, but not others, on some cattle of a particular gender but not the rest. There are bans on beef possession in some states and no clarity on this in other states, and bans on transport in some places, regulations on time and temperature and carrying conditions elsewhere. There is little logic or coherence to any of it.

The Congress, as in the case of Punjab and elsewhere, initiated the process of total bans on cow slaughter in the north but it was under the BJP that the laws have become unhinged. The desire to punish has become deranged and the laws exist primarily to victimise and brutalise Muslims, the majority of those in the butchery trade. Uttar Pradesh liberally uses the anti-terror National Security Act on Muslims for cow slaughter ('In Uttar Pradesh, more than half of NSA arrests this year were for cow slaughter', *Indian Express*, 11 September 2020) because the preventive detention law allows it to jail people without trial or formal charge. Gujarat's life imprisonment for cow slaughter passes no test of reasonableness.

Even for murder and rape the burden of proof is on the State. Innocent until proven guilty is a fundamental principle of justice. India has reversed it here. The penalty in states like Gujarat, where the offence attracts life imprisonment and a minimum of ten years with a fine of Rs 5 lakh, shows that the intent of the law is not economic. No white collar crime in India attracts life imprisonment.

And the state is keen to use these laws. The *Indian Express* reported ('Gujarat man gets 10 year jail term for cow slaughter', 7 July 2019) that a man accused on 29 January by his neighbour of stealing his calf and slaughtering it to serve at his daughter's wedding was tried and convicted not for theft but for cow slaughter. The prosecution had no evidence to show that this had happened and the Forensic Science Laboratory at Rajkot couldn't even prove that the meat served at the wedding meal was in fact beef.

However 'in such a scenario', Sessions Court judge Hemantkumar Dave noted, 'It is incumbent upon the accused to prove that the meat found in the biryani was not obtained by slaughtering the said calf.' This was the reversal of burden of proof in the law under which the man was jailed for ten years. On 19 September, the sentence was suspended by an embarrassed Gujarat High Court with the judge using 'judicial discretion' and the man was ordered to be freed. The government said it would appeal.

All the laws make the pretence of preserving cows, bullocks and buffaloes for economic reasons. There is no reference to religion though the reason is evident from the language used to promote them and the violence they generate.

Under the BJP and Modi especially, the laws can be said to have fully revealed the fiction that they are aimed at 'organisation of agriculture and animal husbandry' as Article 48 seeks to achieve.

There is no relationship between milk production and cow slaughter. The world's largest producer of cow milk, the United States with 97 million tons a year, also slaughters the most cows, over 32 million each year.

According to the National Dairy Development Board, India produces 176 million tons of milk but of that about 100 million tons is buffalo milk compared to 76 million tons of cow milk a year. This is because buffalo milk contains twice the fat of cow milk and is therefore more valuable.

But Article 48 does not seem to apply to the buffalo and India slaughters four times as many buffaloes as it does bullocks and cows, according to the Modi government's report on animal husbandry statistics of 2019.

There is no protection for the beast even in Gujarat, which has more buffaloes than cows because they are more productive. The laws written by the BJP in Madhya Pradesh, Rajasthan, Haryana, Jharkhand, Uttarakhand and Delhi exclude buffaloes though the intent of the constitutional directive and presumably, the laws, is the preservation of cattle for promotion of animal husbandry and production of milk. And most of India's buffaloes are in the Hindi heartland. Writer Kancha Ilaiah has said that this is because of the inherent bigotry of Hindutva. It doesn't like the buffalo, though it is more useful than the cow, because it is black. It also shows that the economic argument is a lie.

Bulls and bullocks are commonly regarded as being useless for anything other than work as draught animals, meaning those bearing loads. That is why the laws initially exempted them from protection. Today, these animals are a burden on the agriculturalist. They have to be housed and fed but offer the farmer no income or useful productive capacity.

In 1951, India had a total of 8500 tractors. In 2019 alone India produced 878,000 tractors. There are millions of tractors across the country today and no economic need to have criminal laws to protect animals who do draught work. Between 1971-72 and 2009-10, the estimated share of draught animals in total power deployed in Indian farms fell from 53 per cent to below nine per cent, according to writer Harish Damodaran, and its share has fallen significantly further in the decade since.

Article 48 wants the State to 'organise agriculture and animal husbandry on modern and scientific lines' and to 'take steps for preserving and improving the breeds.' Even if we assume that the intent was not Hindu sentiment but scientific, that was a time when there was no breeding possible without bulls. Today, breeding is selective and scientific.

Writing in the *Indian Express* ('In thrall to the holy cow', 6 April 2018) Damodaran pointed out that artificial insemination began in India in 1946. In 2016-17 more than 7 crore artificial inseminations were performed, more than a quarter of all cows and buffaloes. The national plan for dairy development proposes to raise that that to 65 per cent by 2021-22.

The use of manure as fertiliser was also one of the reasons cited in the debates. In 1959, India began production of urea. India today produces 25 million tons of fertiliser. Also, Damodaran writes, 'Thanks to the Pradhan Mantri Ujjwala Yojana, there were 21 crore active domestic LPG connections as on 1 January 2018, corresponding to an estimated coverage of 79 per cent. That has made dung cakes practically redundant as a source of cooking fuel even in rural India.'

One of the arguments pushed in the Constituent Assembly for the ban on cow slaughter was that milk was vital for the health of the nation. Thakur Das Bhargava said that the reason for India's high infant mortality rate was a lack of milk. 'How can you improve your health and food position, if you do not produce full quota of cereals and milk?' he asked. India produces more than its full quota of milk. In 2018-19, India's dairy exports rose 126 per cent to 1.2 lakh tons, according to the Ministry of Animal Husbandry, Dairying and Fisheries.

The concern for the wellbeing of cows is the reason for the laws, but the fact is that cows are among the most ill-treated of all animals. Bullocks are castrated to make them docile. There are over 14 million of them (1.4 crore) dragging carts across India, a report in *Down To Earth* in June 2015 said.

In his work *Sapiens*, Yuvan Noah Harari said of draught animals that their life is 'completely alien to their urges and desires. It's reasonable to assume, for example, that bulls prefer to spend their days wandering over open prairies in the company of other bulls and cows rather than pulling carts and ploughshares.'

Milk, butter and ghee are part of religious ritual in India but the production of milk is one of the cruellest things man does to animals. Harari writes that the milk producing cow is almost constantly pregnant and fertilised within two and three months of giving birth in order to maximise milk production. Calves are kept near their mothers, but prevented from suckling too much milk. 'The simplest way to do that is to allow the kid or calf to start suckling, but drive it away once the milk starts flowing.

This method usually encounters resistance from both kid and mother,' Harari writes.

The *Hindu Businessline* ('FIAPO report on dairy industry leaves a bad taste in the mouth', 27 October 2017) carried a story on the Federation of Indian Animal Protection Organisations describing conditions in India on this. It found that 'cattle are separated from calves (male calves died within the first week in 25 per cent of dairies surveyed) and receive little to no veterinary care'.

Dead calves were stuffed with hay, a system known in India as khalbaccha: 'Because of strong maternal bonds, the mother often stops lactating if the calf has died. Hence a khalbaccha is routinely used to mimic the presence of a calf and continue milking,' the report said.

The cows 'spend their lives in cramped, poorly ventilated and dark enclosures in more than one quarter of the dairies, where injuries from slipping in their own excreta are a common occurrence; 64 per cent of the dairies had ill, injured and distressed cattle,' the report said.

There is no attention paid to the concerns of the cow being abused in this fashion among cow lovers in India. Their passion for Article 48 shows itself mostly in violence against Muslims.

A 2018 report by the Centre for Justice and Peace (CJP) said that a specific part of the state laws was being weaponised by Hindutva groups. Many included text like this one from the law in Karnataka: 'Appointment of competent authority: The Government may, by notification, appoint a person or a body of persons to perform the functions of a competent authority under this Act for such local area as may be specified in such notification.'

The CJP report said the laws 'empower private parties, to help enforce the State's draconian cattle laws. Similar is the case for Maharashtra and Gujarat. And Haryana Gau Seva Ayog, established to oversee implementation of cow protection laws in the state, has members that run cow vigilante groups, with several accusations of vigilante attacks.'

Across India, gau raksha samitis have been formed which act as quasi-official bodies. *Hindustan Times* reported ('In Jharkhand, a "Hindu helpline" to check beef sale, cow slaughter', 2 November 2015) of the setting up of one such group by Hindutva groups. 'We will have to go out on the ground and stop the illegal slaughter since the police are not serious about the issue,' one of them told the newspaper.

The Supreme Court has lapsed quite easily into Hindu majoritarianism on the issue of cow protection. It first heard the case in 1958 when butchers and hide merchants from Bihar challenged the initial laws prohibiting cow slaughter. The butchers said their Fundamental Right under Article 19 was being violated. Article 19(1)(g) reads: 'All citizens shall have the right to practice any profession, or to carry out any occupation, trade or business.'

Thakur Das Bhargava, who had spoken of no coercion and of making a compromise on the cow having Fundamental Rights, joined the litigation and now told the court that the Directive Principles regarding the cow were superior to the fundamental rights of Indians. The court had to decide whether the fundamental rights could be curtailed by the qualifying 'reasonable restriction' on it which said that the State could make any curtailing law that was in the interests of the general public.

The court concluded that India was short of milch cattle, breeding bulls and working bullocks, which needed protection. And so a total ban on the slaughter of cows of all ages and calves of cows and calves of buffaloes was declared valid. A total ban on the slaughter of productive she-buffaloes or breeding bulls or working bullocks was also valid. But 'the total ban on slaughter of she-buffaloes, bulls and bullocks after they cease to be capable of yielding milk or of breeding or working as draught animals cannot be supported as reasonable in the interest of the general public'.

Note the distinction that the Supreme Court made between cows that stopped being productive and buffaloes. The judgment specifically admits that it had taken Hindu sentiment into consideration when arriving at the reasonableness of the restrictions.

Chief Justice Sudhi Ranjan Das said: 'There can be no gainsaying the fact that the Hindus in general hold the cow in great reverence and the idea of the slaughter of cows for food is repugnant to their notions and this sentiment has in the past even led to communal riots. It is also a fact that after the recent partition of the country this agitation against the slaughter of cows has been further intensified. While we agree that the constitutional question before us cannot be decided on grounds of mere sentiment, however passionate it may be, we, nevertheless, think that it has to be taken into consideration, though only as one of many elements, in arriving at a judicial verdict as to the reasonableness of the restrictions.'

Till 2005, the Indian courts had held that a total ban on the slaughter of bulls and bullocks for their entire lives was an unreasonable restriction on the fundamental rights of butchers. In 2005, the Supreme Court said Gujarat's total ban on all cows and all their progeny including bullocks of all ages was reasonable. The judges found that bullock dung and urine was useful, environmentally friendly and a ban on slaughter was an act of compassion. In this fashion, the Supreme Court lent its voice to the tenuous claim made in the Constituent Assembly that the ban was for reasons other than Hindu sentiment.

What has happened in India in the time of Modi is predictable and a natural consequence of the decades-old Hindu sentiment on cow slaughter pretending to be a secular principle. Modi pushed for harder cow slaughter laws in 2014 after taking power and BJP governments in Maharashtra and Haryana responded. The fervour generated began a spate of lynchings which targeted Muslims some of whose murders were even recorded on phones by onlookers.

The Muslims in the Constituent Assembly had asked the Hindus to go ahead with a full ban honestly, and had said that they would accept it, but this offer was waved away with the assurance that there would be no coercion. It would have been better had the Hindu conservatives been honest and straightforward about their reasons for the pushing for the ban. Their subterfuge has harmed India and its citizens and damaged its reputation as a nation founded on modern, secular principles.

14

HOW TO FIGHT IT

'The arc of the moral universe is long, but it bends towards justice.' (Dr Martin Luther King Jr)

This is a beautiful line of course, made more attractive by the truth that it carries.

The trajectory of humanity is towards more equality, more freedom, greater individual liberty, less discrimination if we observe the history of our times and of the times immediately before ours.

In the half century between us and Dr King, who was killed in 1968, we have made progress on such things as the rights of women over their bodies, on the rights of people to love whom they want and marry whom they want, the softening and lifting in the United States of laws and practices intended to harass and humiliate African Americans, the abolition across most of the world of the death penalty, the recognition of the problems of state-inflicted torture and many other things that were as problematic and as obvious in the 1960s and the times before that, but left unaddressed.

In the century before Dr King, the world witnessed the abolition of slavery, the ending of colonialism, the signing up by nations to the Universal Declaration of Human Rights, and also the development of an international framework that has made war between nations less likely. If we seem to despair much more than exult at what we see happening around us and fear things are in general decline, it is because progress disappoints in the short run, but surprises in the long run.

If we were to think of things that have gone the other way and seen deterioration, it is not easy to list those that are not specific to a few nations. There has been extreme violence visited on some populations, and genocide which has gone unpunished. There are many parts of the world where representative democracy is not practised, and many where even the limited victories referred to above have either not come or not come fully. New problems of inequality and abuse linked to economic, social and cultural rights have also come to light.

The arc of justice does not bend itself: it is through work, diligence and intelligent intervention that rights have come to large parts of the human race, and that trajectory is visible to us.

In India, as elsewhere, the locus of justice and individual liberties and equality is in three places: in the Constitution, in government, and in laws and policies. The reality in India, which is in many ways unique to us, is that we do not have a problematic Constitution even though we have a deeply unequal society. This is something that other nations around us cannot say. Pakistan has a problem with its Constitution that must be addressed at some point if they are to make progress in meaningful fashion. A nation that constitutionally places the status of its minorities at a lower rank in terms of political equality, social equality and religious equality will need legislative correction. The fact is that this is not required in India.

There remain however at least three issues in the Indian Constitution that do require addressing and have become the points of contention because they violate our basic principle of secularism and also that of fundamental liberties.

Two of them, on cow slaughter and prohibition, are in the Directive Principles and not enforceable. Cow slaughter is in any case prohibited by many states at the level of the province. But there are states, especially in the Northeast, where it is permitted because it is a local custom unrelated to religion.

The lack of sufficient slaughterhouses of industrial scale in India, the caste-based occupation of butchery (in the hands, because of their caste, mostly of certain Muslim communities) and the ghettoisation and segregation of Muslims around India has also meant that the slaughter and sale has more or less continued without regulation and without being touched by the law even in some states where there is a ban. The fiction in the Constitution, that Article 48 seeks a ban on cow slaughter to organise agriculture and animal husbandry on modern and scientific lines needs to be accepted and addressed meaningfully. At this point that can only be done by the judiciary. A nation cannot allow Directive Principles to encroach on the justiciable rights of individuals, including the right to livelihood, to freedom of religion, and the right under Article 19 to carry out any profession, any trade and any occupation. The Directive Principles are vague statements often observed in the breach.

How seriously do we take for instance Article 39, directing the State to ensure that the operation of the economic system does not result in the concentration of wealth? Or Article 42, asking the State to secure just and humane conditions of work in a nation where hundreds of Dalits die cleaning gutters?

What about Article 51 which says the State will 'encourage settlement of international disputes by arbitration'? From Nehru down, we have done exactly the opposite and discouraged and resisted the settlement of our international disputes through arbitration. It should not be difficult to decriminalise the laws against slaughter and beef consumption.

Prohibition is not a communal issue and the states that have dabbled in it have done so as much for general social reasons as moral ones. And they usually tend to succumb and lift it in time because of the economic implications that B.H. Khardekar, the only Constituent Assembly member to push back against prohibition warned of. The large numbers of India's poor mean that unlawful distillation happens even in states not under prohibition. Prohibition remains in the Constitution as a relic of an upper caste Hindu moralism on this issue that no longer exists in society.

The third issue is more problematic because it is in the fundamental rights (Article 22). It says no person can be detained except through due process, which includes access to a lawyer and production before a magistrate. The reality is that this is observed in the breach and there are few rights for an accused who in India is no different from a convict.

However, dangerously, even these safeguards do not constitutionally apply for those held in preventive detention. The State has, and makes full use of, a terrible power to hold anyone without crime, charge or trial. This power has been used disproportionally against minorities in particular but the underprivileged and marginalised generally. India cannot transition to being the sort of modern progressive democracy that surely most of us want it to be without eliminating the sort of absolute power that Article 22 gives the State.

Elsewhere, reservations for Muslims who are backward was introduced through the Mandal Commission and, while it has not been as beneficial to them and it needs to be expanded significantly, it exists in law. Freedom of religion, curbed severely through the restrictions we have seen in the Chapter 8, can be regained through legal challenge in those states where it has been eroded. The route to rolling it back exists, through an emphasis on the fundamental rights and a de-emphasis on the State's regulations and restrictions. In general, then, we can conclude that on the side of the Constitution, what has to be defended and safeguarded in India, unlike in some of its neighbours, is the existing basic structure. If there is a remaining hurdle, such as Article 22, it can be addressed through this basic structure.

The second place where justice and equality need to be preserved is in government. Indian history has shown that while injustice and discrimination and even violence have been a constant feature in the past, it has been the case that the government at least pretends to take an inclusive position. This has changed since 2014. The language of the government of India is officially majoritarian.

The Hindutva project and the BJP are inseparable from bigotry. As we have seen in the chapters on their garbled texts and party history, their only consistent and true ideology is their hatred of other Indians. Their presence in government means that their hostility to minorities and pluralism will continue to be expressed visibly, vocally and through their prejudices.

What they have introduced into the polity will only be removed when they leave. It can only be addressed and corrected meaningfully when they are not in office. The way to do that is naturally through the vote.

Thus far, it has not be easy to put together coalitions that oppose the BJP for the threat that it poses. It has been easier to stitch together something that is less fundamental and more opportunistic. The caste-based parties of Uttar Pradesh, led by the Yadav family and Mayawati, coming together for the general election in 2019 appeared to be an indication of a union that was fundamental but turned out to be one that was opportunistic, breaking up immediately on news of their defeat.

In previous times, it used to be the Communist bloc that proposed an anti-BJP union of so-called secular parties, but its slide, apparently permanent, in popularity, has more or less removed this ideological bulwark.

There is limited scope for voters to urge parties to unite against majoritarianism, because the undeniable fact is that our problems are not limited to mischief and division purely on matters of religion. Poverty, inequality, justice, education, opportunity, safety, healthcare, and access to all manner of things provided by the State and many such things weigh as much on the minds of voters as do the danger of majoritarianism. And it is not the case that the parties that are cognisant of the BJP's danger to Indian society have articulated a meaningful departure and demonstrated competence on these things.

The first-past-the-post system, a fragmented society that usually votes in tribal fashion, and the competence of the BJP at attracting people towards it have made the vote of the secularist less effective. The BJP is also the only party with a nationwide grassroots presence at the level of the neighbourhood. It can convert into voters more effectively the people that it attracts, and it has the ability in the present times to attract more people towards it.

So the vote is one instrument of democratic pushback against the BJP but it is not the only one and it is often not the most effective one. One has to reckon with the BJP in office. This brings us to the third way in which injustice and inequality show themselves: through laws and policies.

To understand how to push back against these, let us examine what democratic tools are available to the individuals and groups that stand against bigotry and discrimination. Two are the justice system and activism.

One of the more visible effects of the rise of Hindutva has been how easily the justice system has succumbed to an overt majoritarianism. India's judiciary has never been of the quality expected of a major liberal democracy. The chapters on religious freedom, Kashmir, cow slaughter and the Hindutva judgments demonstrate this. Our Constitution makes lofty promises which the State cannot fulfil for various reasons, but more damagingly, it is often the case that the court either ignores or encourages the deliberate damage Hindutva does.

The condoning of the capture of absolute power by individuals and using the Constitution as a prophylactic has been done elsewhere in our parts. Pakistan's judges thought up a 'doctrine of necessity' to justify the taking over by the army of government. India's judiciary once professed such unshakeable faith in a former prime minister, that they allowed her to suspend habeas corpus. Under this current prime minister, equally charismatic, the judiciary has again undermined the importance of habeas corpus to the extent that it is all but suspended. In hundreds of thousands of incidents, preventive detention has been allowed across India over the decades. All states continue to have laws that let bureaucrats, policemen and politicians determine which citizen can be picked up and locked up without having committed a crime.

Judgments have been sent down that have permanently scarred India's society and its standing in the world such as the one in 2019 that handed over the site of the Babri Masjid to those who vandalised it. And yet the law and the legal system exist and for that reason must be approached. One's faith in the justice system and in the judiciary can be low, and certainly one has been given sufficient reason in the recent past to justify a lack of faith. But other than the expectation of justice, the court is also a forum for the presentation of the case. At a time when this has become difficult to do in the media, it is necessary and important that the courts be approached, even if this is done with scepticism.

And so onto activism, that part of democratic politics that is rarely practised. In India, we have had civic activism written into our democratic history. India's freedom was the climax of a four-decade agitation that introduced methods and tactics and a grand strategy that was applauded and emulated globally, including by Dr King. It involved non-violent protest and mass mobilisation around innovative actions.

The achievement of freedom did not end activism in India but the scale became smaller from then on: either regional, for instance in the agitations demanding linguistic states, or even community-based, as was the case for the demand in the late 1980s for reservations for backward classes. On occasion when it was national, such as in 1975, it was led by political parties and not by civil society.

It should be acknowledged that one of the most successful and largest agitations was the one that led to the demolition of the Babri Masjid. The Hindutva force was able to mobilise hundreds of thousands of people, many of them on the street, to support its demand of vandalism. But it should also be acknowledged that mobilisation on the basis of religion and often against other religions is relatively easy on the subcontinent. Similar mass movements against minorities similar to the anti-Babri campaign have been seen elsewhere in our geographical neighbourhood.

The State in India is seen as soft, meaning it is unable to monopolise the use of force and often succumbs to pressure on the street. Capacity is low, and the tools available to control the population limited. The recourse to lethal violence by the State against citizens, usually a means of last resort in democratic nations, is frequent here for this reason of lack of State capacity and the agitators know it. One way that is all but guaranteed to bring engagement with the State if not outright capitulation is to have numbers on the street.

Large-scale peaceful agitation is necessary to get the State in India to be interested even in talking to its citizens, which it can otherwise ignore. Even large agitations that are not physical, meaning conducted online or through letters, can be and are usually ignored by the State.

The production of evidence is not a requisite as it might be in another democracy. A manifest and public violation of law by the State and its officers does not produce immediate remedial and corrective action. The State is the primary violator of the Constitution and the law in India. More crimes are committed by the State and its agents than by the citizenry. Such a State must often be goaded and pushed and pressured peacefully into doing the right thing by law.

The way in which this can be done best is through targeted activism. This is a craft which must be learned and deployed in the right fashion. It is not something that is taught in civics courses in our schools but it should be. The effective, peaceful and meaningful engagement of the citizen and of groups of citizens with the State is what makes and keeps democracies vibrant. Civic activism is a democratic engagement, as deep as, and it could be argued even deeper than, voting.

The most visible and the most effective recent illustration of such activism is fortunately one of recent times. It is the movement against the change in citizenship laws, known as 'No CAA No NPR No NRC', addressing the Citizenship Amendment Act, the National Population Register and the National Register of Citizens. It is a beacon and a shining light.

Let us look at activism and how it works through the example of this movement, which succeeded in getting the Modi government to back off from a plan that it had promised to implement several times. In this, it has been unique, and particularly so, because its success was achieved by the community that Modi despises. If they can prevail against discrimination and bullying, with fewer tools and almost no sympathy from their fellow Indians, it offers the rest of us a model and a pathway. Their campaign must be studied, understood and emulated.

A campaign is a means to achieve change. Usually, this is a change that is hard to achieve. Say it is a law or a policy that needs to be reversed by getting the State to withdraw it. The opposition to withdrawal, because it will come from the authority in power, is many times more powerful than the campaigners.

That is actually why activism gives it the military term 'campaign', which evokes heroic Caesarian or Napoleonic imagery. And this is not for romantic reasons. A civic campaign usually requires the sort of planning and effort and often even the scale that a military campaign does.

The 'No CAA No NPR No NRC' protest became a campaign even though it was not planned as one when it began. It took on the meaning and nature of a full campaign by the time only four weeks or so had gone by because so many people joined in, from so many parts of the world, that they added and kept adding to the elements that built it from a protest to a full campaign. And its success can be measured by the fact that by the time it paused itself, it was the government which was forced to say it would not take the next step that it had wanted to before the protests began.

A background to the issue may be appropriate here. The root of the problem lay in Assam, where the Congress under Rajiv Gandhi over three decades ago had promised the eviction of refugees who came into the state before the Bangladesh War (1971). How would these individuals be identified? Where would those marked as being foreign then go or be sent, given the absence of treaties with neighbouring nations? This was not given much thought, and having signed the treaty, the issue was then put in cold storage.

In 1998, the governor of Assam, a retired military man named S.K. Sinha, sent a note to the president of India where he referred to the situation in alarming language: 'Large-scale illegal migration from East Pakistan/Bangladesh over several decades has been altering the demographic complexion of this state. It poses a grave threat both to the identity of the Assamese people and to our national security. Successive governments at the Centre and in the state have not adequately met this challenge.'

The governor demanded action 'to avert the grave danger that has been building up for some time ... If not effectively checked, (Bangladeshis) may swamp the Assamese people and may sever the Northeast land mass from the rest of India. This will lead to disastrous strategic and economic results.'

The governor acknowledged that he was not basing this assessment on any data. He added: 'Unfortunately, today we have no census report on the basis of which we can accurately define the contours of trans-border movement. Thus, we have to rely on broad estimates of theatrical extrapolations to work out the dimension of illegal migration that has taken place from East Pakistan/ Bangladesh.' In short, he had no evidence to prove this theory but he felt strongly enough about it just the same to raise it with the president officially.

In 2005, Sarbananda Sonowal, who later became the BJP chief minister of Assam, went to the Supreme Court to make the laws governing the identification of individuals suspected to be foreigners harsher. The Supreme Court leaned on S.K. Sinha's note in this case to conclude that Assam was facing 'external aggression' which threatened a constitutional breakdown. This was reckless and unwarranted use of extremist language that reflected the prejudices and bigotry existing against Muslims which exist even in India's highest court.

The judiciary reversed the burden of proof for the residents of Assam, a regular feature it condones as we have seen before. Normally, it is the state that must prove wrongdoing or criminal activity and it must provide the evidence that someone must be punished. This is the meaning of the term 'innocent till proven guilty'.

However the onus of proving they were not foreigners (and for those born after 1971, that their parents or grandparents were not foreigners) was thrust by the judiciary onto the Assamese. They were all guilty until they could prove themselves innocent.

In a nation where many, if not most, are poor and many, if not most, are not fully literate, where documentation is weak, and in a state where flooding is not rare and the total loss of property quite common, this reversal of the burden of proof on such an important matter was cruelty. The other thing that the state did was to have almost no safeguards.

The foreigners' tribunals which would determine whether someone should be set free or sent to a jail, were staffed by people given four days of training. They were advocates and retired civil servants hired on two-year contracts.

It was before such people that the individuals would have to present their case. The Assam government run by the BJP told the tribunal members what it wanted them to do by not extending the contracts of those who had a low rate of declaring individuals as foreigners.*

This was revealed in an affidavit that the government itself submitted to the Gauhati High Court when some of the tribunal members moved court saying they had been let go of from their jobs without any reason. This was not so, the government said, and claimed that all tribunal members had been given a performance appraisal. In 2017, it submitted a note which showed the names of the individuals, a column showing 'percentage of foreigners declared', 'general view of the Government upon the member' and 'whether may be considered for further retention or may be terminated'.

Individuals who had marked fewer than 10 per cent of the total number of people coming to their tribunal as being foreigners were deemed to be 'not satisfactory' and shown to be 'terminated'. The state government was effectively incentivising its tribunal officers to mark more people as foreigners, and punishing those officers who were not doing so. Such injustice

*Affidavit filed by the government of Assam in Mamoni Rajkumari Vs State of Assam http://ghconline.gov.in/Judgment/WPC44762017.pdf

did not receive nationwide much less global notice and the matter was limited to the Assamese media.

The crisis snowballed when an Assamese, Ranjan Gogoi was appointed as the chief justice of the Supreme Court. The state which was under the BJP drew up a first list, excluding over 40 lakh people and then a final list of those who it was satisfied met the criteria that it laid out. This was the so called National Register of Citizens.

The list excluded 19 lakh people from it who would now have to line up before the foreigners' tribunals with their papers and prove their citizenship. The majority of these 19 lakh turned out to be Hindus. This was unexpected because the BJP had believed its own narrative and governor Sinha's theory of a state overwhelmed by illegal immigrants, when there was no evidence to show this was the case.

The BJP government then decided to scrap the Assamese NRC that it had forced India to spend so much resources and effort on, and forced Indians to spend much resource and effort on. The government spent about Rs 1,600 crore on its processes. A report by the Rights and Risk Analysis Group ('NRC-excluded spent crores on hearings: Study', *The Hindu*, 28 August 2019) said another Rs 7,836 crore had been spent by individuals to gather their papers and hire advocates.

The report said the draft NRC had excluded about 13 per cent of the state's 3.1 crore people, most of whom were below the official poverty line. 'Many had to mortgage agricultural lands, sell their cattle, livestock and agricultural products like betel nuts, and paddy or their only means of income like auto-rickshaws while many took loans to meet the expenses for the NRC hearings,' the report said.

All of this had come to nothing as the Assam BJP government itself disowned the NRC findings in November 2019. The BJP at the Centre now quickly moved to say that it would instead conduct an NRC that was nationwide. The BJP had promised this in their manifesto in 2019 under 'Combating infiltration': 'There has been a huge change in the cultural and linguistic identity of some areas due to illegal immigration, resulting in an adverse impact on local people's livelihood and employment. We will expeditiously complete the National Register of Citizens process in these areas on priority. In future we will implement the NRC in a phased manner in other parts of the country.'

This was absurd because there was no history of agitation elsewhere as there had been in Assam, nor had there been any allegations of the nation being overrun by foreigners. There was no reason for now doing this nationwide except to squeeze India's Muslims.

The nationwide NRC would be read in tandem with another one that the BJP legislated in 2019, the Citizenship Amendment Act. This CAA offered fast track citizenship to those non-Muslims who had migrated from either Afghanistan, Bangladesh or Pakistan before 31 December 2014.

Why was the law specific to these three nations? This was not made clear and indeed did not make much sense. A lot of the migration into India has happened from Sri Lanka, whose Tamils have fled the fighting. Between 1983 and 1987, over 1.34 lakh Lankan Tamils came to India ('The ignored plight of Sri Lankan refugees in Tamil Nadu', *India Today*, 9 July 2016). But they were not covered by the CAA. And many refugees have come from Tibet, fleeing Chinese rule. They were not covered either. The rights group National Campaign Against Torture calculated that a total of 6 lakh refugees in India would be excluded by the CAA. It said that 'those who stand excluded from the Act comprise 3,04,269 Sri Lankan Tamils, 1,08,005 Tibetans, some 1,00,000 Chins from Myanmar, 40,000 Rohingyas from Myanmar and 39,619 others recognised by the United Nations High Commissioner for Refugees, ' ('CAA has made 6 lakh refugees forever stateless, says rights group', *The Hindu*, 19 March 2020).

What was the logic of determining persecution by faith and limiting it to the faith of Hindus, Christians, Buddhists, Sikhs, Jains and Parsis (the six faiths the CAA specifically refers to)? This was not explained.

Pakistan has constitutionally excluded Ahmadiyyas as we have seen and Pakistani Shias have faced extreme violence in Karachi and Balochistan, but these groups were not covered by the CAA either. Those repressed because of their sexuality or political affiliation were also excluded. As the historian Ramachandra Guha concluded, the CAA appeared to assume that in South Asia only Muslim states persecuted and only non-Muslims faced persecution.

Supporters of the law said that Muslim refugees in a similar situation who had entered before 2014 were not really excluded and could apply for citizenship under the regular (non-CAA route). This, of course, is discrimination and violative of the Constitutional guarantee for the right to equality. But reporting by journalists proved that even this route for Muslims was being shut off by the changes in regulation.

The point of the exercise was of course a mystery only to those who assume Hindutva acts in good faith against Muslims and who did not listen to what the BJP government's stated intention was. As the CAA bill was going through Parliament, Home Minister Amit Shah made speeches in which he likened immigrant Muslims to termites. In his public declarations he laid out a chronology to assure BJP supporters who were worried about going through the same wringer that the Assamese had just gone through. On 20 November 2019, Shah said that the CAA would first come which would filter out and protect the non-Muslims. Then the government would unleash the NRC and the 'termites' would be sent to concentration camps.

Things moved rapidly now. On 11 December 2019, Parliament passed the CAA bill and made it law. The Lok Sabha had first passed the CAA bill in early 2019, before the general election. This passage had led to protests against the law in the Northeast, where there has been a demand for the NRC but without the CAA, since the residents of those states, ethnically distinct, did not want Indian citizens from other states either. Till this point it had been only some parts of the media that had focused on the issue as being a regional matter. In the absence of a nationwide NRC or even any talk of it, the threat was limited.

After the threats made by Shah, the promise of a national NRC and the passage of the CAA, for India's Muslims, the targets of both the CAA and the NRC, it was a situation that they could not leave for others to manage for them. The faith in the judiciary was always low but almost gone after the Babri judgment which had come in October, only days before Shah made his NRC chronology public. Politically, the space seemed closed for them. The opposition made some noises about the problems with the CAA but it was passed because the opposition didn't stand united and many non-BJP parties voted in favour of it. Agitation and protest seemed the only democratic option available to them.

Four days after the bill became law, protests broke out in Delhi, most notably at Jamia Millia Islamia University. The Delhi Police, under Amit Shah, used extreme violence against the student protestors, vandalising the university library, using sexual violence against women and men, and blinding one student. The media coverage of this was predictably prejudiced and against the students.

The assault on Jamia led to a sit-in protest at a neighbourhood near the university, named Shaheen Bagh. It was led by women and would continue to be led by them all the way to its end in March, by when they were international celebrities and had achieved what they had been protesting for—the shelving of the all India

NRC (the CAA was challenged as being unconstitutional in the Supreme Court).

The sit-in was round the clock, through the day and all through the night and it was in the cold of the Delhi winter. In the evenings, as the protest continued to grow in size and fame, people from outside the neighbourhood came to show their solidarity. Soon these began to include the famous, and this brought more media attention. The protest was full of activity: music and poetry and speeches and all this happened with much flag waving. Here were Muslim women insisting on showing their Indianness to a state that saw their faith and them as foreign.

On 18 December, protestors in Uttar Pradesh, governed by the BJP, were fired on by the police and several died. This escalated the movement which now sprang up all across India and mostly in Muslim neighbourhoods similar to Shaheen Bagh. India is ghettoised and the Muslim professional is usually forced to stay in these ghettos because she is not given accommodation in Hindu-dominated colonies,* or is legally forced into urban ghettos as we have seen in the case of Gujarat's Disturbed Areas Act.

This uniformity in a way helped the quick spread of the protests because mobilisation, space and safety were all accessible and available in these neighbourhoods. The Shaheen Bagh model of the sit-in was quickly emulated all over India and there were around 150 of these round the clock protests in cities by March 2020. They were led by Muslim women with substantial participation by student, civil society groups, actors, musicians, poets, writers and other individuals from the arts. For many, this was their first protest, and for all it was the biggest they had participated in and witnessed.

---

*See 'Muslims not allowed—the stereotypes of Mumbai's rental property market' (*CNBCTV.com*, 21 September 2020) and 'Accommodation available: Muslims don't apply' (*Outlook*, 1 April 2002).

The Shaheen Bagh model of a fixed site, continual and unbroken resistance and a time table of cultural activity made it easy for many to participate. If you felt strongly about the violations and the prejudice in the law, or even if you were merely curious, there was a place in your city or town you could go to and participate in the resistance. For those who attended and took part, one striking thing was that the movement lost no momentum with time. It could be said with accuracy that in fact the opposite happened. More cities, more students, more universities and more people joined in with time. This required the individuals at each protest site to very quickly learn new skills.

The 'No CAA No NPR No NRC' movement produced a generation of talented mobilisers and organisers. Along with a famous civil rights victory and the production of a model for future protest, this is the other contribution that the movement has made. Hundreds of young women and men, most of them in their twenties, were now activists with experience of how to manage a group of 200 or more people, how to raise money and get and distribute provisions, how to represent themselves before the media, how to spread the word and expand the protest, how to respond on social media and so on. They learned how to campaign.

These protestors were asking only for equality. They had no demand but that they not be harassed by a State intent on repeating the inhumanity of what was being done in Assam. They had no other ask and wanted nothing.

This is the reason that the protest became globally problematic for the Modi government. It was seen unequivocally as a State that was bullying and discriminating against its own citizens and, as the protests went on, being deaf to their legitimate concerns and came to be seen as a global problem. On 22 December, a week after the Jamia attack when it became clear that the protests were a real force of resistance, Modi said that the NRC had not been discussed by his government.

This went against the public statements and threats made by Shah only days earlier. However, two days later, the government sanctioned money to conduct a nationwide headcount of people that was unrelated to the Census. Research into the laws and bylaws soon showed that this new headcount, the National Population Register, was actually linked to the NRC.

On 24 December, a report in *The Hindu* ('Fact check: Is the government right in denying the NPR-NRC link') showed that Amit Shah had lied. It said that the 'NPR is indeed the basis for NRC, as Section 14A of the Citizenship Act empowers the government to compulsorily register every citizen of India and issue an identity card and to maintain a "National Register of Indian Citizens". The citizenship register is generated out of the NPR database.'

It was now difficult to believe in the government of India and in what the prime minister was saying. The protests continued and began to take on a global dimension that had not been expected either by the government or even the protestors.

As the sit-ins spread, and there were marches, often of hundreds of thousands of people, and gatherings of tens of thousands, two other things happened. There was a strong and effective social media pushback against Hindutva, which attracted the foreign media and the foreign states.

On 21 December 2019, Malaysia, and later Turkey, Indonesia and Iran publicly engaged the Indian government over the issue. On 23 December, the Organisation of Islamic Cooperation (OIC), the fifty-seven-member grouping of Muslim majority nations, put out a statement saying that it was 'closely following recent developments affecting the Muslim minority in India.' And that it 'expresses its concern over the recent developments pertaining to both the issue of citizenship rights and the Babri Masjid case'.

Such engagement is unwelcome to India which has always made much of what it sees as intrusions into its sovereignty. However the defence that India has especially put forward is that the world need not be concerned about such matters because India is a constitutionally secular and democratic State. The accusations against it must collapse because of this grand fact, and if there was any truth to them it was based on an aberration which went against what the government of India and its Constitution stood for.

Hindutva has captured the Indian State but it sits behind the facade of Nehruvian secularism and inclusion. It pretends to be what it is not. For this reason, it is also vulnerable. Its contradictions are more easily pointed out. A Hindutva government that accepts it runs a Hindu Rashtra would more easily be able to show defiance. A Hindutva prime minister who swears by secularism opens himself to being seen as a hypocrite. Brushing off foreign intervention may be relatively easy to do when the accusers themselves harass their minorities and don't have pluralist laws. But it is more difficult when the perpetrator pretends to not be doing what he is accused of.

India's secularism is used as a carapace under which Hindutva abuses India's minorities. This contradiction is Hindutva's weakness. It is dishonest about its bigotry.

On 22 January 2020, a motion was tabled in the European Parliament and was to be voted on. It was one of only a half-a-dozen or so items to be taken up by the MEPs in that session. It detailed what the CAA was about and listed out the government's rationale for legislating it. The resolution said, 'The indivisibility of human rights, including civil, political, economic, social and cultural rights, is one of the main objectives of the European Union in its relations with India.'

From here it laid out the case against the Indian government in such harsh terms as have not been seen by the Ministry of

External Affairs (MEA). There could be no defence against the unvarnished criticism of prejudice. The text of the motion needs to be quoted at length.

It noted that the CAA extended fast-track citizenship to undocumented migrants from the Hindu, Sikh, Buddhist, Jain, Parsi or Christian communities of Afghanistan, Bangladesh or Pakistan, who entered India on or before 31 December 2014. And noted that India had only an 'informal justification' that Muslim-majority countries were more likely to persecute their minorities.

The motion pointed out that 'Sri Lankan Tamils who form the largest refugee group in India and have been resident in the country for over thirty years, do not, however, fall under the purview of the CAA; whereas the CAA also excludes Rohingya Muslims from Burma, who have been described by Amnesty International and the United Nations as the world's most persecuted minority; whereas the CAA also ignores the plight of Ahmadis in Pakistan, Bihari Muslims in Bangladesh and Hazaras in Pakistan, all of whom are subject to persecution in their home countries.'

It said, 'CAA is explicitly discriminatory in nature as it specifically excludes Muslims from access to the same provisions as other religious groups.' And this was offensive because 'according to the Indian Constitution, India is a sovereign secular democratic republic and including religion as a criterion for citizenship is therefore fundamentally unconstitutional'.'

It pointed out to the Indian government that the CAA Act it had just passed 'contradicts Article 14 of the Indian Constitution, which guarantees the right to equality to every person and protects them from discrimination on the grounds of religion, race, caste, sex or place of birth.' And that it also violated India's commitment to uphold the Universal Declaration of Human Rights, the International Covenant on Civil and Political Rights, and the International Convention on the Elimination of All Forms of Racial Discrimination to which India was a State Party and which prohibited discrimination on racial, ethnic or religious grounds.

The motion noted the protests, the twenty-seven deaths from police firings, the thousands of arrests and the internet shutdowns and curfews being used to curb peaceful assembly. It mentioned events in Uttar Pradesh, the attack on Jawaharlal Nehru University and the impunity to the attackers.

After this, it said that 'the CAA sets a dangerous precedent and represents an intensification of the government's Hindu nationalist agenda' and that 'both the contents of the CAA and the violence it has encouraged, both from the police and pro-government groups, are clear breaches of the human rights of residents of India and its neighbouring countries'.

The motion noted that the UN had also expressed concerns, as had the Office of the United Nations High Commissioner for Human Rights, which said that the CAA was 'fundamentally discriminatory in nature'. It said that the CAA was linked to the NRC and that Shah's statements showed that 'the NRC process aims to strip Muslims of their citizenship rights while protecting those of Hindus and other non-Muslims'.

It noted the detention camps in Assam and others coming up elsewhere, including in Bangalore and said it was 'difficult to view the CAA in isolation, as both the amendments and the NRC could deprive minorities of their citizenship of India; whereas only Muslims excluded from the NRC will have difficulty winning their cases at foreign tribunals'.

It concluded its observations by noting that many Indian states were now saying they would not implement the law, including Kerala (which filed the petition against the CAA in the Supreme Court).

The motion called CAA fundamentally discriminatory and condemned it. It regretted the fact that 'India has incorporated religious criteria into its naturalisation and refugee policies'. It called on India to 'immediately engage in peaceful dialogue with the protestors and repeal the discriminatory amendments'.

As mentioned, this sort of public hiding on human rights was not something the Indian government has received before. The MEA diplomat abroad is not trained to defend the country against such direct attacks, especially from institutions which it wants to be on the right side of, such as the organs of the European Union.

The harshness and directness of the attack was not something that India could ignore. It made the government squirm enough for it to try and block the resolution. What it succeeded in doing was to get the MEPs to table the motion but agree to a delay on the vote, which Modi feared, correctly, would be in favour of the resolution. This, the Members of European Parliament agreed to, putting off the vote for a session a few weeks down the road, which was then delayed by the Covid-19 epidemic. It remains dormant, because the actions have ceased at the Indian end.

However, this unprecedented international concern about Hindutva nastiness unfolding in India came with consequences. After the EU MEP motion, anti-CAA protests had broken out across Europe by Indian groups mobilised locally, many of them academics and professionals upset by what India was doing and how because of the State's bigotry the nation was being perceived globally.

On 26 January, a pamphlet was circulated calling for a protest outside the United Nations building in Geneva. It read: 'We, a group of Indians in Europe (Germany, Netherlands, Sweden, Switzerland, Poland, Finland, and France) have organised a protest at the United Nations, Geneva on the 1st of February. There have been several protests all over Europe and the idea was to unite at the UN. We stand against the CAA on grounds that it violates our Constitution and goes against the secular nature of our country. We also stand against the possible implementation of NRC. It is inhumane, unnecessary, arbitrary, prone to be being abused, and will disproportionately affect the minority communities, and poor people in our country. We condemn the brutal attacks on protesters by the UP and the Delhi police, and we stand in solidarity with the protesters in India.'

On 29 January, there was a coordinated protest in eighteen European capital cities. This had never before happened, when groups of concerned Indians around the world were taking on their own government and doing so publicly. The relationship the expatriate has had with India has always been one of unconditional reverence. Any criticism of happenings in the country is usually defended, but not this time.

Protests in India and activism related to protests can be seen in some ways as following a formula. If there is mobilisation it is for a march, a rally or, rarely, for a limited period sit-in. An open-ended and always-on movement, such as the one represented by 'No CAA No NPR No NRC', was not something the State had any experience in managing. And neither was it something that any protest group ever had experience in organising.

One of the amazing things about it is that 'No CAA No NPR No NRC' was that it was and remained spontaneous and leaderless. It was anarchic in the purest sense of the word, meaning without a leader ('archon' in Greek, from where the term is derived). Shaheen Bagh was the most prominent site of the protests but it was not the only one. The strength of the movement came from its spread and its numbers and the resolve. If credit can be given, it must be given to Muslim women first and then to student groups. The firmness of the pushback against the discriminatory laws was because of the weight they put behind it.

Political parties were wary of throwing their weight fully behind what seemed for the most part a protest by Muslims. But it was that absence of organised political participation, which we must also accept was mandated by the protestors who did not want their movement hijacked, that gave it even more credibility.

The levers that made the 'No CAA No NPR No NRC' campaign strong were mass mobilisation and external pressure. Legal intervention was attempted but the conclusion of this writer and others is that the judiciary is pliant in India. If it is independent it is not on the issues that are hard or where a powerful State has interests. Where there is conflict and passion, it sides with the majoritarian view and comes around to it, as the Babri judgment and the disinterest in the rights of Kashmiris shows. It kicked the CAA legality question down the road and did not hear it with the urgency it can demonstrate in cases it has an interest in. So not much was expected from India's Supreme Court and not much came of it at the moment in time when it needed to show its quality and its independence.

The support that came from provincial legislatures that passed resolutions against the citizenship laws was important but it came later, as a result of the protests. Without large numbers of people in their cities gathering and remaining mobilised, the states would not have had any reason to defy the Centre on an issue which was not of importance to them. In that sense even the foreign intervention came because of the local mobilisation. Everything that fell into place came later and came because of sheer numbers, which were irresistible.

The 'No CAA No NPR No NRC' movement multiplied quickly and successfully across India because the Shaheen Bagh style sit-in was easy to emulate and also because millions of people were willing to be mobilised. Citizens, most of them Muslim, but also including others, took to marches across India in their hundreds of thousands to show their opposition to the laws and to seek the support of others. The most difficult part of a campaign is what activists call offline mobilisation. The word used is offline because the usual way of gathering people around an issue ('mobilisation') is online, which is relatively easy. Campaigns put out something on social media or through a phone number where interested individuals give a missed call.

This missed call number is recorded and gives the campaign a database to get engage with its supporters. The usual sequence is then to ask the person who called to take another action, such as signing a petition. When that happens, the database logs it and there is a record of which supporters appear to be more committed. These are then again approached and asked for more commitment. This is often in the form of seeking a donation. Rarely, especially in our part of the world, are such supporters asked to come to the street and physically participate: in a march or a rally, let alone a sit-in. It is rare because this level of commitment is unusual among large numbers of people. The sit-in is the rarest of them all because it requires sustained commitment and sacrifice. The Union and state governments in India are so wary of sit-ins that they are given allocated spaces in Delhi and in state capitals where people can come and sit and, usually, be forgotten.

A sit-in is meaningful and effective only when it is defiant. Shaheen Bagh and protests like it became relevant because the State and its media did not want them to do what they were doing, where they were doing it. The State had the power and the authority to evict the women by force. The protestors dared the State to do it, and their defiance was not just an irritant but almost intolerable for the State and its majoritarian support base. This produced a fairly nasty narrative against the women and the protests in the media, especially, the television media.

Supporters of the movement are often disconsolate when examining the media and the hostility from the government towards a non-violent movement. But that very hostility is a sign that a movement is effective. And effective 'No CAA No NPR No NRC' was.

Modi had not expected the resistance that he found. It was unprecedented. And in his experience, when bullied and harassed, Muslims did not push back. Such counter-mobilisation to majoritarianism was new. He had no response to the movement as it built. After saying the NRC had not been discussed, he went silent on the subject, as is his wont when things are not going his way (something similar happened after China took land in Ladakh and Modi chose not to acknowledge the loss—it appears to be a character flaw). He went silent on the issue of the NRC after this.

In the face of what was by then a nationwide movement, the Modi government deprioritised the NRC from January. On 24 December, Amit Shah had said that the NRC and NPR were not linked. On 15 January 2020, Kerala challenged the constitutionality of the CAA in the Supreme Court. The following day the Centre removed the linking of PAN (Permanent Account) numbers in the NPR, trying to show that it was benign. On 17 January, West Bengal refused to participate in an NPR meeting and the same day the Centre said that parents' details on the NPR form were voluntary and could be done away with. On 28 January, Odisha said it could not include parents' details in the NPR form. On 25 February, the Bihar Assembly, which the BJP leads in an alliance, passed a resolution against the NRC.

The protest of the Muslim women was so effective that it forced reluctant political parties to take a position against the Centre and in the case of Bihar, even against their own party's central leadership. It was clear by now that Modi and Shah had been defeated. The threats to rid India of Muslims through the NRC went away and the termites and chronology phrasing was never repeated. There was no explicit statement saying that the NRC would be put off, and even the postponing of the NPR was done through a statement released by a bureaucrat. After all the brave words on the NRC, neither Shah nor Modi took ownership of the retreat.

It is how bullies and cowards slink away from a confrontation, without apparent resolution. The government simply stopped talking about the citizenship laws, and Hindutva instead turned to what it usually does when it is angered: violence against other Indians.

The riots that were instigated by the BJP and its associates in Delhi in February 2020 cost over fifty lives, mostly Muslim and the vandalism of hundreds of homes and shops and the desecration of mosques.* It was the impotent lashing out of the defeated. The persecution of activists who had participated in the 'No CAA No NPR No NRC' protests on the false accusation that they had instigated or participated in violence shows that the government felt the sting of defeat. The Modi government has been vicious in using the Covid pandemic to lock up those who had shown resistance. It had no compunction in jailing even pregnant women, again with little or no resistance from a pliant judiciary.

However, this is how civil rights victories are won. The great American activist John Lewis called it 'good trouble', the actions that invited the negative attentions of a prejudiced State. In the long term, the fact that the movement has produced so many successful activists who are now household names will hold us as a nation in good stead. We have the steel to be able to defend constitutional values in a peaceful and democratic manner and much of that steel was forged in the cauldron of the 'No CAA No NPR No NRC' movement.

So what lies ahead for us now? How is it that Indians can push back against Hindutva majoritarianism? We need to understand what tools we have available to us and how they can be used.

*See 'The roots of the Delhi riots: A fiery speech and an ultimatum' (*New York Times*, 26 February 2020) https://www.nytimes.com/2020/02/26/world/asia/delhi-riots-kapil-mishra.html

Article 19 says that: 'All citizens shall have the right
(a) to freedom of speech and expression;
(b) to assemble peaceably and without arms;
(c) to form associations or unions;
(d) to move freely throughout the territory of India;
(e) to reside and settle in any part of the territory of India; and
(g) to practise any profession, or to carry on any occupation, trade or business'.

The reality is that today we have no such rights. Do Indians have the right to 'assemble peacefully and without arms'? No. We have the right to apply for permission for peaceful assembly to the local police station. The police has the right to approve, deny or not respond. That is where the real right is held. Scenes of groups of protestors, some as small as half-a-dozen, holding placards and chanting slogans outside business establishments and government offices, and even political rallies, are common in the United States and Europe. In India, such a gathering would be broken up or not allowed to happen. India has criminalised protest. Where it is allowed, after written permission, it is usually in specific spaces allocated for 'protest'. Jantar Mantar in Delhi is such a place, a land cordoned off at both ends with stalls of protests, some of them there for months, unseen and unheard.

In Bangalore, you have Town Hall and Freedom Park, in Mumbai Azad Maidan, where protest after permission may be allowed during specific periods of time. This does not constitute the right to peaceful assembly. It is denial of a fundamental right given to us by the Constitution. We have to take the right lawfully back.

Freedom of speech and expression is qualified by so many laws that it is hard to know where to begin. India has criminalised free speech through sedition, criminal defamation and criminal contempt of court. The mother country we borrowed these laws from no longer has them. There is no right to dissent in India and anything offensive to majoritarian Hindutva is called anti-national. The Kashmiri can teach you a thing or two about freedom of speech and expression if you claim that India is free.

Forming associations is not easy in India and registration can be denied or cancelled. Those who work in the organised civil society space, meaning professional NGOs, know just how difficult the State makes it for them to exercise this fundamental right.

We have seen the problem with the right to carry out a trade, which has been struck off for butchers and by extension, for restaurants. Many of these rights have become ossified. The State has strong investment in denying them to us, and we have not been as strong in claiming them.

The footnote under Article 19 reads 'Nothing shall affect the operation of any existing law, or prevent the State from making any law, in so far as such law imposes reasonable restrictions on the exercise of the right...'

The question is whether the restrictions imposed are reasonable. They are not.

Reclaiming our fundamental rights is the answer to the problem of Indian majoritarianism and also the only way to realise and unlock the value of our Constitution. We have to peacefully reclaim our rights both at the level of the individual and the level of civil society.

India has a weaker civil society than other democracies. It is vibrant, yes, and it is defiant and it is brave. But it is small.

India needs to create a bigger space for that part of our nation which is not government and not business corporations. That is civil society. It is groups, formal and informal, and individuals, and the space that they create with their actions.

The dictionary defines it as 'society considered as a community of citizens linked by common interests and collective activity'. The World Health Organisation defines civil society as 'the space for collective action around shared interests, purposes and values, generally distinct from government and commercial for-profit actors. Civil society includes charities, development NGOs, community groups, women's organisations, faith-based organisations, professional associations, trade unions, social movements, coalitions and advocacy groups.'

These are at the heart of our society because outside of politics they are what we express ourselves through. India has excessive expression from our political parties. That is their right. But we have almost no counter to them, even when they are violating the law and when our government, which the parties control, trample on our rights.

The RSS is the civil society of majoritarianism. The RSS is an NGO—by some accounts, the largest in the world. Its affiliates, the ABVP, the Bajrang Dal, the Durga Vahini are also civil society groups. They do at the campus and neighbourhood level the same lumpen mischief that the BJP does in national politics. The Sangh's Hindutva majoritarianism manifests itself through ensuring that its perspective has dominance in the fields it enters. While it has entered many fields, its concerns are purely majoritarian and narrow. The agenda is limited though the damage is immense.

The opposition to them must come from a civil society that pushes back not against them alone, but in favour of a general secular pluralism that our Constitution stands for. It must stand not just against the majoritarianism alone but for the wider liberal constitutional values. This is what must be strengthened. How? To illustrate this let us look at a recent example that touches our lives directly.

On 12 August 2020, the *Indian Express* reported ('Asha workers protest at Jantar Mantar demanding better pay, face FIR') on the protest of India's six lakh Accredited Social Health

Activist (ASHA) workers. Paid Rs 2,000 a month, this group of all-female workers are the ones doing contact tracing of Covid, while not been given protective clothing. They had gone on strike to demand better conditions for work.

ASHA workers helped eradicate polio and reduced the number of Indian women dying during child birth. The *Express* report of their protest (from Jantar Mantar, of course) said that they had been booked for unlawful assembly and an FIR filed. They had been protesting since 21 July but had been unheard.

Whom does it benefit that these women are given their rights? All of the nation. We cannot win over Covid if those actually fighting it are saying they are handicapped in their fight. It is undeniable that their cause is just and their demand is correct. But they are alone, and for asking for their rights they are persecuted by the Indian State.

This is a group that is standing up for its rights on its own. In another democracy such a large number of women in such a vital role at a time of a pandemic would generate public and media interest of a very high level. Why did this not happen in India? Even when our individual interest is aligned with a group's, we did not extend it support. Why did we not? What might have happened if a large number of middle class people had? This is something we have to ask ourselves and answer honestly.

The 'No CAA No NPR No NRC' protests showed us more than a glimpse of this. There were youth who were knowledgeable and enthusiastic about the movement, who had no personal motive to be involved save their love for their nation and its people and their rights. The other side doesn't have this asset. It would not be easy to get youth to be enthusiastic about the mass incarceration of fellow Indians in concentration camps or the denial of justice.

We must try and take an action daily in favour of expanding our civil society. It doesn't matter if the action is online, offline, a donation, attending a talk or even just learning about the new environment law and how it will affect India. Our actions mean something. Participation expands civil society.

It is through mass individual participation in everyday activism, through raising of voices, through funding just causes and funding organised civil society groups, through supporting progressive calls for engagement and supporting those who need that the Western democracies have become the open societies they are. It is our dream as well to be there, and most of us agree that we want an India that is prosperous and resembles those nations whose people have the most freedoms.

We are not alone in wanting this. The world also wants to see a secular and plural India and especially, that part of the world that the Indian State cares about. Civil society can use this global interest in our progress as a lever. The opportunities will continue to come, as Hindutva majoritarianism pushes ahead with its agenda.

Majoritarian intolerance in India was first flagged by the United States government officially in 2004. The US Commission on International Religious Freedom (USCIRF) looked at the post-Godhra riots situation in Gujarat and recommended to the George W. Bush administration that Atal Bihari Vajpayee's government be classified as a 'Country of Particular Concern' (CPC).

The report observed that Vajpayee 'had not condemned the massacre of Muslims unequivocally' for more than a year. It noted that there was no justice for the victims, mostly Muslims, in Gujarat, and it also noted the anti-conversion legislation that was passed, also in Gujarat. The following year, the Vajpayee government fell and the report, noting that Manmohan Singh had taken over, dropped India from the list. However, the issues raised in the report remained.

In March 2005, the Commission issued a statement encouraging the US State Department to prevent Modi's planned visit to the United States, citing evidence presented by India's National Human Rights Commission and numerous domestic and international human rights investigators of the complicity of Gujarat state officials in the mob attacks on Muslims. This was of course, the famous visa ban on Modi, and he did not visit the US from then on, till he won the 2014 election.

On 28 April 2020, India was again marked as a country of particular concern, with five dozen references in the report (the highest in the twenty-two-year history of the bipartisan body). On the first page of the annual report, India's record is nailed to the cross.

It reads: 'India took a sharp downward turn in 2019. The national government used its strengthened parliamentary majority to institute national-level policies violating religious freedom across India, especially for Muslims.' This is the first time that the USCIRF accused India's Union government of not an act of omission, as was its observation on Vajpayee's condemnation of the Godhra massacre, but of commission.

It said the Modi government's prejudice against India's Muslims was showing through India's actions on citizenship, cow slaughter, Kashmir and conversions. The report notes the Ayodhya ruling, and the conduct of the Uttar Pradesh chief minister Yogi Adityanath. It recommended to US President Donald Trump that he designate India as CPC, 'for engaging in and tolerating systematic, ongoing, and egregious religious freedom violations, as defined by the International Religious Freedom Act'.

It wanted Trump to 'impose targeted sanctions on Indian government agencies and officials responsible for severe violation of religious freedom by freezing those individuals' assets and/ or barring their entry into the US'. It seeks to 'strengthen US Embassy's and consulates' engagement with religious communities, local officials, and police, especially in regions impacted by religiously motivated violence; increase US partnerships with Indian law enforcement to build capacity to protect religious minorities, houses of worship, and other holy sites, and confront religious-based hate crimes; and allocate funding to support civil society to create a monitoring and early warning system in partnership with police to challenge hate speech and incitement to violence'.

This portends intervention, which will come. How deep the intervention is, whether it will be limited to behind the scenes arm-twisting or sanctions, will depend on who is in charge of the United States and how the Indian government behaves from here on. The day the USCIRF report was released, social media reported a BJP legislator hectoring a Muslim vegetable vendor and his son, and another BJP legislator telling his constituents to boycott Muslims.

India's official response to the report was quite breezy and brisk. It read: 'We reject the observations on India in the USCIRF Annual Report. Its biased and tendentious comments against India are not new. But on this occasion, its misrepresentation has reached new levels. It has not been able to carry its own Commissioners in its endeavour. We regard it as an organisation of particular concern and will treat it accordingly.'

This doesn't mean anything. India has no leverage on the bipartisan body. The government's hope is that Biden does not take the recommendation. But even if they do not, the US president will have that leverage over Modi in this matter. The report also opens up linkages between rights activists, non-government organisations and the US, which will irritate and alarm the Indian State.

The USCIRF recommendations came after a series of public meetings with Indian academics and activists, including Aman Wadud, a young lawyer who has worked with the victims of the NRC in Assam, and Ashutosh Varshney, who has studied communal violence in India, meaning that the recommendations are based on the findings of Indians themselves, against the majoritarianism that is plaguing India.

Of course, this is interference in our internal affairs, but we have to accept that we brought it on. The Trump administration has little interest in human rights in India, and as such Modi should have had an easy pass. But even the USCIRF chair, Tony Perkins, who was nominated by the Republicans, weighed in against India. What has transpired in the USCIRF will not end with the releasing of the report recommending action against India.

Unless the Modi administration shows great change of direction, India will figure again in next year's report. The current mention will stay alive till then, and incidents of bigotry and discrimination and violence against Indian minorities will be flagged to the USCIRF and the Western media. This will give leverage to the activists and Indian civil society over a government that has thus far been dismissive and contemptuous of them and their work.

It opens up for them the space to try and pressure the Modi government in a way that is not possible purely through politics locally or through the compromised justice system. It adds substantial leverage in a vulnerable place. And any probing here will produce some favourable result and some gain.

The Ministry of External Affairs is not monolithic. It has senior diplomats who would have agreed with Modi here that India can absorb some international censure and get away with it. There will be some who don't agree but will go along. There will be some who don't agree and will express themselves within the government. There will be some who may rebel. Indians have been brought up on a narrative of inclusion. It is not easy for the State to discard this overnight as Hindutva wants done.

The stronger the pressure there is on the structure, the more likely it is to fragment in its opinion and the less likely it is for the government to push something through that is extreme. Civil society can and must mobilise so that this pressure on the government is kept up when it abandons secularism and pluralism.

The State in India has little interest in constitutionalism. No awards are given for it, and on the other hand, the judiciary and the system does not punish errant and often even criminal behaviour. The State can, for example, harass activists with bogus cases and there will be no punitive action against those who did the framing. Such things as wrongful detention, excessive use of force, harassment and malicious action by the State are not penalised.

Civil society must get the State to be more invested in constitutionalism. We have to ensure that where the State and its agents bend or break the law or the values of the Constitution, they are held to account and called out. These attempts may fail, and that is fine. Structural change requires construction at the foundation. Effort is the critical investment. Results will follow.

Constitutional space has been given to us. Even if it has been severely restricted over time, it exists. The space needs to be appropriated in a way that it has not been, and especially not been by the urban middle class. And it has to be expanded. We have to fray the 'reasonable restrictions', we have to unravel them and we have to let the true meaning of the fundamental rights shine through.

Progress on rights is inevitable. History is with the progressives: the future is also with us. Conservatives seek to conserve a past that is not possible to hold on to. Change is inevitable and constant, and the arc of the moral universe is headed in the direction of progress on individual rights and dignity. Our task is to hasten the arc along on its path towards justice.

INDEX